Legal Research

for Beginners

Sonja Larsen and John Bourdeau

DEDICATION

From Sonja Larsen: To my parents, Torbjørn and Ingeborg Larsen, and to my brother and sisters–with thanks for all their support.

Also to Professor Nancy Savage for being such a bright spot in law school; and to the memory of Patricia Patton, who showed me that combining a legal career with a concern for others is possible.

From John Bourdeau: To my parents, Alice and Leo Bourdeau, and to my brothers and sisters, for all their patience and encouragement. Thanks for helping me find my way.

All inquiries should be addressed to:
Barron's Educational Series, Inc.
250 Wireless Boulevard
Hauppauge, New York 11788

International Standard Book No. 0-8120-9768-8

Library of Congress Catalog Card No. 96-39398

Library of Congress Cataloging-in-Publication Data

Bourdeau, John.
Legal research for beginners / John Bourdeau, Sonja Larsen.
p. cm.
Includes bibliographical references and index.
ISBN 0-8120-9768-8
1. Legal research—United States. I. Larsen, Sonja. II. Title.
KF240.B69 1997
340'.07'2073 dc21 96-39398
CIP

PRINTED IN THE UNITED STATES OF AMERICA
9 8 7 6 5 4 3 2 1

CONTENTS

HOW TO USE THIS BOOK

We know that the prospect of doing your own legal research can be daunting, even downright frightening, but by picking up this book you've already taken your first step toward alleviating that fear and answering your legal questions. There really is nothing to be afraid of. You've probably done some library research in the past, and legal research isn't all that different—only the books and the terminology are unfamiliar. Reading materials that you've gathered, taking notes, and organizing your notes and thoughts into usable form are all things you've done in the past. You already have most of what it takes to do legal research, and this book will provide you with or inspire you to get the rest.

This book is intended to show you a methodical and cautious way to do legal research. By "methodical and cautious," we mean that we want your search to be initially as broad as is necessary for a research beginner—you can always narrow your search later, when you start to understand which information is relevant for your purposes and which is not. There are three advantages to our method: First, it lays a strong foundation on which all your subsequent work can build; second, by being so inclusive in the beginning stages of your research, you won't miss out on any important information; and third, it allows room for you to make mistakes and pursue a couple of minor detours or complete dead ends without letting these errors derail your progress.

There are a few things about the set-up of this book that we want to explain before you use it. We didn't think that it was enough to tell someone how to do legal research; we wanted to show you how it is done, much in the same way that an experienced golfer takes you through that first difficult swing by putting your hands on the club and swinging it with you. To accomplish this we take you through actual research problems—leading you every step of the way. Due to the ever changing nature of the law and the frequent supplementation and updating of law books, however, it may be possible that the materials on the shelves will not always match our descriptions of them in the text. Our remedy for this problem is to provide you with copies of the pages that we are discussing, so just in case the books have changed you will still be able to see what we are talking about.

Another thing we want to mention is the use of italics. Where you see a word *italicized*, like this, in *Legal Research for Beginners* it means that a definition of that term extracted from *Barron's Law Dictionary* has been provided in a handy appendix in the back of this book. We suggest that you consult it when you want to know a traditional legal definition of a term. Furthermore, if you want legal advice, we suggest that you seek a lawyer. This book is designed to teach you how to conduct your own legal research, it does not attempt to give legal advice.

Likewise, to help you with your research we have provided sections called Chapter Highlights at the end of each chapter. These highlights are like the bare bones of the book. They can be used before, during, or after reading each chapter to underscore what is important and to help you remember what steps to take in your research process.

Finally, before you start your research, we suggest that you always have a pen and paper (or a computer) handy. This is because good legal research technique requires you to take notes that you can later use to find other materials and, when you finish your research, to summarize the answers you find on issues. In fact, even keeping a separate folder or notebook for all of your notes is suggested.

Now, there's no time to start like the present. You won't need to venture into a law library until after you read the first two (or three) chapters, so read these chapters in a place that you feel comfortable. After the first couple of chapters, find a law library, and you'll be ready to get down to work.

Good luck!

CHAPTER 1

FIRST THINGS: THE LAW AND THE AMERICAN LEGAL SYSTEM

Look for it, it cannot be seen . . .
Listen for it, it cannot be heard . . .
Grasp at it, it cannot be held . . .

—*Tao Te Ching, verse 14*

THE LAW

This quotation from the *Tao* does not describe the *law*, but for first-time legal researchers the law can seem just as mysterious. There are three basic reasons for this confusion:

- The law tries to be all things to all people.
- There is a lot of stuff that we call the law.
- Everything is confusing when it is new.

On a personal level, we know that it is not a good thing to try to be all things to all people. It causes confusion, feelings of betrayal, and backlashes of resentment. Sound familiar? For the law, however, it's a necessary state of affairs. The law is supposed to be for everyone. The law has to govern whole societies. It has to be fair and impartial while being stable and responsive, harsh to wrongdoers but comforting to the wronged.

It's no wonder then that there is a lot of stuff that we call the law. To hold the balance for society, legislatures enact statutes, which create the need for agencies to write rules and regulations to enforce the statutes, which leaves to the courts the job of interpreting the law and filling in the gaps where, inevitably, there are no statutes, rules, or regulations to settle disputes. All of this material has been written down for ages, with the result that law libraries are filled with hundreds of thousands of volumes. But don't be discouraged.

Everything is confusing (and scary) when it is new. Remember what it was like the first time you drove a car, went out on a date, or tried to solve a problem in algebra class. You made it through all of these trials, and with a little patience, you can learn to do basic legal research too. With this in mind, let's looks at some necessary background information on the American legal system.

THE AMERICAN LEGAL SYSTEM

Common law

The legal inheritance of the United States was drawn from numerous sources: English law, Roman law (the Justinian Code), French law (the Napoleonic Code), Native American law, the Bible, local custom, and common sense. The most influential of these, however, was the English common law that the colonists brought with them to govern their affairs.

Common law is a system of judge-made law. It developed because early on most laws were not written down by legislatures. For the sake of stability and uniformity, judges began to follow the decisions of other judges who had heard similar cases in the past. This made sense because otherwise each judge could have made up the law any way he wanted. From following these past decisions, known as precedent, rules of law developed.

This process of following precedent evolved into a doctrine called *stare decisis* (pronounced, star-ray duh-sigh-sis). Stare decisis is a Latin term meaning to stand by that which was decided. In operation, stare decisis demands that a court in a particular jurisdiction (we'll explain jurisdiction a little later on) must follow a legal rule passed down from a higher court in its jurisdiction if the court faces an identical legal problem. For example, if a dispute is brought to trial in Alabama involving an individual who was hit by a train at a crossing, and in the past the Supreme Court of Alabama decided a case in which a person was hit at a train crossing, but it denied recovery to that person because she did not stop, look, and listen for a train before attempting to proceed across the tracks, then in the later case the trial court in Alabama must rule that the person who was hit at the train crossing cannot recover if that person did not stop, look, and listen for a train before attempting to proceed.

Stare decisis is important because it adds stability to the law, yet it is also flexible. Although the doctrine generally demands that a former decision be followed, it can be ov... other words the *precedent* can be abandoned and a n... law established—if there is a good reason to do so.

In the past, following precedent through stare decisis was ... most of American law was created. America is still considered ... common-law country. Nevertheless, civil law is playing an ever increasing role in our legal system.

Civil law

Civil law is what most people think of as law. It consists of things like constitutions, statutes created by the legislature, rules and regulations created by government agencies, treaties signed by the president, and ordinances created by local governments.

LAW FACT

The term *civil law* can also refer to the law that does not deal with criminal law; for example, the sort of law that is applied when you slip and fall in a grocery store. This is not the kind of civil law we're discussing here.

The civil law must be followed by the courts; it is binding on them, so long as it is constitutional and is not preempted by a higher level law.

For a law to be constitutional it cannot violate the rights of citizens and it must further one of the powers granted to the government by the constitution. The constitution, whether state or federal, is the highest law within the jurisdiction, and any law, common or civil, in violation of it is unenforceable.

A law's constitutionality, however, is not the only concern; to be valid it must not be preempted. *Preemption* takes place when state legislatures pass laws that are inconsistent with federal law or that are in areas of concern in which the federal government does not want them to act.

LAW FACT

The federal government's power of preemption is based in the *Supremacy Clause*, found in Article VI, Section 2, of the U.S. Constitution.

For example, suppose the U.S. Congress passed a law declaring a 55 mile-per-hour speed limit on all interstate highways. Now suppose a state government attempted to set the speed limit at

40 miles-per-hour on the interstate highway that passes through the state. The state legislature would be preempted from doing so, and the state statute would be invalid.

Helpful Hint

t would be a mistake to think that because of preemption there can't be valid federal, state, and local laws all in the same area. For example, the Securities Act of 1933 and the Securities Exchange Act of 1934 are federal laws that govern the issue and trade of corporate securities, such as stocks and bonds, but state laws —called blue sky laws— also validly regulate corporate securities. This means that even if you've found a federal statue that is relevant to the outcome of your case, you can't be entirely sure that your research is done until you've checked state and local law too.

Jurisdiction

Where there is a federal system of government in which states and the national government share power, it's absolutely necessary to have a mechanism that helps to decide which courts will have the power to act in a particular circumstance. Otherwise, a person instigating a suit could bring it in more than one court, the courts could reach different conclusions on the same issue, and there would be no settlement of the problem, which is the whole reason to go to court in the first place.

In the United States this confusion is avoided through the exercise of *jurisdiction.* Jurisdiction limits the power of a court over people, subjects, and territories. Deciding which court has jurisdiction to hear a case is extremely important because a decision handed down by a court without jurisdiction is unenforceable. If you bring a case in the wrong jurisdiction, then all the time and money (precious to both you and the court) you use to pursue the case is wasted.

Helpful Hint

You may know more about one type of jurisdiction —territorial jurisdiction— than you are aware. You've probably heard the term used on television cop shows or courtroom dramas, where the prosecutor complains that someone has escaped and is outside the jurisdiction. What they are really saying is that the person is physically outside the territory in which the court has the power to enforce its punishment.

FEDERAL COURTS

Although many people think that the federal courts have their hands in just about everything nowadays, their jurisdiction is primarily limited to cases that involve conflicts over violations of the U.S. Constitution or the laws created by the U.S. Congress; cases in which the United States is involved in the suit as plaintiff, prosecutor, or defendant; and cases in which there is a conflict between two states, or a state and a citizen of another state, or citizens of two different states.

LAW FACT

The jurisdiction of federal courts is created and limited by Article III, Section 2 of the U.S. Constitution.

The federal courts' power is also defined by its level and the territory over which it presides. At present, there are thirteen federal circuits and three principal levels of courts.

Each circuit is divided into territories called districts where district courts preside over trials. If either party in a case feels that it has received an unfavorable decision, it may, in limited circumstances, attempt to *appeal* the case to the court of appeals for the circuit in which the district court is found. Finally, if one or both of the parties is still unsatisfied, they may, again under limited circumstances, attempt to have the decision reviewed by the highest court in the land, the U.S. Supreme Court, which can hear appeals of cases brought in any of the circuits.

For instance, if someone violated a federal law, say a law against mail fraud, from his office in Harrisburg, Pennsylvania, the case could be brought to trial against the defrauder in the Third Circuit District Court for the Middle District of Pennsylvania. An appeal of the decision reached by the district court could be taken to the Third Circuit Court of Appeals, and if this decision was disputed, then it could end up being argued before the U.S. Supreme Court.

LAW FACT

This is just a basic, not a complete, explanation of the federal court structure. There are many other specialized federal courts such as the U.S. Court of International Trade, Bankruptcy and Tax courts, and Military courts.

LAW FACT

A person does not have an absolute right to appeal a case to the Supreme Court. The Supreme Court generally gets to choose which cases it hears by granting or refusing certiorari (pronounced, sir-shore-are-ray).

UNITED STATES COURTS OF APPEALS

First Circuit: Maine, Massachusetts, New Hampshire, Puerto Rico, Rhode Island

Second Circuit: Connecticut, New York, Vermont

Third Circuit: Delaware, New Jersey, Pennsylvania, Virgin Islands

Fourth Circuit: Maryland, North Carolina, South Carolina, Virginia, West Virginia

Fifth Circuit: Louisiana, Mississippi, Texas

Sixth Circuit: Kentucky, Michigan, Ohio, Tennessee

Seventh Circuit: Illinois, Indiana, Wisconsin

Eighth Circuit: Arkansas, Iowa, Minnesota, Missouri, Nebraska, North Dakota, South Dakota

Ninth Circuit: Alaska, Arizona, California, Hawaii, Idaho, Montana, Nevada, Oregon, Washington

Tenth Circuit: Colorado, Kansas, New Mexico, Oklahoma, Utah, Wyoming

Eleventh Circuit: Alabama, Florida, Georgia

District of Columbia Circuit: District of Columbia

Federal Circuit: Based in District of Columbia, but hears cases from all regions.

STATE COURTS

State courts have jurisdiction within the borders of their particular states and have an appeals process similar to that of the federal court system.

In the state system, cases are first heard by judges (and sometimes juries) in the trial courts, the decisions of the trial courts can then be appealed to intermediate appellate courts, and final appeals can be taken to the "court of last resort," usually called the state supreme court.

Helpful Hint

Just because the person that you wish to sue isn't located within the borders of the state doesn't mean that your court of choice can't acquire jurisdiction over her. State courts can sometimes invoke *long arm statutes* to reach outside of their borders and get jurisdiction over out-of-state defendants.

LAW FACT

Not all of the highest courts in the states are called the Supreme Court. For example, in New York the highest court is called the Court of Appeals and the trial court is called the Supreme Court.

One major distinction between state courts and federal courts is that state courts are courts of general jurisdiction. This means that they can hear almost any type of case, not merely the cases that federal courts are limited to hearing. This is not to say that questions of jurisdiction don't matter when you attempt to bring suit in state court. Jurisdiction is always something to be concerned about, so you will want to check practice references (see Chapter 10) to make sure that you are bringing your case in a court that has the power to hear it and render a valid judgment.

LAW FACT

This discussion of jurisdiction in terms of state and federal courts isn't meant to imply that jurisdiction is an "either or" proposition. It is possible for courts to have concurrent jurisdiction, which means that two different court systems, state and federal, can have jurisdiction over a case at the same time. Where there is concurrent jurisdiction, the plaintiff usually has the first say as to where a case will be brought.

Hierarchy of laws

You're probably thinking, "O.K., I know that courts only have power in their jurisdictions; I know that there are a number of courts, both state and federal, and that there is both civil and common law. But what law should I be looking for? Which law will win my case?" The answer will depend on the facts of your case, but there are some guiding principles that can help you to decide which law is strongest.

First, let's look at civil law, in this instance constitutions, statutes, regulations, and ordinances. Constitutions carry more legal clout than statutes, and statutes carry more clout than regulations. The reasons for this are simple. In principle, a constitution is the law from which all other laws are derived. If there is no constitutional provision saying that the legislature has the power to create a certain statute, then it cannot do so, plain and simple, and if it tries to do so, the statute will be invalid. Furthermore, regulations can only be issued by agencies if the statute that gives the agency the power to act says that it can do so. If the agency tries to overstep these bounds, then the regulation is invalid. For instance, if a statute says that an environmental agency can create a regulation to protect the numbers of fur seals killed and the agency then issues a regulation prohibiting the importation of live baby seals to aquariums, the courts will probably find this regulation to be invalid because it exceeds the agency's power to regulate the killing of seals rather than their importation.

Like regulations, ordinances are also on the hierarchy below statutes. The validity of ordinances, however, is controlled by the doctrine of preemption, which was mentioned in the discussion of civil law, pages 3–4 of this chapter. What this means is that a local government can only pass ordinances in areas of concern that the state legislature has not already occupied.

Now, how does all this fit together with the common law? Good question, because the common law and civil law are not entirely separate and distinct. The common law is supposed to be applied in basically two instances:

– where there is no statutory law on the subject, or
– where there is statutory law but it needs to be explained.

LAW FACT

Judges and lawyers sometimes call these gaps in the civil law interstices (gap was obviously too short a word), which literally means a tiny space, like a crack or crevice.

What this implies, as you may have guessed, is that civil law generally has more clout than common law. Because all statutory law needs to be explained (has a legislature ever passed a law that didn't need to be explained?), you can never entirely escape from the common law. Even if your case is the first one to invoke a particular statute or section of a statute—what is known in the legal world as a case of *first impression*—you will need to have a court interpret it. Your case then will become precedent and from then on stare decisis will operate, governing other cases dealing with the same issue. There's a kind of circularity to the whole thing.

The hierarchy of judicial opinions, from strongest to weakest in precedential value, goes from the court of last resort (the highest court) to the intermediate appellate courts to the trial courts to the administrative courts.

In combining civil and common law, the strongest case that you can find is a supreme court case agreeing with your interpretation of a constitutional provision, statute, or regulation. If you can't find this, then the next strongest authority is an appellate court that agrees with your interpretation of the law at issue. If this search fails, then you should try to find a trial court decision of the law at issue or an administrative interpretation of it.

Helpful Hint

Because constitutions, both state and federal, are the weightiest form of law, courts don't like to invoke them without good cause. Instead, they will decide issues that come before them by using some other law if they can and will generally invoke constitutions only when all other avenues of settling a dispute are closed. For example, a number of federal civil rights statutes have been passed by Congress, and even though a court could invoke the Fourteenth Amendment to guarantee civil rights in a particular case, it will not do so if it can base its decision on particular provisions of the civil rights statutes instead.

A final note on administrative law

Administrative law, the law created by government agencies, may be the first wave of law that you run into, and it is slightly different from other forms of law because the agency has the power to create both civil law (rules and regulations) and common law (decisions and orders). Like the law discussed in the preceding sections, the civil law itself holds greater weight than the decisions and orders, but the decisions and orders are

Helpful Hint

An administrative decision is given less weight than a state or federal court decision, but courts often defer to the interpretation of rules and regulations by the agency that created them because these agencies are considered experts in their field.

needed to act in the gaps left by the rules and regulations and to interpret them. Administrative decisions can be appealed to regular courts, usually once all attempts at remedying the situation have been exhausted with the agency.

LAW FACT:

According to the doctrine of *exhaustion of administrative remedies*, a person within the agency's jurisdiction has to go through all of the agency's channels, board reviews, administrative hearings, and the like before he or she can appeal an unfavorable decision by the agency to state or federal court.

With this brief legal background discussion in mind, let's move on to the next step: developing a legal research strategy.

CHAPTER HIGHLIGHTS

Classifications of American law

- Common law
  - Derived from English law
  - Created by judges writing opinions in cases
    - Rules of law developed over time when judges decided to follow opinions from previous cases.
    - Practice of following rules from previous cases evolved into a requirement to follow past precedent, embodied in the doctrine of stare decisis

- Civil law
  - Law created by legislative bodies
    - Consists of constitutions, statutes, treaties, regulations, rules, and ordinances
    - Civil law, if valid, must be followed by the courts
  - For a law to be valid it must be constitutional
  - For a law to be valid it must not be preempted by a law from a higher authority

How American law functions

- Jurisdiction
  - Doctrine used to reduce confusion between courts in the American system
    - Helps to decide which courts can act in particular circumstances
    - Limits the power of a court over people, subjects, and territories
  - Federal courts
    - Jurisdiction is limited primarily to cases involving the U.S. Constitution or laws created by the U.S. Congress; cases in which the United States is a party; and cases in which there is a conflict between two states, a state and a citizen of another state, or citizens of two different states
    - Jurisdiction of federal courts is also divided by territory and level of court
      1. Courts are divided into 13 federal circuits, each encompassing certain states and U.S. territories
      2. Courts are divided into three principal levels of courts: Supreme Court (the federal court of last resort), circuit courts of appeal, and district courts
  - State courts
    - State courts are courts of general jurisdiction, not limited like federal courts in the types of cases that they can hear
    - State courts have power, generally, within the borders of their states
    - State courts are generally divided into three principal levels of courts: court of last resort, intermediate appellate courts, and trial courts

- Hierarchy of laws
  - Constitutions have more authority than statutes, and statutes have more authority than regulations and ordinances
  - Generally, civil law carries more authority than common law
  - Common law is applied where there is no statutory law controlling the subject or where there is statutory law but it needs to be explained

- The opinions of the court of last resort are the most authoritative type of common law, followed by the opinions of intermediate appellate courts, followed by the opinions of trial courts, and finally the opinions of administrative courts

CHAPTER 2

GETTING FROM HERE TO THERE

All that is necessary for a student is access to a library and directions in what order the books are to be read.

— *Papers of Thomas Jefferson, 1790*

PRELIMINARY THOUGHTS

By now you have some idea of how the legal system is organized. Now it's time to learn how to navigate that system by learning how to do legal research.

These are the steps you'll be following:

- Find a law library open to the public.
- Summarize the problem and define the legal issue.
- Consult a legal encyclopedia.
- Read initial cases.
- Find more cases!
- Update cases.
- Investigate statutory law.
- Do computer research (optional).
- Organize your research and findings.
- Decide what to do with your research.

We'll discuss each step briefly before you plunge into your work.

Words of comfort

With so many legislatures passing laws and so many different courts interpreting those laws, researching a legal issue can be difficult, frustrating, and time-consuming, even for seasoned researchers. If you don't believe us, just take a moment to look around once you're in the law library. Sure, there are plenty of people who look completely at ease, even sleepy. But look closer and you'll see the harried expressions of many others. You're in good company.

This chapter should relieve some of your anxiety—it will give you a good idea of where you're headed and how you'll get there.

> **Helpful Hint**
>
> If you don't understand something now, don't sweat it. Later chapters will go into greater detail and tell you what you need to know to research your particular issue.

For now, we'll look at the big picture and leave out the details. Meanwhile, relax and read on to get familiar with some of the soon-to-be well-traveled legal turf.

To help explain each step in the research process, we're going to include examples of other beginners, like you, who are embroiled in their own legal research problems. As we take them through the process of researching their topics, you'll get a clearer idea of how to tackle your own topic.

Where do I go to do research?

Unless you have a fully equipped collection of legal encyclopedias and case reporters in your home, you'll have to find a law library in order to do your research. Even legal research on the computer can't replace a trip to the law library (at this point in the evolution of on-line research).

Perhaps the easiest way to find a law library is to ask the librarian at your city or county library where the closest one is. Another way to find a law library is simply to look in the government pages of your phone book and track down your county law library. If you live in a county that has one, call and find out when the general public has access. (Some county law libraries allow access to nonlawyers only during specified hours.)

Alternatively, if there is a law school nearby, call the librarian there and see if the law school will allow you to use its library. A local bar association or a courthouse (if you happen to live in a city where one of these is located) may also have a law library that you can use.

Keep looking until you find one. You might have to make a few phone calls, but eventually you'll find a library which you can use. In fact, you can consider this your first lesson in learning about legal research: Persistence pays off.

Once I've located a law library . . .

Don't be shy about using it! You have just as much right to use these facilities as any lawyer does, at least during the hours you're allowed access. Still, those first hesitant steps toward the library, where you mistakenly pull the push door or push the pull door, are probably the most intimidating steps you'll take in the course of your research.

Another possible monster of a problem might be asking the law librarian for help. Given that you've already gotten this far, and perhaps feel a small measure of confidence in having done so, why not slay that dragon now, metaphorically speaking, by politely requesting some help from the librarian?

You can either ask the librarian for a map to the library, which explains where various volumes are found or ask for something you'll be using early on anyway: a legal encyclopedia. If you choose to ask for a legal encyclopedia, ask for either *American Jurisprudence 2d* (Am. Jur. to most librarians and lawyers) or *Corpus Jurus Secundum* (C.J.S).

Whichever alternative you pick, you'll find that your law librarian probably isn't a dragon and, if not actually willing to help you find every resource you may need for your research, is at least not interested in intimidating you. In fact, some librarians may even ask you what subject you're researching so that they may direct you to specific sources. Just tell him or her that you're at the beginning of your research and learning about the library at this point, but that you're sure you'll have questions for them later on. Don't worry, you will.

Relax and read

At this point you should be sitting snugly in a corner of the library, surrounded by lawyers efficiently skimming through impressive-looking volumes as if they've done this all their lives. Don't let this discourage you. After a few days of research, you will look exactly the same way (though the fancy suit is optional).

SUMMARY OF RESEARCH STEPS

Meanwhile, the following description of what you'll do in the course of your research should give you a rough idea of what's ahead.

STEP 1. SUMMARIZE THE PROBLEM AND DEFINE THE LEGAL ISSUE

Your first step can be made either in the library or in the privacy of your own home, even before you crack your first legal volume. Figure out in everyday language what it is you want to research. Try to reduce your problem to a concise statement. A one-sentence summary of the issue is best. While you'll want to forget the minor details at this point and focus on the big picture, you'll also need to include enough detail so that there is, in fact, an issue. Once you have a summary of the problem you're grappling with, you'll be ready to start applying the law to your facts.

This one-sentence summary is now ready to be categorized as a particular legal issue. Is it a landlord-tenant dispute? Are two business partners deadlocked in deciding the future course of their business? (You might decide the latter example is a partnership problem or a business relationship situation.) Is it a question of a deadbeat dad who doesn't pay child support or alimony? (Divorce and child support might be the legal terms to look up.) With some legal terms or legal keywords to describe your facts, you're ready for some background research.

Step 2. Consult an encyclopedia

Remember when you were in grade school and were assigned to write a report on England or Abraham Lincoln? Chances are, you immediately turned to an encyclopedia, which you no doubt used extensively in writing the report.

The encyclopedias may not look the same and the topics may be slightly different, but this step is just like the one you took in your grade school days.

You'll use your legal issue to find articles on your subject. These articles will give you a good overview of the law, and possibly some references to some cases you'll look at later. For now, you'll be familiarizing yourself with some of the terminology in your area and the different legal viewpoints on your issue.

Once you've read an entry (or several entries) in the encyclopedia, you may also find cross-references to other sources, which we'll discuss in fuller detail in Chapter 4.

> **Helpful Hint**
>
> Sometimes you might have a pretty obscure issue and then you'll have to look up quite a few topics before you find an article that discusses your situation. For instance, if you're wondering whether a court would find you liable to your neighbor after your pet snake bites your neighbor's pet ferret in your backyard, you might find yourself looking up "boa constrictor," "pets," "nuisances," "snakes," and "animal companions" before you discover the information you want listed under "wild animals."

Step 3. Read the cases

Now you're ready to study firsthand information, directly from the horse's mouth. This is the part where you read what the courts actually have to say about situations similar to your own. How did courts analyze the problem in the past? Are there any general trends in the cases? What are the important policies behind their decisions?

LAW FACT

A court's decision is called a holding. Sometimes, a court will discuss hypothetical fact patterns and how it might decide a related issue that's not involved in the case before it. In a variation on that theme, a court may also digress to a deliberation of how the issue might be affected by a different fact pattern. Law students and beginning researchers may have some trouble separating a court's holding from its discussion. Remember to focus on the bottom line of the case—the court's holding or holdings—and ask yourself which part of the court's discussion was necessary to reach the holding. The discussion that isn't necessary to the court's holding is not binding on future courts.

As you read, you'll find that there are plenty of cases your research turned up that aren't really on point, or relevant. Don't worry. Put these aside and focus on those cases which seem analogous to your own facts. Often, a court will refer to other cases on the same subject that it decided previously. Sometimes, courts will refer you to cases decided in other jurisdictions. Any or all of these references can be valuable, and you'll find that just by reading a handful of cases, you have a much greater knowledge of how courts treat such problems. You also might discover helpful references to other cases.

This step can take the lion's share of your research time, so be prepared for a lot of case reading, especially while you are just getting familiar with how to read a case and learning the special terminology that might be applied to your issue.

STEP 4. FIND MORE CASES

We've already mentioned two ways you might find relevant cases:

- reading legal encyclopedias, which point you toward other cases decided with facts similar to your own, and
- being referred to other cases by the courts that decided those cases you've already read.

But there's also a third way you can find even more cases, which we'll discuss now:

- using West's key numbers.

Briefly, almost any case you find will contain West headnotes, organized under one or several topics and further organized by *key numbers*. *Headnotes* are located at the beginning of the cases and are short paragraphs summarizing the cases' legal points. Most often, the headnotes you find are prepared not by the courts but by the publisher of the case, and are preceded by a topic. Key numbers are simply West Publishing Company's way of further organizing these headnotes under certain subtopics. This system is designed so that cases won't be forever buried in a mountain of volumes and never heard from again. (What would happen to stare decisis if we couldn't find the cases that provide the precedents on which current law is based?) A sample West topic might be "Animals" (or "Constitutional Law" or "Negligence"), which would be further organized by key numbers. The topic "Animals" might be divided by key number into "1. Wild animals," "2. Dog bites," "3. Rabid animals," and so on. Don't worry, you'll learn more about it in Chapter 6. Meanwhile . . .

STEP 5. UPDATE YOUR CASES

Finally! You've found the perfect case—the one where someone just like you brought the same complaint against someone just like your adversary and won her case. It seemed impossible that you would ever find such a gold mine, but there it is—you've got a foolproof case, you think. But what happens when that case you're depending on to win is *reversed*, *quashed*, *overruled*, or otherwise annihilated? More importantly, how do you know that has happened?

LAW FACT

Reversal occurs when a higher court sets aside, annuls, vacates, or changes a lower court's (or administrative tribunal's) decision. A court can also quash a lower court's order or decision, which means to annul, overthrow, or vacate by judicial decision. When a case is overruled, its holding is overturned. A case can be overruled by a higher court or the same court that decided the overruled case originally. As you can imagine, in casual conversation, these terms are often used interchangeably.

You'll have to consult an updating service, the most widely available of which is *Shepard's Digests* and is found in all law libraries. When you look up a case in the Shepard's volumes, which are updated alarmingly frequently, you'll find exactly what's happened to the case since it was originally published. Sometimes a case will have been slightly modified, clarified, or followed by other courts (always a good thing!), but whatever the scenario, updating your cases is a must if you're to avoid the embarrassment of discovering that your elaborate legal theory is actually a fragile house of cards waiting to be knocked over by your opponent.

LAW FACT

A court can modify, clarify, or explain its prior holding in a subsequent case, which simply means that the court makes the prior holding clearer by applying the holding to the facts that it has at hand.

This can be one of the most frustrating aspects of legal research. Don't fret though, because Chapter 6 will demystify some of the intricacies of the updating process.

STEP 6. CONSULT CIVIL LAW

If you were wondering what happened to the civil law we mentioned earlier (remember that civil law, as we discussed in Chapter 1, refers to statutes, ordinances, and regulations), look no further. While it's possible to research statutory law earlier on in the research process, we've found that by waiting to investigate the statutes, you allow the courts, which have perhaps addressed your issue in the past, to decide whether a statute applies to your situation. While it might seem a simple matter to figure out whether or not a statute applies to you, in practice it can be difficult and the courts (rather than you) are often better equipped to deal with that question. This way, you don't end up in a wild goose chase at the beginning of your research trying to decide whether a particular statute does or does not pertain to your case. In most instances, if there's a statute that has an impact on your issue, you've almost certainly seen it mentioned in your case reading. You may have read about the statute in a legal encyclopedia, or one of the cases you may have read will have said something like "As the plaintiff points out, and the court agrees, the question of whether the plaintiff has a case against the defendant is clearly addressed by the Florida Statute."

If this happens, you'll have to hunt down the text of the relevant statute (we'll help you with that later) and read it to make sure the legislature hasn't done something annoying like repealing the statute or changing it so that it no longer applies to ferrets or snakes. You'll also read the statute to see if perhaps there isn't a section that is even more attuned to your fact situation, like, for example, a section on the liability of snake owners where the pet snake kills an animal on the owner's property.

Just like cases, relevant statutes can change or become invalid quickly and noiselessly. Looking at the latest version of the statute (as well as updating all your cases as explained in Chapter 6) should help keep you abreast of the latest developments in the law.

Of course, one way to read cases as they are handed down by the courts is by getting a hold of a computer, which Chapter 8 will explain.

STEP 7. PERFORM COMPUTER RESEARCH

The world of on-line research is, as of this writing, changing rapidly, and will probably continue to change often, leaving most nonlawyers (and many lawyers!) in the dark as to how to connect to the cases they need. The two most complete computer-research systems are the Westlaw system (brought to you by the same people who gave you West key numbers) and the LEXIS system (owned by Reed-Elsevier, an international publisher).

Both services will give you a fairly reliable list of cases on any topic you might be researching, albeit at a pretty steep price, especially for the one-time researcher. Prices for connect time are quite expensive, and you will probably spend at least 30 to 45 minutes on the system the first time you use it, even if you prepare a research query beforehand. Moreover, if you did the job right in your search for cases in the first six steps, you probably will receive only a marginal number of new cases by using either LEXIS or Westlaw.

The fastest-growing (and less expensive) areas of on-line research are those that are sponsored by university law schools, the federal court system, or various state supreme courts. We'll discuss these avenues of research in Chapter 8.

STEP 8. ORGANIZE YOUR RESEARCH AND FINDINGS

It may be hard to believe, but you're almost done. This is the point where you write yourself a legal memorandum, which begins by explaining your legal issue (or issues), and then proceeds to answer the question raised by the issue. What recourse, if any, does a recipient of social security benefits have when his benefits are terminated? Can he file a case in court or must he first bring his case before the Social Security Administration? Can he recover the money he had to pay when he was forced to move from his apartment because he was unable to pay the rent?

Your memo will answer these questions by referring back to those cases and statutes you've read and applying helpful precedents to your situation. For instance, if you discovered a case in which someone who owned an alligator had to pay a Chihuahua owner for the Chihuahua's death at the hands of the alligator, your memo might evaluate whether a boa constrictor is treated in the law the same way that an alligator is and if the alligator situation was otherwise analogous to yours.

This is the step where you'll have to bring your analytical powers to bear. Argue both sides of the issue unflinchingly, keeping in mind that an outlandish argument probably wouldn't be too persuasive in most courts. You might have to look back at some of your cases again and decide which ones are most pertinent.

Of course, if you can work out a dispute without going to court and simply wanted to know your legal rights or options so that you could negotiate with someone in an informed way, congratulations! You've finished your work and can pat yourself on the back for a job well done.

If you're going to go to court, mediation, or arbitration though, you are ready to complete the last, and perhaps most nerve-racking, step.

Helpful Hint

Don't ignore relevant cases that fail to support your own legal theory of the facts. Courts certainly won't do that, and this is one time when ignorance certainly isn't bliss. If there's a case that seems to decimate your position, then read the case again carefully. Be prepared to accept that your argument may be too tenuous to be convincing. Also ask yourself if a case has facts that may be analogous to yours. Before you give up, remember that even if a case you found while researching seems on point with yours, you could possibly make an argument (if it's an argument made in good faith) that a prior case (as you will have realized by now!) should either be reversed or is distinguishable from yours. Who knows? Maybe your case is one that will satisfy the court that an outdated precedent should be abandoned.

Step 9. Decide What's Next

At this point, you are familiar with the law on your subject and any cases pertinent to the issue. If you are going to appear before a judge, a mediator, or an administrative tribunal, you should have the substantive information you need to make your case, if you performed your research well (kind of makes you want to repeat all the above steps, doesn't it?). If you decide to represent yourself and not hire a lawyer (also known as appearing *pro se*), you'll need a practice guide, some of which focus specifically on laypeople. In Chapter 10, we'll point you in the direction of the appropriate resources that address the nuts and bolts of presenting your own case in court. Just how do you file a complaint or defend a suit, anyway? And is there any prescribed way to do it?

Luckily, there are companies that publish everything from the form used in your state to file complaints to real-life examples of how lawyers prove their points in their cases. Plus, there are resources that tell you what sort of peculiar rules your particular court may have, like a rule setting forth deadlines for submitting various legal papers to the court (called filing) after you've already filed your complaint. And then there are a bevy of other edifying books that talk about trial procedure as well.

A word before we begin

Even if Step One is already becoming hazy in your mind, you now have an overview of the work that is just ahead. Although the task of researching your issue might seem monumental now, we can assure you that your efforts offer their own built-in rewards when you find yourself on the right track, cruising through the library and finding relevant cases. Plus, researching your own issue gives you the satisfaction of knowing that you are competent to look up and study the law without necessarily having to call a lawyer and ask for help.

But we should caution you that this book is not intended to teach you how to practice law. Nor can it turn you into an attorney. In most states, you need three years of law school to accomplish that. Moreover, this book is not a substitute for legal advice from an attorney, and if you find that your questions aren't getting answered by your research, that may be the time to hire a lawyer.

But, if you want to know what the law says firsthand, and wish to research a legal problem for yourself, this book is intended for you. That said, let's turn to the next step: summarizing your problem and defining the issue in legal terms.

CHAPTER HIGHLIGHTS

Locate a law library using one of the following methods

- Ask a librarian at your local public library where the closest law library is
- Look in your phone book for a county or city law library
- Call a nearby law school to see about obtaining access there
- Call a local bar association or courthouse to find out whether they have law libraries open to the public

Summary of research steps

- Start by summarizing the problem and defining the legal issue
- Consult a legal encyclopedia for background information regarding the issue
- Read the cases you find mentioned in the legal encyclopedia
- Find more cases using West's digests
- Check to see whether your cases are still valid in light of possible later changes in the law
- Find applicable statutory law, ordinances, or regulations
- Research using a computer (an optional step)
- Organize your research and findings; and
- Assess your case and decide whether to pursue it or not

Advantages of performing your own legal research

- Acquire a firsthand understanding of what the law says
- Know that you performed a thorough and exhaustive search of the law
- Develop the confidence to research other legal questions in the future
- Approach the legal system with the confidence that comes from understanding an area of the law

CHAPTER 3

DECIDING WHAT THE ISSUE IS

Training is everything. The peach was once a bitter almond; cauliflower is nothing but cabbage with a college education.
—*Mark Twain, Pudd'nhead Wilson, 1894*

TRANSFORMING A PROBLEM INTO A LEGAL ISSUE

For your dispute or problem to become a full-fledged legal issue, it must be transformed into one by rephrasing your problem using the correct legal terminology. To do this, you'll first have to narrow your problem down to its essentials. Then, you'll fit it into a legal category, which will help you to think up legal terms to use for your index searching (see Chapter 4). This chapter will help you to classify your dispute, problem, or question into a legal category (or, if your problem is more complicated, into several legal categories). By learning how legal matters are categorized, you'll feel more oriented within the legal world. And with a map of the terrain, you'll be able to chart a provisional path to your destination. Your destination, still just a flicker on the horizon, is to understand the legal implications of your problem. Keep in mind that no strategy is foolproof. Even the most well-planned trips can hold unexpected false starts and pitfalls, so just be prepared to rethink your strategy if you discover that you're heading to a deadend.

To this point we've only discussed what research entails, but now we've arrived at the planning stages for the trip ahead (the jumping-off place is just around the corner in Chapter 4). To help you plan this trip, we're going to give you a list of legal categories, like landlord-tenant law, environmental law, and so on, and you'll have to decide under which categories your legal problem fits. Just because you find one category that seems suitable, don't stop searching the list. We can't emphasize enough how important it is that you survey the entire legal terrain. If you narrow your research options down to one path before looking at every category, you may needlessly take a more arduous path than necessary to get to your destination. So read all the categories before choosing one, and check off all those that seem to be matched to your facts.

SUMMARIZING YOUR PROBLEM

To classify your problem into a category, you have to first figure out what the problem is. Ask yourself what you want to research and then try to reduce your problem to a concise question, phrased in everyday language. While you'll want to forget the minor details at this point and focus on the big picture, you'll also need to include enough detail so that there is, in fact, a problem to be solved.

To illustrate how to summarize your facts, we'll introduce you to Kristin. Kristin lived on the first floor of a house with her boa constrictor, Max. Dave rented the upstairs apartment from Kristin and lived there with his ferret, Devil. Although Dave's lease didn't allow him to use the yard, Kristin and Dave were on good terms, so several months ago she informally offered him the use of the yard so that he could take Devil outside to run and hop in the sun. One day, while Dave and Devil were outside, Max slipped out of the house, slithered over to Devil, and swallowed the ferret whole. Kristin ran out to the yard when she heard Dave, yelling and chasing the snake with a rake. The next week, Dave confronted Kristin and threatened to sue her (though not specifying what his grounds were) if she did not buy him a new ferret and reimburse him for the therapy that he had promptly begun to help him get over his traumatic loss. Kristin, bewildered and scared, is considering paying for the ferret and the $100/hour therapy, but she first wants to find out whether Dave has a case against her.

Now, using this example, let's summarize Kristin's dilemma so that we can address her problem.

Include enough details in your summary

The trick to creating a useful summary is to include enough details to make it interesting. For instance, Kristin's legal question might be too broad if she frames it like this: Can someone sue me when my pet kills his? This is too broad because the question is not specific enough to get a meaningful response. On whose property were the pets when one was killed? Was the attack provoked?

A question like this is more helpful: Can my tenant sue me for the cost of his ferret and therapy, where the tenant witnesses my boa constrictor killing his ferret in my yard, if the tenant's lease does not allow him to use the yard, though I gave him permission to be there?

Although inelegant, this question is admirable for including most of the details of the case. Keep in mind, however, that even though you are able to phrase your facts in one sentence, this doesn't always mean that you'll find your particular situation indexed and extensively discussed in any legal encyclopedia or other resource. After all, there aren't any "landlord-tenant and animals" topics in any legal encyclopedia.

Tricks of the trade

One good rule of thumb is to imagine you're asking your lawyer friend to run to the law library and get some background information for you (always a time-saving device, by the way). If this were the case, you'd want to be specific enough in explaining the particular scenario so that he or she would have a rough picture of what happened and what sort of issues might be involved.

Another useful rule of thumb is to label all the characters who are involved in your fact pattern. For example, instead of referring to the character as Dave and Kristin, call them tenant and landlord. Similarly, instead of writing about Joe, Susan, Jeff, and Margaret, call them mortgagor, construction contractor, doctor, and driver. When you use a person's title, position, or role, sometimes the conflict in the situation becomes easier to understand.

Phrasing your problem isn't a precise science. There will no doubt be a number of ways to describe the situation, some of which use fewer details and others which use more; but omissions of minor facts in your phrasing shouldn't make the difference between a bungled investigation and good research. For instance, a less detailed version of the matter would be this: Does my tenant have a case against me for his ferret's death, where my boa constrictor kills the ferret on my property, and I have given the tenant permission for it to be on my property?

There will often be more than one problem to be researched in your statement of the question, but at least you will have a manageable problem to get you started.

CIVIL LAW OR CRIMINAL LAW?

The legal world is split into two major categories: civil law and criminal law. By civil, we mean noncriminal law (how's that for circular reasoning?), such as tort law or divorce law or labor law. In Chapter 1, we discussed civil law in its primary meaning, that is, as a legal system based on code law. We then contrasted civil law with common law, the model followed by 49 states in the United States (Louisiana remains a renegade). But the civil law we're discussing here is civil law in the noncriminal sense. Roughly speaking, civil law applies to all legal matters that don't involve criminal fines, criminal penalties, or imprisonment.

At this point, you should try to decide whether your facts involve a criminal or a civil issue. Ask yourself whether you or anyone else involved could be in trouble with the law because of some deliberate harm you've done, such as drunk driving, stealing, cheating on a tax return, or hitting or hurting someone.

Helpful Hint

Some legal issues have criminal as well as civil aspects. For instance, a father who kidnaps his son in order to keep his ex-wife from getting custody of the child is subject to criminal penalties as well as a potential civil suit, if his wife chooses to bring such an action. Likewise, someone who punches another at a bar may be subject to two suits as well: first, a civil suit, by the person who was punched and perhaps had to undergo surgery after the incident, and second, a criminal suit, brought by the state. And don't forget O. J. Simpson, who first was tried in criminal court for murder and then had to defend himself in a civil suit for the same act. If you fall into a category that you think might involve both criminal and civil suits, read both Criminal Law, Briefly Explained, which categorizes criminal law issues, and Civil Law Explored, which discusses civil law issues, so you can be sure to explore every aspect of your issue.

CRIMINAL LAW, BRIEFLY EXPLAINED

Crimes have traditionally been divided into two types: *felonies* and *misdemeanors*. Some states are starting to abandon this distinction and instead classify crimes in terms of degrees. Note that those states that retain the felony/misdemeanor distinction may nevertheless employ the degree system within the felony and misdemeanor classifications. Whatever classification system your state uses, it's important to have at least a fleeting acquaintance with the meaning of a felony and misdemeanor, because the terms are tossed around so much in the research material and by the courts.

A misdemeanor is a class of criminal offenses that are less serious than felonies and which are subject to less severe penalties than felonies. Many states no longer employ the distinction between misdemeanor and felony. An example of a misdemeanor is the crime of breach of the peace.

Felonies are penalized more severely by the law and include more serious crimes. Although all felonies were originally punishable by death, not all states use the death penalty anymore, and even in the states that do, only a few crimes are punishable by death. Felonies include crimes like murder, rape, arson, and kidnapping.

Although crimes can be classified into other theoretical categories as well, we're not going to focus on these categories here for one simple reason: Such classifications won't help with your research.

Instead, a commonsense approach to criminal law, which draws upon the knowledge you've probably accumulated just from watching television shows like *Perry Mason*, *L. A. Law*, and any number of other series, will probably serve you best here. (And you thought that information would never come in handy!) What follows is a list of crimes (and definitions where necessary) that might be related to the question you want to research. Check off any topic that seems appropriate and underline any other terms in the descriptions of the crime that seem related to your question; you'll use the terms as keywords when you start researching.

Crimes

- **Abortion** (Premature termination of a pregnancy; although a protected right, abortion can in some instances be a criminal act. Other keywords include birth control and contraception.)
- **Adultery**
- **Aiding and abetting another in committing a crime** (Actively or knowingly assisting another in the commission or attempted commission of a crime. Mere words may be enough to constitute this crime, but presence at the scene of a crime, alone, is not enough; you can be guilty of aiding and abetting another to commit, or to attempt to commit, a crime.)
- **Aiding or allowing escape**
- **Assault and battery** (Intentionally or recklessly injuring or touching another or causing one to fear imminent injury; for other keywords, try aggravated assault, aggravated battery, mugging and attack; see mayhem below.)

- **Attempt to commit crime** (An overt act, beyond mere preparation, moving directly toward the actual commission of a crime; for most crimes, if you can commit the crime, you can attempt to commit it as well, which in itself can be a crime. There has to be some act that the defendant made in attempting the crime; mere thought is not sufficient.)
- **Bigamy** (Being married to two people at once.)
- **Breach of peace** (Conduct that unreasonably threatens the public peace; keywords under this category might include loitering, prowling, disorderly intoxication, cross burning, and disorderly conduct.)
- **Bribery** (Voluntary giving of something to influence the performance of an official duty.)
- **Burglary** (Unlawfully entering a building with the intent to commit a crime within.)
- **Conspiracy** (A combination of two or more persons to commit an unlawful act; murder, rape, arson, and practically any other crime can be the subject of a conspiracy.)
- **Criminal fraud** (For instance, using false pretenses and impersonation to obtain or gain access to property; obtaining a mortgage through false representations; engaging in insurance-related fraud; making false claims of having an academic degree; the keywords false pretenses and false impersonation or false personation may be helpful here.)
- **Criminal mischief, nuisance, and trespass**
- **Defamation** (Libel and slander; the publication of anything injurious to the good name and reputation of another; printed defamation is called libel and spoken defamation slander; use libel and slander as additional keywords.)
- **Embezzlement** (The fraudulent appropriation of property already in one's possession to one's own use.)
- **Extortion** (The taking of property by threatening someone with some future harm; try also the keyword blackmail.)
- **False imprisonment** (The unlawful confinement of a person or unlawful knowing restraint which interferes substantially with a person's liberty; another keyword is false arrest.)
- **Forgery and counterfeiting** (The fraudulent making or altering of a writing, with the intent to prejudice the rights of another; for another keyword, try uttering forged instruments.)

- **Gambling** (Paying some amount in the hope of winning a prize.)
- **Homicide** (Any unlawful taking of life; this crime is divided into four types.)
  - **Felony-murder** (When one who is committing a felony kills another.)
  - **Manslaughter** (Manslaughter can be voluntary or involuntary and generally does not involve the kind of cold-bloodedness usually associated with murder.)
  - **Murder** (Unlawful killing with a premeditated intent to kill; even if the killer forms the intent to kill seconds before doing so, the killing can still be found to be premeditated.)
  - **Vehicular homicide** (This is a fourth classification of homicide and is not used in all states; some states classify this crime as manslaughter.)
- **Incest** (For other keywords, use also statutory rape, rape, molestation, child molestation, and child abuse.)
- **Income tax evasion**
- **Kidnapping** (Unlawfully confining and either moving or secreting another; as another keyword try abduction.)
- **Larceny** (The taking of another's property unlawfully with the intent to deprive the owner of its use; see the topic theft.)
- **Lewd and lascivious conduct** (Another keyword is obscenity.)
- **Mayhem** (A battery where the attacker permanently maims or disables the victim; try aggravated assault, aggravated battery, and assault and battery as other keywords.)
- **Obstructing justice** (Impeding or obstructing of those who seek justice in a court, or those who have duties or powers of administering justice therein; justice is obstructed where a person tries to influence a jury, a witness, or a judge; this crime involves interfering with the judicial process.)
- **Perjury** (Making a false statement while under oath.)
- **Possession of narcotics and other controlled substances**
- **Prostitution**

- **Racketeering** (An organized conspiracy to commit extortion; definition has broadened as state and federal governments have vigorously begun to prosecute those involved in organized crime; as a keyword, try RICO [Racketeer Influenced and Corrupt Organization Act].)
- **Rape** (Unlawful sexual intercourse with a female without her consent; certain sex crimes do not require intercourse. Other keywords include sexual offense, sexual battery, statutory rape, rape shield statute, rape trauma syndrome, sodomy, and marital rape.)
- **Receiving stolen property** (Receipt of stolen property, knowing that it has been stolen; in some jurisdictions, the recipient must also have had wrongful intent in accepting the property. Another keyword is fence.)
- **Riots and unlawful assemblies** (A meeting with intent to carry out a plan that would result in a riot, intent to commit a crime by open force, or intent to execute a plan that would cause others to apprehend a breach of the peace.)
- **Robbery** (The unlawful taking of property from another in his or her presence by using force or putting the person in fear.)
- **Solicitation** (Requesting another to commit a crime; consent of the second person is not required for the request to constitute a crime.)
- **Stalking** (Many states now have antistalking laws designed to target those people who harass or annoy others. Keywords include antistalking laws, restraining orders, temporary restraining orders, battered women, domestic violence, and battered woman syndrome.)
- **Subversive activities** (Another keyword is treason.)
- **Theft** (The taking of property unlawfully; a general term used to describe larceny, embezzlement, burglary, robbery, receiving stolen property, and extortion. See any of the above terms in this list.)
- **Weapons offenses** (Includes illegal possession of weapons, possession by felon, or by one engaged in a felony or under indictment, illegal carrying of a concealed weapon, alteration or removal of firearm serial number, and leaving a loaded firearm within a minor's reach or easy access; other keywords include assault weapons and concealed weapons.)

- **Wiretapping** (Acquisition of the contents of any wire or oral communication through the use of any electronic, mechanical, or other device; other keywords include surveillance, eavesdropping, and electronic eavesdropping.)

Defenses to crimes

- **Abandonment of criminal intent or criminal activity** (Also called renunciation; this defense can be used as such only when someone is charged with attempting to commit a crime, and then voluntarily abandons the purpose; try also the keyword renunciation.)
- **Alibi** (A provable account of one's whereabouts at the time a crime was committed such that it would have been impossible or impracticable for the person to commit the crime.)
- **Coercion and duress** (When one person compels another to commit a crime through mental pressure or physical force. The force used or threatened must be sufficient to overcome the will of the other.)
- **Collateral estoppel** (A doctrine that recognizes that facts which were decided at a previous trial cannot be decided differently at any future trial; for example, if someone is charged with robbing six people at a poker game and is found not guilty in the first trial involving only one of the supposed victims because the jury finds that she wasn't even at the game, the state is estopped from retrying her alibi with respect to the five other victims.)
- **Consent of victim** (Informed consent by a victim to what would otherwise be a crime; while consent of the victim is a good defense for some crimes, for others, it falls flat. For example, someone charged with statutory rape cannot effectively claim consent of the victim; because the essence of statutory rape is having sexual relations with someone who is underage, the underage person's consent has no effect on the fact that a crime was committed.)
- **Defense of others** (The use of force to defend others from imminent danger of bodily harm; see also the topic self-defense.)
- **Defense of property** (The use of nondeadly force to prevent another from entering on one's property or taking one's personal property.)

- **Double jeopardy** (This defense is used when the defendant has already been tried for the same crime in a criminal trial.)
- **Entrapment** (The use of governmental trickery or persuasion to induce a defendant to commit a crime; for example, entrapment occurs where an undercover police officer induces someone to commit a crime.)
- **Guilt of another person**
- **Ignorance or mistake of the law** (Warning: as long as the law is clear and unambiguous, this is no defense.)
- **Immunity from prosecution** (Agreement by a prosecutor not to prosecute the defendant, usually in exchange for information which leads to the prosecution of others.)
- **Impossibility** (Defense that states that even if the perpetrator committed an act, it could not possibly constitute a crime; for example, one cannot be guilty of receiving stolen property if the property was never stolen in the first place.)
- **Intoxication** (Drunkenness or inebriation which may be a defense to a crime; but when a crime requires that the defendant have specific intent when committing it, intoxication can serve as a defense.)
- **Mental condition or capacity** (A mental state which shows a lack of criminal responsibility; for instance, one may be too young to be capable of forming the mental intent necessary to constitute an offense, or one may be suffering from insanity such that one isn't capable of forming the intent to commit a crime; other keywords include insanity and infancy.)
- **Necessity** (The compulsion to commit a criminal act because of the circumstances; for example, a person sets fire to a building in order to prevent the spread of a raging fire into a community.)
- **Recantation** (Withdrawal or repudiation, usually of a confession; in most cases, this defense is applicable only to the crimes of perjury and obstructing justice.)
- **Res judicata** (Doctrine very similar to collateral estoppel and is often grouped together with it; it states that a final judgment by a court of competent jurisdiction is conclusive upon the parties in any subsequent trial involving the same action.)
- **Selective prosecution** (The singling out of certain defendants for prosecution of a particular crime; also known as discriminatory enforcement.)

- **Self-defense** (Defense of oneself against the unlawful use of force.)
- **Statute of limitations** (A statute declaring that no criminal charge may be made unless brought within a specified time period after the right of action occurred. Although for certain felonies there is no statute of limitations, for most, the law prescribes a certain time period after a crime is committed in which a person can be prosecuted for that crime.)

Of course, besides the crimes themselves and defenses to crimes, there are other issues that arise in the criminal law area. Juries may have been improperly chosen (on the basis of race for example), the police could have executed an illegal search and seizure, or an arrest might have been made without probable cause. In addition to any of the above topics that you jotted down, add any of the following terms that seem connected to your topic. Your list of terms are the keywords which you'll use to search the encyclopedia indexes.

Related terms

- **Actus rea** (The act necessary for the completion of a crime)
- **Arrest**
- **Constitutional law** (See this topic under "Civil Law Explored," below.
- **Civil rights** (See this topic under "Civil Law Explored," below.
- **Cruel and unusual punishment**
- **Drugs and narcotics**
- **Habitual offenders** (Also called career criminals)
- **Mens rea** (The mental state necessary for the commission of a particular crime)
- **Miranda rights** (The police must read you your rights when they arrest you, and a failure to do so could invalidate a conviction.)
- **Remedies** (In criminal cases, if a prisoner feels that he has been wrongfully convicted and placed in jail, he may request the court to issue a writ of *habeas corpus* [pronounced hay-be-us core-pus] to the state demanding that the state set him free. Other keywords include punishment, sentence, mandatory sentence, habeas corpus, writ of habeas corpus, mandamus, writ of mandamus, and writ of error.)

- **Search and seizure** (The police aren't allowed to search a house, car, or you without first having some reason to believe that you have committed a crime.)
- **Sentence and punishment**
- **Youthful offenders** (Specific laws may apply to very young offenders.)

If after reading this list of terms you still can't decide whether you have a criminal or civil issue, read on. First, don't be fooled into thinking the matter is a criminal one just because a fine is involved. Not all fines or penalties are criminal in nature. For instance, you might be fined for illegal parking, but this is not defined as a crime in most states. Many aspects of our public lives are regulated by ordinances and statutes, but the violation of these laws and regulations will often only lead to the imposition of an administrative fine or some other penalty, but not a criminal penalty. As a bizarre example of a civil penalty, a fine may be exacted from a funeral director for the director's refusal to follow state procedures for embalming bodies, but the violation of these procedures may only call for an administrative fine, not a criminal one. Remember that the size of a penalty has nothing to do with whether it is an administrative or criminal penalty; it's the statute itself that will tell you whether the fine constitutes a criminal or a civil penalty.

If all this confuses you and you're still not sure whether you're dealing with a criminal or civil issue, don't worry. Any problem with classification at this point may mean that you're looking at an issue that involves both civil and criminal matters. A little research will clarify things. If you're worried that you might be starting on the wrong path, take comfort in knowing that the worst that can happen is that you will get back onto the right research path later rather than sooner. Your resources will eventually reveal the criminal or civil character of the issue you're addressing.

In the meantime, keep reading to find out whether your facts contain civil law elements.

CIVIL LAW EXPLORED

The civil law area is so broad that we'll have to discuss a mass of categories in order to cover this area adequately. Check off those categories that seem appropriate so that you can include them in your list of keywords. For each category, we'll also include ideas for other keywords that you should underline for later use when you start consulting the indexes of your legal resources. Don't hesitate to write in your own keywords if you can think of other ones that describe your topic.

LAW FACT

Almost every legal resource—collections of statutes, legal encyclopedias (often called jurisprudences), case reporters, form books, trial aids, *American Law Reports*, legal periodicals—can be accessed through indexes. Although in one sense this is good news for the layperson (after all, who doesn't know how to use a cookbook index or a textbook index?), these indexes provide their own source of confusion. Instead of every legal resource using the same terms for the same concepts, they will often perplex and bewilder the most seasoned researcher by seemingly hiding a topic in their indexes. For instance, in some encyclopedia indexes alimony issues might appear under the heading alimony, while in other encyclopedias, the same topic is listed under divorce or support. More frustrating still, even within the same publishing company, most of the volumes published do not have a standardized legal index. This means that even when you are using volumes that the publisher designed for you to use together, the legal indexes for those volumes are still inconsistent. This is why it's so important to have many keywords in mind when searching the indexes. Even if one fails, there's always another (and another, and another . . .) you can try.

Although you may think that there is a distressing amount of information just ahead, take comfort in the fact that somewhere in this morass lies the category you need. So let's get started!

– **Administrative law**

Administrative law is an area that affects many other legal matters. For instance, zoning matters are first contested at the administrative level, as are workers' compensation cases and, often, discrimination cases. At this point, however, unless your issue directly concerns an administrative tribunal, a decision by an administrative law judge, or the process of bringing a case before an administrative tribunal, don't linger too long on this topic. This is because, if your facts will require you to file a case before an administrative tribunal, you'll find out soon enough as you sift through your research matters without ever having to consult a volume on administrative law. Keywords are administrative law and exhaustion of remedies.

– **Adoption**

Adoption issues can generally be found under that very term in the indexes. However, consider other keywords like constitutional law (for example, can homosexuals or single people adopt a child and if not, why not?)

– **Bankruptcy**

There are different types of bankruptcy a person (or organization) can declare, which have different repercussions. Under one type, the debtor is allowed to keep certain possessions, while under another the debtor must get rid of all assets. Whichever you are interested in, keywords to note are bankruptcy, insolvency, dissolution, receivers, and receivership.

– **Child support and custody**

Child support and custody problems are among the most frustrating legal problems. A refusal by one person to allow an ex-spouse to exercise visiting rights and failure by one spouse to make support payments or to make them within the appointed time are common areas for dispute among divorced people. Even if the relationship between ex-spouses is amicable, misunderstandings or ambiguities in a divorce decree can give rise to a lot of tension. For this topic, keywords include child support, child custody, custody, children, support of children, family law, divorce, separation, modification, and arrears.

– **Civil rights law**

Civil rights law includes such issues as affirmative action, discrimination on the basis of age, sex, race, nationality, ethnic origin, disability, marital status, and perhaps sexual orientation. Discrimination can occur in such areas as employment (see the "Employment and labor law" topic), government programs, housing, club memberships, and public accommodations. Affirmative action concerns on the part of governments have led to the enactment of legislation in many jurisdictions that aims to help minority and small businesses by informing them of bidding times and requirements for government projects and by distributing helpful information on running businesses and receiving financial grants. Keywords here include housing law, public accommodations, civil rights, minority businesses, private clubs, affirmative action, gender, race, racial matters, sexual discrimination, racial discrimination, ethnic discrimination, homosexuals, AIDS, AIDS-based discrimination, handicapped persons, disabled persons, the American with Disabilities Act, discrimination, and Title VII.

– **Computer issues**

In the past couple of years, computers have seemed to open up a Pandora's box of ethical, privacy, and community issues, not to mention legal issues. On the legal front, computers have precipitated controversy in areas ranging from constitutional free speech rights to criminal law, copyright law, and public access laws. Obviously, this is a burgeoning legal field, with new laws being enacted every day to regulate computer users and abusers. For keywords, see the topics "Constitutional law" and "Intellectual property law." Other keywords might include privacy, right to privacy, computers, software, and computer crimes.

– **Consumer protection law**

In the case where a consumer feels that he or she may have been taken advantage of, there is a large body of law designed to deal with fraudulent practices by manufacturers or vendors. Did you buy a new car that turned out to be a lemon? Were you promised one product, but then the seller gave you an inferior one? Have you not been given a refund that was promised to you? Keywords include Deceptive and Unfair Trade Practices Act, consumer protection, Consumer Product Safety Act, fraud, misrepresentation, breach of contract, and contract.

– **Constitutional law**

Constitutional law is an intricate legal area, with application to every area of the law. Constitutional law works on two levels: First, all areas of law contain statutes that can potentially be declared unconstitutional if they don't pass constitutional muster (that is, they violate some provision in the Constitution). Second, you can be treated unconstitutionally in the sense that the law, as applied to you, is unconstitutional. For instance, a zoning law that is otherwise constitutional might be struck down in whole or in part, because in your case, it has the effect of discriminating against a protected group, like African-Americans or women. Keywords include constitutional law, equal protection, due process, religion, freedom of speech, speech, organizations, associations, bill of rights, minorities, privacy, zoning, disabled persons, handicapped persons, poor persons, poverty, and standing. See also the topic "Civil rights law."

– **Contracts**

Contracts don't have to be written to be enforceable; even spoken agreements can be enforced in many circumstances. Contracts can be broken in situations ranging from hiring someone to do household repairs for you to selling a multimillion-dollar company or a house (see the topic "Property law," however, for a broken contract to sell a house). Whenever you sign an agreement for services or goods, the resulting contract can be broken. If you are a consumer who signed a contract with a company and the company broke the contract, you should look at the "Consumer law" topic; if you are a party to a landlord-tenant contract, see the "Landlord-tenant" topic. Keywords include contract, agreement, breach of contract, liquidated damages, oral contract, specific performance, offer, acceptance, consideration, impossibility of performance, statute of frauds, covenants, adhesion contracts, impairment of contract, and parol evidence.

– **Corporate, sole proprietor, and partnership law**

Disputes might center around business relationships, like partnerships or family corporations. Can one partner obligate the partnership to a contract with a third party even if the other members didn't agree to the contract too? How does one dissolve a partnership? Add members? Resign? In the case of a close corporation (you'll know if you're a shareholder whether your corporation is a close one or not), what happens when the directors are deadlocked? What rights do regular shareholders to a corporation have? For these types of dilemmas, keywords that could be helpful are partnership, corporation, sole proprietorship, business relationships, joint-stock companies, joint ventures, dissolution, shareholders, directors, stock, shares, and nonprofit corporations.

– **Divorce and related matters**

Do you want to get divorced or separated or draft a property settlement between you and your spouse? Does your ex-spouse refuse to pay alimony or consistently pay it late? Or do you want to modify the amount of alimony payable under your divorce settlement? Even if you're not married, you might be entitled to support payments (called palimony in lawyer slang) if you have lived with someone for a certain length of time. Keywords under this category include divorce and separation, property settlement, alimony, maintenance, spousal support, lump-sum alimony, family law, marriage, prenuptial agreements, arrears, and no-fault divorce. (See also the topic "Child Support and Custody" regarding support and arrangements for children of divorces or separated parents.)

– **Employment and labor law**

Employment status or relationships might be a concern. Were you demoted, laid off, fired, or unfairly disciplined? Was your job not held open for you after you took a leave of absence even though your employer promised to do so? Were you harassed at work, either verbally or physically? Were you fired for union activity? Employment difficulties can mean either that employment discrimination is lurking in your issue or that labor law problems are involved. If you are fired after filing a workers' compensation claim, that topic should be thoroughly checked instead. Unemployment compensation claims that are denied can also frustrate the unemployed person; this is a heavily regulated area, and the topic has its own heading in the encyclopedias. Keywords to consider include labor law, unemployment compensation, sexual harassment, employment discrimination, employment law, retaliation, layoffs, Workers Adjustment and Retraining Notification Act, collective bargaining, union, public employer, dress and grooming requirements, domestic employment, demotions, discharge from employment, closing of business, clerks and clerical employees, closed shop, leave of absence, Family and Medical Leave Act, insubordination, Labor Management Reporting and Disclosure Act, lockouts, longshore workers and stevedores, machinists, mechanics, maternity, nepotism, group insurance, overtime, minimum wage, pension and retirement, occupational safety and health, outside employment, and moonlighting.

– **Environmental law**

Environmental matters are regulated by a slew of state and federal laws designed both to protect our environment and sometimes to exploit the environment for limited purposes. The battles between business and environmental interests have been highlighted in the press lately, as both sides seek to gain control of, or influence over, public lands for their own reasons. Environmental law areas include regulations governing water and air pollution (look under the "Nuisance" topic as well), and laws governing endangered species and the disposal of toxic, nuclear, and other wastes. Keywords in this area include environmental law, pollution, standing, environmental regulations, air pollution, water pollution, pollution, waste disposal, nuclear waste, endangered species, Clean Air Act, eminent domain, strip mining, Comprehensive Environmental Response, Compensation, and Liability Act.

LAW FACT

Note that in this area, an important issue concerns *standing*, or the legal right of a person or group to sue someone else. To assert standing, you are required to show that you are somehow affected by a violation of the law, enough so that you have a personal stake in the outcome of a case. The concept of standing is especially important in the environmental law area because a private person or group may not be able to sue, say, a logging company that is expanding its operations or a factory that is building its facility in a protected wildlife area. Instead, the statutes might permit only the government to sue an alleged violator of the law. Still, private citizens and groups may be able to show that they are affected by the violation of environmental laws and may nevertheless be able to bring a suit. If not, the subtopic **nuisance** (found under the topic **Tort law**) sometimes provides a viable alternative to environmental suits based on environmental statutes.

– **Evidence**

After you finish researching your topic, you might find yourself wondering whether certain evidence you have would be admissible in court. Is a contract between you and the guy who broke the contract admissible in court? What about evidence concerning an oral contract between you and another? To make matters spicier, what if the other party to an oral contract is now dead—is the contract still admissible? And how convinced does a judge or jury have to be before you've proved your point? Then there is the general question of what sort of evidence is considered relevant and material and what evidence is not. Finally, who has the responsibility to prove a disputed matter—you or your opponent? Keywords: evidence, best evidence rule, materiality, relevance, proof, burden of proof, and standard of proof.

– **Infants and minors**

Like any class of people who are treated in a special manner by the law, children are subject to more regulation than most other members of society. School searches, juvenile courts, and child neglect laws are just a few of the special rules and institutions that have arisen with respect to children. Children are also subject to special rules when it comes to their negligent or intentional wrongs committed against others. Under the infants and minors topic are those situations in which children either have done something that has exposed them to legal action (carried drugs to school or hurt another child, accidentally or purposefully) or are being acted upon by the legal system in cases where their parents have neglected or abandoned them. (As to matters of child support and custody, see the topic "Child support and custody"). For keywords, consider the following: children, infants, minors, delinquent children, schools, private schools, public schools, divorce and separation, child custody, child support, juvenile delinquency, juvenile courts, and family court.

– **Insurance law**

Insurance issues may be of interest to you if your insurance claim has been denied and you believe it shouldn't have been, if you were inadequately paid for a claim, if your insurer disputes the time of coverage, or the type of coverage you have, and if there is a disagreement as to whether you had a preexisting condition or not. Keywords to underline are insurance, insurance law, insurers, preexisting conditions, and insurance claims.

– **Intellectual property law**

This area of law includes patent law, copyright law, trademark infringement issues, and trade secrets. If someone plagiarizes another's work without getting permission first, then the issue might be one of copyright infringement. Similarly, patented inventions and innovations or trade secrets can be "stolen," while trademarks can be copied or mimicked to such an extent that they have in effect been stolen. See the keywords patents, intellectual property, copyrights, trade secrets, and trademarks.

– **Landlord-tenant law**

Does the problem involve a landlord and tenant, involved in a dispute over rental property? (If the dispute concerns something totally unrelated to the rental issue, for example, a grill that the landlord borrowed from the tenant last summer and then lost, this is *not* a landlord-tenant issue). Any dispute between the two involving rent, repairs, an injury to the tenant on the property, security deposits, destroyed premises, broken leases, evictions, and the like will fit under this category. Even if the issue involves another party, like a guest of the tenant who is injured while visiting the tenant, consider this a landlord-tenant problem. Some keywords to remember under this topic are: landlords and tenants, and premises liability

– **Occupations and professions—regulations**

Certain professions require licenses or certifications in order to practice them. Special taxes or permits may be needed before one starts to work in these occupations. Physicians and lawyers, for example, need licenses in order to practice, as do undertakers and certain health workers in hospitals or nursing homes. Keywords include business professions, occupations, licenses, licensing, business franchise tax, undertakers, cemetery companies, building contractors, contractors, physicians, doctors, lawyers, attorneys, and nurses.

– **Poverty issues and the law of benefits**

People who are poor face all of the legal issues mentioned in the other categories as well as problems unique to the impoverished. Their problems range from trouble obtaining benefits which are wrongfully withheld to civil rights issues. Public housing conditions may also provide grounds for legal action. Keywords include poverty, poor persons, welfare, benefits, Medicaid, Medicare, social security benefits, Aid to Families with Dependent Children (AFDC), landlord-tenant, civil rights, discrimination, entitlements, public assistance, legal aid, and human rights.

– **Prisoner law**

Just as the poor face legal issues unique to their situation, so do prisoners. Prison conditions, parole, and probation can be administered unfairly or unconstitutionally. Even medical assistance and access to prison law libraries can be dispensed illegally. Keywords include prison law, prisoners, constitutional law, parole, and probation.

– **Procedural issues**

Civil procedure, which tells us how, when, and where to file a complaint in court, and then how the case will be conducted, is generally a matter of form, as opposed to the other substantive topics listed here. Because procedure can impact the substantive law, however, it is listed here. For instance, statutes of limitation (the laws that tell us how long we have to file certain cases in court) are procedural issues, but if you file a case one day too late, your case is probably lost before it even begins. In certain instances, the period of limitations is halted for reasons like the other party is hiding or you haven't figured out yet that you've been injured by someone. At any rate, procedure might be of interest to you if you are wondering if there's still time to file a complaint against someone, if you want to know in what court complaints like yours are filed, or if you're wondering whether you have to sue every possible defendant under the sun from the beginning of a case, or whether you can start by suing just one or two. Keywords here include terms like civil procedure, statutes of limitation, jurisdiction, venue, process, service of process, parties, joinder of parties, necessary parties, claim, counterclaim, ancillary claims, third-party defendants, interpleader, and impleader.

– **Property law**

Property law embraces everything from real estate dealings to adverse possession, landowners' liabilities, easements, and bailments. And, of course, real estate covers a whole host of topics all by itself, including mortgages, zoning (see the "Zoning and eminent domain" topic), deeds, adverse possession, quiet title actions, and land use regulations. Property law also involves personal property issues, such as bailments (suppose you give your property to another to keep and control for you and they lose or destroy it?). Keywords to look up are property law, personal property, real property, real estate law, landowners' liability, easements, bailments, municipal regulation, land use regulation, mortgage, foreclosure, zoning, construction permits, adverse possession, quiet title, quit claim deed, warranty deed, and deed.

– **Remedies**

If you're already pretty certain that you've caused someone to suffer harm or they've caused you to suffer harm, and you're interested in finding out what you (or they) would have to do or pay to rectify the situation, then your issue involves remedies. The most common remedy at law consists of *damages*. Damages simply refers to monetary compensation that the law awards to one who has been injured by the actions of another. In civil suits, wrongs are often compensated for with money, because, for example, it is impossible to have a company restore the use of a hand that was caught in one of its machines, or for the builder of a building to restore a loved one to life after a roof caved in. There are, however, types of relief other than money. Plaintiffs may ask for an *injunction*, an order from the court telling the opposing party to stop doing something or not to start doing something. Keywords include injunction, restraining order, temporary restraining order, permanent injunction, mandatory injunction, damages, actual damages, compensatory damages, consequential damages, special damages, exemplary damages, punitive damages, incidental damages, liquidated damages, specific performance, and nominal damages. (Before using all these words as keywords, look them up in a law dictionary to see whether you can rule out some keywords right off the bat.)

– **Tort law**

Have you injured (or been injured by) someone else, either mistakenly or intentionally? If the injury was job related, check off workers' compensation as well. If the injury occurred on rented premises, look at the landlord-tenant topic. If you are being plagued by a neighbor's nuisance (or you are plaguing your neighbor), see the "Nuisance" topic. And if an injury occurred because of the suspected malfunctioning of a product (like a car, ladder, lawnmower, child car seat), check "Products liability." Where one of the parties involved is insured, check "Insurance law." If you suspect that an injury was intentional, make a note to yourself to check "Criminal law" as well. The area of tort law is huge, as you no doubt realize. See other subheadings below to find a more manageable topic within the tort law area. Keywords include torts, negligence, premises liability, products liability, pain and suffering, mental distress, emotional distress, strict liability, and malpractice.

- **Legal and other professional malpractice**

Accountants, lawyers, and many other professionals are required to abide by certain rules of professional responsibility within their profession, but this in no way ensures that they always do so. Clients are frequently allowed to make complaints to the professional association to which the erring professional belongs. Besides the disciplinary action that the governing body of the profession (a state bar association, for example) may take, a client may also sue the professional in court to recover fees the client has paid, punitive damages, and other amounts. Keywords here are accountants, architects, attorneys, lawyers, professions, professional responsibility, occupations, business occupations, professional malpractice, and malpractice.

- **Libel and slander**

Perhaps one of the raciest areas of tort law (think of the number of lawsuits brought against tabloids for reporting scandalous and untrue information), libel and slander occur when someone makes a false and malicious statement for the purpose of harming someone else's reputation or business. Libel consists of a printed statement, while slander involves the spoken word. For keywords, see libel, slander, defamation, and first amendment.

- **Medical malpractice**

If a doctor misdiagnosed your condition, causing your medical state to worsen, or was careless in performing surgery or informing you of your medical options, you'll want to look carefully at the medical malpractice area of the law. Despite the many waivers and releases from liability that patients may be required to sign, a patient can sometimes make a good case if his or her doctor was grossly negligent. Keywords here are medical malpractice, physicians, physicians and surgeon, and discovery rule.

- **Nuisance**

Nuisance is an area of tort law that is complete in itself.

Nuisances can stem from air pollution, noise pollution, and eyesores. A new building that blocks out the view of others or a funeral parlor that spews air pollution at its neighbors are two examples of nuisances. On a smaller scale, neighbors can leave their garbage out for weeks without having it removed (in which case you might check out the "Zoning" topic as well), or they can run a kennel on the side, which causes smells and barking to pervade your home. For any of these problems, see the keywords nuisance, air pollution, noise pollution, pollution, air and light easements, zoning, and injunctions.

- **Products liability**

Have you been injured because of the unsafe condition (or negligent design or defective condition) of a product you were using? Even if a product was not defective, the fact that it does not include safety features or includes only inadequate features can be enough to impose liability on its manufacturer and the retailer from whom you bought the product. Besides the more obvious products like cars, space heaters, or chainsaws, these products can include pajamas (which aren't flame resistant) and almost any other product that can injure you. Keep in mind, though, many courts will demand that the user (that's you) use the product for the purpose for which it was intended in order to make a valid claim. More on that later. Meanwhile, keywords include products liability, and strict liability.

– **Tax law**

If you have a problem with your taxes, or your business taxes, this is a fairly easy issue to categorize. Your questions might range from what your rights are at a tax audit to penalties for tax evasion or misrepresentation (this introduces a slight overlap with criminal law, by the way). Additionally, you might wonder how to fight an unfavorable audit or how to appeal an adverse administrative decision. Keywords to note are taxation, tax law, state taxation, state tax law, federal taxation, federal tax law, taxpayers, and taxpayers' rights, local taxation, municipal taxation, administrative law, Internal Revenue Service, real estate taxation, and sales tax.

– **Unemployment compensation disputes**

Whether a worker has been fired for just cause or laid off can affect whether the worker can collect unemployment compensation benefits. Sometimes an employer will insist that a worker has been fired for good cause and that therefore the worker should not be able to collect benefits. When researching this area of law, remember that administrative law concepts play an important role in understanding the processing of a worker's claim, because a worker is usually required to make a complaint at the administrative level before he or she can appeal to the courts (the administrative law topic is listed above, but don't worry about researching that issue until it appears that you need to). Keywords include unemployment compensation, and benefits.

– **Wills and estates**

This topic will interest you if you are writing a will, inheriting property from someone who never wrote a will, receiving property under a will, or not receiving property under a will and think you have a right to do so. This area of law has attracted increasing attention from laypeople in the past 10 to 20 years, as more and more people tackle the task of writing their own wills or decide whether to avoid probate by putting their assets into living trusts. Happily, there are a wide collection of forms and step-by-step guides for writing a will and devising a strategy to avoid writing one. Better yet, you can probably even find forms specifically tailored to the laws of the state in which you live. If your interest concerns questions of tax, how your marriage affects the way in which you can distribute your assets, and your state's law regarding wills, see the keywords: estates, wills, estate planning, living trusts, and inter vivos trusts.

– **Workers' compensation law**

Workers' compensation is carefully regulated by laws and government agencies. This area is of interest to those who have been injured while doing job-related activities or someone who feels that he or she has been retaliated against (fired, demoted, passed over for a promotion) by an employer for bringing a workers' compensation claim. Keywords include workers' compensation, workmen's compensation, and retaliation.

– **Wrongful discharge**

Although wrongfully discharging someone from their job sounds like a topic that you would find under the "Employment and labor law" heading, this area of the law is properly considered a tort. An employee is wrongfully discharged when he or she is fired for impermissible reasons. Keywords are wrongful discharge, employment law, employees, retaliatory discharge, and hiring and firing.

– **Zoning and eminent domain**

Are you facing a zoning issue or the threat of eminent domain? If property located near your own property is about to be developed into a high rise or a paper factory, you might have grounds for a suit. The fact that your neighbors are breaking a zoning ordinance or running a business from their homes might also be grounds for a complaint. The government's right of eminent domain can be defined as the right to take private property for public use. Though a strong right, it is not totally unconditional. Property owners have a right to contest the state's right of eminent domain, or at least to contest the amount which the government is offering the owner. Keywords to note are zoning laws, eminent domain, condemnation, nuisance, and property law.

EXAMPLE: CHOOSING TOPICS

Let's check back in with Kristin, whose boa constrictor killed her tenant's ferret. Kristin has carefully considered the topics and decided that her issue doesn't involve criminal law. Instead, she determined that the topics most relevant to her own situation were "Landlord-tenant law" and "Tort law." Though she's not sure that her fact pattern truly involves a landlord-tenant issue, it's perfectly fine for her to explore the possibility that her status as a landlord might play a role in the legal issue.

BRAINSTORMING FOR KEYWORDS

Brainstorming is a great way to come up with more keywords to search. To brainstorm effectively, start by looking at the actors and actions involved in the case. Ask yourself the following questions:

1. Who are the people or entities (like corporations or departments of government) that are involved in the case you are thinking of bringing? Obviously, here you would be using more general terms like employer, landlord, tenant, worker, school board, student, counsel, inmate, prosecutor, and prison, not Bill Smith or Florida Board of Prisons. It's unlikely that the indexer has heard of your prosecutor, Bill Smith (no matter how infamous he is in your town), or has included the specific prison system where you are being

unfairly held (even if its past mistakes have made the national news).

2. What things or devices were involved that led to your problem? Make sure that the things you choose here are actually related to the problem. Your car may have been at the scene of an accident, but unless it was involved in the accident, it shouldn't be listed. Say you were driving your car when you saw a huge pothole on the other side of the road. You stopped your car and got out to check and see how deep it was so that you could report it to the state department of highways or some such organization, and you slipped and fell into the pothole and broke your leg. In this instance, your car was at the scene of the accident, but it was not involved in the accident, so you wouldn't use it as a keyword. On the other hand, if you were driving in your car and the car went into the pothole and was wrecked, then you should include *car* as one of the terms in your search.

Helpful Hint

It might also be a good idea to think of synonyms for the words that you chose, or if you can't think of any synonyms, look in a thesaurus. Most indexes, like most lawyers, tend to be a little formal. So, following our example in the text, you are more likely to find the term *automobile* or *vehicle* in the index than *car*, or if you do find *car* it will say something like "see automobile."

3. Why did the problem occur? This will probably encompass your issue. In Kristin's case, she might ask, "Why should I have to pay for Dave's therapy and a new ferret?" And she might answer, somewhat defensively, "Because I failed to warn him that my boa constrictor was also in the yard (after all, I didn't know he was there either!) and because a boa constrictor is a dangerous animal." Terms like *failure to warn* and *dangerous animal* are popular terms in indexes, and Kristin should jot them down.

Another matter that you may want to look into under the why category is why would the plaintiff possibly lose? In other words, how would you (if you were accused of the wrongful act or omission) or the opposing party put up a defense? For instance, a state agency in the pothole example may say that it cannot be sued because it's protected by *sovereign immunity*, a doctrine that declares, essentially, that you can't sue the state for its negligence.

In Kristin's case, Kristin might argue that Dave assumed the risk of danger befalling his ferret if the ferret played in her yard, because Dave knew she had a boa constrictor. Assumption of risk is an excellent keyword.

4. Where did the problem occur? This one can be important to both the substance and procedure of the case. For example, if a problem arises at work, then it could imply that *workers' compensation acts* (or *workmen's compensation acts*) might be involved and could control the outcome of the case. On the other hand, where a business has its offices may also affect questions of jurisdiction.

In Kristin's case, the alleged injustice took place on her premises. The fact that the accident occurred on Kristin's own property might affect her liability for Dave's costs, so she might add premises liability to her keywords, if it's not already on her list.

LAW FACT

In the past, workers' compensation acts were referred to as *workmen's compensation acts*, and sometimes they may still be referred to in this way. With a change in workplace demographics earlier in this century since the passage of many of these acts, most legislatures have changed the names of the acts to incorporate the gender-neutral term.

5. When did the problem occur? This question may not be all that helpful, unless you have a *statute of limitations* problem. A statute of limitations is just that, it is a statute created by the legislature which limits the span of time within which an action can be brought, usually beginning from the time the problem was, or should have been, discovered, and ending with the date one year, two years, three years later (or whatever) that the legislature has chosen. The logic behind this is that it would be unfair to hold a person, company, or agency perpetually responsible for past actions. In other words, if you have a gripe against someone then you should do something about it within a reasonable amount of time.

LAW FACT

Murder is one of the few exceptions to statutes of limitations. Generally, there is no time after which an individual is free from prosecution for murder.

6. How do you want to rectify the problem? This question deals with the question of damages in the case of civil suits, or punishment, in the case of criminal suits.

Kristin already knows how Dave wants to rectify the problem —by getting her to pay damages for his therapy and to buy him a new ferret. But can she legally be required to do so? Damages is an excellent keyword if you're wondering how much you can be made to pay for the costs someone else incurs after you harm him or her. It's also a good keyword for those who are wondering how much someone else can be made to pay for their expenses after they're harmed by him or her.

YOU'RE READY TO GO!

At this point, you've summarized and condensed your problem into something you can tackle and you have a few good keywords to start your search. At least one of your keywords will hopefully lead you toward the relevant headings in the encyclopedia index. Go back over the criminal and civil law sections and jot down all the checked and underlined keywords to compile a keyword list. Add any other keywords that you might have thought of during the brainstorming exercise. If you're worried that you might have a lot of useless words, worry no further: The worst that can happen is that your keywords aren't of any use; the best thing is that you open up a floodgate of information by finding one or more of them in an index.

Your list of keywords will come in handy throughout the rest of the book. Add keywords as you discover more about your topic, and use the improved list to further research form books, practice references (Chapter 10), loose-leaf services (Appendix 2), and other legal references you're interested in.

Congratulations! You've done some important legwork and now are ready to apply your ideas to finding some concrete legal information. Before you set off for the library, though, you may first want to read the next chapter at home and then set aside an entire day to hunt through indexes and encyclopedias at the library.

CHAPTER HIGHLIGHTS

Summarize the problem you want to research

- ➤ Reduce your problem to a question
  - – Include enough detail to be helpful in your research
  - – Leave out extraneous trivialities, which only cloud the important facts
  - – If in doubt about whether to include a particular detail, you should generally keep it in

Develop a list of keywords—those terms you'll use to search the indexes of the legal resources

- ➤ Use the list of criminal and civil law topics in this chapter
- ➤ Brainstorm your own list of additional keywords, using the particular facts present in your own case
  - – Who are the people or entities involved in my case?
  - – What things or devices were involved that led to my problem?
  - – Why did the problem occur?
  - – Where did the problem occur?
  - – When did the problem occur?
  - – How do I want to rectify the problem?

CHAPTER 4

LEARNING ABOUT YOUR TOPIC

Attempt the end, and never stand to doubt;
Nothing's so hard but search will find it out.
—*Robert Herrick, "Seek and Find" (1591-1674)*

PREPARING FOR THE PLUNGE

Armed with your summary and your keywords, you're ready to take your first steps exploring the encyclopedias. This exploration will start with an index search. Although an index search will eventually lead you to the information you need, this search can be a major headache. Be sure to have plenty of patience on hand, because you'll probably spend at least one day reading encyclopedia entries and indexes, following several different avenues of research, rereading encyclopedia entries, writing down case citations, hunting vainly through yet more indexes, and reading still other encyclopedia entries.

Even if you venture down a few paths of research that you later decide aren't really applicable to your situation, remember that none of this time spent is time wasted, because it can be just as important to discard certain topics as it is to find useful ones. We assure you that you'll find the information you need, as long as you persevere with your search.

EXAMPLE OF BACKGROUND RESEARCH: COLLECTING ALIMONY

Louise is supposed to receive alimony and child support from her ex-husband, John, every month. He was laid off from his job six months ago, however, and stopped making support payments five months ago. Because Louise felt sorry for him, she decided to let the payments slide while he was looking for a new job. Then, two weeks ago, she learned from a mutual friend that John had found another job three months earlier and is earning much more money than he earned at his first job. Louise is furious because he said nothing to her about his new job, and she is wondering whether it's too late to recoup the prior months' payments. In fact, while she's at it, she'd like to examine whether she could also get higher alimony and child support payments. Before she spends money hiring a lawyer, she'd like to find out under what circumstances other ex-spouses have managed to get back such skipped payments and what her chances are of getting the payments increased.

Louise has already categorized her issue under the headings "Divorce and related matters" and "Child support and custody" (see Chapter 3) and gathered these keywords: divorce, property settlement, alimony, spousal support, separation, lump-sum alimony, family law, marriage, prenuptial agreements, child support, child custody, custody, children, support, family law, and divorce and separation.

Her first step is to get rid of any keywords that are obviously unrelated to her situation. Louise knows she is not arguing over the property settlement in her divorce decree, nor is she arguing about a prenuptial agreement. She's not really certain what lump-sum alimony means, so she opts to keep that as a keyword and perhaps discard it later if it turns out to be unrelated to the matters at hand. Otherwise she keeps her list intact and is ready to start looking through the encyclopedias and other reference materials.

LOOKING IN AN ENCYCLOPEDIA

After you find out where the *American Jurisprudence 2d* (Am. Jur. 2d) or *Corpus Jurus Secundum* (C.J.S.) are located in the library (they should be situated fairly close to one another, because both are national encyclopedias), walk up to them jauntily and pick out a volume, any volume. If you glance around the library once you're back in your seat, you'll probably notice that no one is paying any attention to you (unless you tripped and fell during your journey). Breathe a sigh of relief. Even though you're new to this, don't worry about looking like a novice or appearing silly. After all, by definition, good research on any matter involves delving into unfamiliar sources and hunting around the library (and sometimes through the computer) to find information. What all this means is that researchers are frequently lost and look confused. After awhile, they (and you) stop looking confused, because they (and you) just *expect* to get lost in rows and rows of bookcases.

Anyway, with your book firmly in hand, flip through it and read a few sentences here and there. Assuming that you didn't pick up a federal taxation volume, you'll probably notice that many of the sections are pretty straightforward and easy to read. (By the way, don't assume that all legal encyclopedias are necessarily boring reading: For instance, they contain such politically incorrect articles as "Common Scold, and such ridiculously rubberneck titles as "Dead Bodies.") Although the footnotes to the texts will all look like gobbledygook to you right now, keep in mind that once you start to make sense of the case cites (which you'll do in Chapter 5) and can decipher the accompanying references to other resources, you'll have a wealth of information at hand. Meanwhile, the encyclopedia you're looking at right now should do much to allay your research-related anxieties. Most of it shouldn't be too difficult to read, and if you turn to the table of contents for any given article, you will see that each topic in your volume is logically divided into parts, which are further subdivided into subparts and finally organized into sections that should (we hope) be grouped rationally together.

Helpful Hint

How do you choose which set to use? Keep in mind that the C.J.S. volumes tend to include all cases that might possibly be relevant to the reader on any given topic, with the result that C.J.S. is heavily referenced and the footnotes often run much longer than the text. Am. Jur. 2d tends to be more condensed, its philosophy being to include only those cases which will be of interest to most lawyers. If you want to read a more detailed encyclopedia, go to C.J.S., but if you're satisfied with fewer footnotes and more generalized information, use Am. Jur. 2d.

If you want a little more of an introduction to the encyclopedias, pick out volume 24 of the Am. Jur. 2d set. This is the volume that contains the topic "Divorce and Separation" and, incidentally, the volume Louise needs to research her alimony and child support questions. Keep it on hand so that you can follow along with Louise as she researches her topic.

LAW FACT

In recent years, a movement had sprung up among lawyers and judges to use "plain English" in their briefs, memos, communications, and cases. This movement is a reaction to the legalese that peppered so many of the cases and sources in earlier days. Phrases like hereinabove mentioned and null, void, and of no effect (isn't one word enough?) as well as needless Latin phrases and excruciating writing that forced the reader to reread a paragraph five times to understand it are generally frowned upon nowadays. This is good news for us, because by using "plain English," judges and research writers are forced to focus their thoughts more clearly in order to explain complicated facts and legal concepts in a straightforward manner. Granted, the effort sometimes fails because certain complicated concepts by their very natures cannot be neatly encapsulated for the reader. Then too, when writers are building on case law which is sometimes hundreds of years old, they cannot always neatly sum up for today's audiences antiquated ambiguities from yesteryear, which were puzzling even when they were written. Centuries of labored and archaic legal language form the building blocks of the cases that in turn built the edifice of the common law: Some of these ancient ruins are just too intricate to convert into neat and tidy suburban American homes. At any rate, by reading just a few of these older cases (dating from the Middle Ages and hailing from Britain), you'll start to appreciate the plain English movement.

Another note: Sometimes ambiguous language is deliberately used by courts, even today. The courts will dance around an issue, hinting at what they might conclude under different circumstances ("it would appear, where the plaintiff asserts a right to inherit all of his mother's estate, he could undeniably do so if the mother's will which disinherited him had been clearly revoked rather than burnt in a house fire . . . ."). In this case, you might wonder what the court really concluded in the end. Don't worry. Sometimes judges don't want to commit themselves irrevocably to a decision; just remember that your confusion may actually be a question of interpretation—you're not necessarily being dense when you wonder what the court was getting at.

DECIPHERING AN ENCYCLOPEDIA INDEX

Article tables of contents and indexes

Some of the articles are spread out over two or more volumes (Criminal Law and Corporations, for example). In cases where an article is contained in more than one volume, the table of contents for the article will be listed in all volumes in which the article is found. For instance, if the Criminal Law article is found in two volumes, the complete table of contents will be listed at the beginning of the article as well as in the beginning of the volume that continues the article. If you want to use the article index (each article has its own index, by the way), you'll have to turn to the back of the volume to find it, not to the end of the article in the volume, which makes sense because most indexes appear at the backs of books. An article that is contained in more than one volume will have an index only in the back of the volume in which the article concludes. In other words, if the article "Automobiles and Highway Traffic" is contained in two volumes, the index will only be found in the second of the two volumes.

General indexes

Each encyclopedia also has an index for its entire set of volumes, called the general index. Am. Jur. 2d has a general index contained in five paperback volumes. C.J.S. has a set of general index volumes as well, divided into three paperbacks. It's best to start with these indexes because looking through each article's index for your keywords would be a staggeringly time-consuming process.

Do you have your list of keywords with you? If so, pull them out and trot over to the general indexes for whichever encyclopedia you're using. Pick out the appropriate indexes (you might need them all) and start searching for your keywords!

Finding your keywords in the index will doubtless be your first taste of the frustrations of research. If this part goes smoothly, consider yourself lucky. It's almost inevitable that you'll be cross-referenced to other headings and find yourself reading at least a few pages of small type below some of the headings. This is to be expected, so you might as well resign yourself to hunkering down and spending a lot of time at this stage.

Keep your pencil ready to write down the articles and sections that the index will direct you to. A lot of the encyclopedia articles the index will refer you to are abbreviated in order to save space—if you're looking for laws relating to the regulation of cemeteries by the state, for instance, the index might

Helpful Hint

The terms infra and supra are frequently used in indexes when cross-referring the reader to other headings. For instance, if you're looking under the heading "Children" in the index and beneath it, you read the entry "Education and schools, infra," the term infra means that you have to flip forward in the index to find the heading "education and schools." Similarly, if you read the entry, "Babies, supra," you'll know to flip back in the index to find the heading "babies." The truth is, because all the headings, subheadings, and subsubheadings are alphabetized, the words infra and supra are simply redundant, because by knowing your alphabet, you can quickly conclude whether a topic will appear later or earlier in the volume.

If you're looking under the heading "Children," and you find an entry that reads "Rash, diaper, see diaper rash, this heading," this simply means to stay within the "Children" heading and look under "diaper rash." Pretty simple, we know, but any confusion on these points could send you flipping fruitlessly through the index with no results to show for your work.

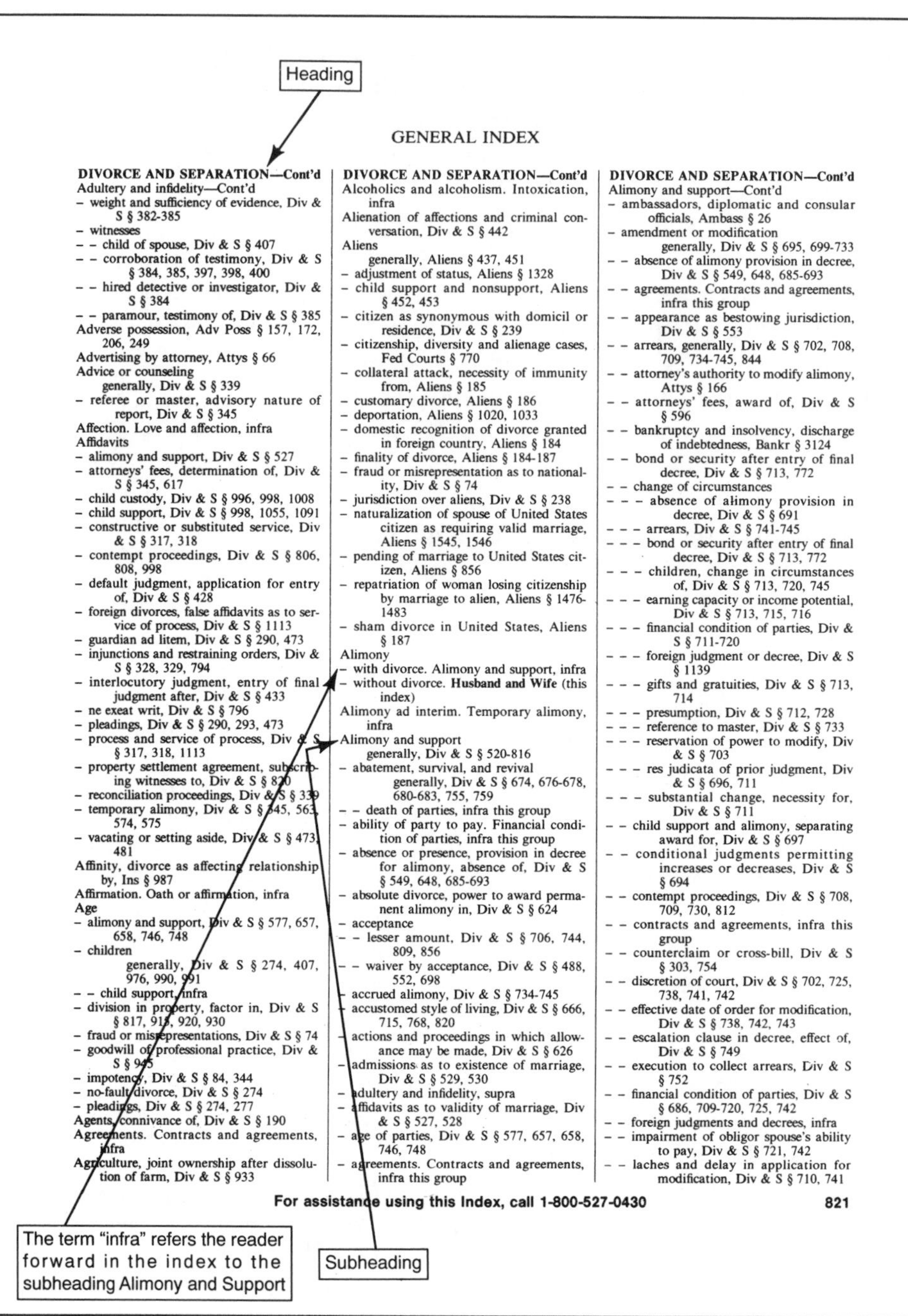

GENERAL INDEX

DIVORCE AND SEPARATION—Cont'd
Adultery and infidelity—Cont'd
- weight and sufficiency of evidence, Div & S § 382-385
- witnesses
- - child of spouse, Div & S § 407
- - corroboration of testimony, Div & S § 384, 385, 397, 398, 400
- - hired detective or investigator, Div & S § 384
- - paramour, testimony of, Div & S § 385
Adverse possession, Adv Poss § 157, 172, 206, 249
Advertising by attorney, Attys § 66
Advice or counseling
generally, Div & S § 339
- referee or master, advisory nature of report, Div & S § 345
Affection. Love and affection, infra
Affidavits
- alimony and support, Div & S § 527
- attorneys' fees, determination of, Div & S § 345, 617
- child custody, Div & S § 996, 998, 1008
- child support, Div & S § 998, 1055, 1091
- constructive or substituted service, Div & S § 317, 318
- contempt proceedings, Div & S § 806, 808, 998
- default judgment, application for entry of, Div & S § 428
- foreign divorces, false affidavits as to service of process, Div & S § 1113
- guardian ad litem, Div & S § 290, 473
- injunctions and restraining orders, Div & S § 328, 329, 794
- interlocutory judgment, entry of final judgment after, Div & S § 433
- ne exeat writ, Div & S § 796
- pleadings, Div & S § 290, 293, 473
- process and service of process, Div & S § 317, 318, 1113
- property settlement agreement, subscribing witnesses to, Div & S § 820
- reconciliation proceedings, Div & S § 339
- temporary alimony, Div & S § 545, 563, 574, 575
- vacating or setting aside, Div & S § 473, 481
Affinity, divorce as affecting relationship by, Ins § 987
Affirmation. Oath or affirmation, infra
Age
- alimony and support, Div & S § 577, 657, 658, 746, 748
- children
generally, Div & S § 274, 407, 976, 990, 991
- - child support, infra
- division in property, factor in, Div & S § 817, 918, 920, 930
- fraud or misrepresentations, Div & S § 74
- goodwill of professional practice, Div & S § 945
- impotency, Div & S § 84, 344
- no-fault divorce, Div & S § 274
- pleadings, Div & S § 274, 277
Agents, connivance of, Div & S § 190
Agreements. Contracts and agreements, infra
Agriculture, joint ownership after dissolution of farm, Div & S § 933

DIVORCE AND SEPARATION—Cont'd
Alcoholics and alcoholism. Intoxication, infra
Alienation of affections and criminal conversation, Div & S § 442
Aliens
generally, Aliens § 437, 451
- adjustment of status, Aliens § 1328
- child support and nonsupport, Aliens § 452, 453
- citizen as synonymous with domicil or residence, Div & S § 239
- citizenship, diversity and alienage cases, Fed Courts § 770
- collateral attack, necessity of immunity from, Aliens § 185
- customary divorce, Aliens § 186
- deportation, Aliens § 1020, 1033
- domestic recognition of divorce granted in foreign country, Aliens § 184
- finality of divorce, Aliens § 184-187
- fraud or misrepresentation as to nationality, Div & S § 74
- jurisdiction over aliens, Div & S § 238
- naturalization of spouse of United States citizen as requiring valid marriage, Aliens § 1545, 1546
- pending of marriage to United States citizen, Aliens § 856
- repatriation of woman losing citizenship by marriage to alien, Aliens § 1476-1483
- sham divorce in United States, Aliens § 187
Alimony
- with divorce. Alimony and support, infra
- without divorce. **Husband and Wife** (this index)
Alimony ad interim. Temporary alimony, infra
Alimony and support
generally, Div & S § 520-816
- abatement, survival, and revival
generally, Div & S § 674, 676-678, 680-683, 755, 759
- - death of parties, infra this group
- ability of party to pay. Financial condition of parties, infra this group
- absence or presence, provision in decree for alimony, absence of, Div & S § 549, 648, 685-693
- absolute divorce, power to award permanent alimony in, Div & S § 624
- acceptance
- - lesser amount, Div & S § 706, 744, 809, 856
- - waiver by acceptance, Div & S § 488, 552, 698
- accrued alimony, Div & S § 734-745
- accustomed style of living, Div & S § 666, 715, 768, 820
- actions and proceedings in which allowance may be made, Div & S § 626
- admissions as to existence of marriage, Div & S § 529, 530
- adultery and infidelity, supra
- affidavits as to validity of marriage, Div & S § 527, 528
- age of parties, Div & S § 577, 657, 658, 746, 748
- agreements. Contracts and agreements, infra this group

DIVORCE AND SEPARATION—Cont'd
Alimony and support—Cont'd
- ambassadors, diplomatic and consular officials, Ambass § 26
- amendment or modification
generally, Div & S § 695, 699-733
- - absence of alimony provision in decree, Div & S § 549, 648, 685-693
- - agreements. Contracts and agreements, infra this group
- - appearance as bestowing jurisdiction, Div & S § 553
- - arrears, generally, Div & S § 702, 708, 709, 734-745, 844
- - attorney's authority to modify alimony, Attys § 166
- - attorneys' fees, award of, Div & S § 596
- - bankruptcy and insolvency, discharge of indebtedness, Bankr § 3124
- - bond or security after entry of final decree, Div & S § 713, 772
- - change of circumstances
- - - absence of alimony provision in decree, Div & S § 691
- - - arrears, Div & S § 741-745
- - - bond or security after entry of final decree, Div & S § 713, 772
- - - children, change in circumstances of, Div & S § 713, 720, 745
- - - earning capacity or income potential, Div & S § 713, 715, 716
- - - financial condition of parties, Div & S § 711-720
- - - foreign judgment or decree, Div & S § 1139
- - - gifts and gratuities, Div & S § 713, 714
- - - presumption, Div & S § 712, 728
- - - reference to master, Div & S § 733
- - - reservation of power to modify, Div & S § 703
- - - res judicata of prior judgment, Div & S § 696, 711
- - - substantial change, necessity for, Div & S § 711
- - child support and alimony, separating award for, Div & S § 697
- - conditional judgments permitting increases or decreases, Div & S § 694
- - contempt proceedings, Div & S § 708, 709, 730, 812
- - contracts and agreements, infra this group
- - counterclaim or cross-bill, Div & S § 303, 754
- - discretion of court, Div & S § 702, 725, 738, 741, 742
- - effective date of order for modification, Div & S § 738, 742, 743
- - escalation clause in decree, effect of, Div & S § 749
- - execution to collect arrears, Div & S § 752
- - financial condition of parties, Div & S § 686, 709-720, 725, 742
- - foreign judgments and decrees, infra
- - impairment of obligor spouse's ability to pay, Div & S § 721, 742
- - laches and delay in application for modification, Div & S § 710, 741

For assistance using this Index, call 1-800-527-0430 821

Figure 1

refer you to "Cem § 5", which simply means you should look at section five of the article "Cemeteries." Each volume of the general index has a table of abbreviations near the beginning of the volume, which alphabetically lists the abbreviations and matches them to the full title of the article. Check this table if you're unsure of any abbreviation in the index.

FINE-TUNING A GENERAL INDEX SEARCH

Let's check back with Louise—she's gotten a hold of the indexes and is busy looking for her keywords (alimony, spousal support, separation, lump-sum alimony, divorce, family law, marriage, child support, child custody, custody, children, support, family law, divorce and separation, arrears). After a few false starts, she tries the keyword divorce in the general index. Success! She finds the heading "Divorce and Separation" in the Am. Jur. 2d General Index (C-E). Finding that the heading spans 61 pages (!), she decides to pinpoint her search even more, rather than read 61 pages of small print.

To do so, she focuses her topic by using her other keywords. First, she tries the keyword alimony, looking for the term as a subheading under the general "Divorce and Separation" heading. Success! She finds the subheading "Alimony and Support" under "Divorce and Separation," and starts to scan the entries below it. First, she writes down the article and section numbers listed under the entry, "generally," which is "Div & S §§ 520-816." By checking the table of abbreviations at the front of the volume, she learns that "Div & S" is the abbreviation used by Am. Jur. 2d to stand for "Divorce and Separation." Sometimes the abbreviations for the articles are not as obvious as this one, and in those cases, you'll be more appreciative of the table of abbreviations.

Louise decides that reading almost 300 sections of information about divorce and separation is too much. Using her keywords, she'll try to pinpoint her search even more. Staying within the "Alimony and Support" subheading, she tries a few keywords before finding "modification." Under the "modification" entry, she finds "—modification. Amendment or modification, supra this group." As we just discovered (see the helpful hint above, supra means that the heading "amendment or modification" will appear earlier in the text, but what does "this group" mean? It means that the "amendment or modification" heading is found within the same subheading, "Alimony and Support." Staying within the "Alimony and Support" subheading, Louise locates "amendment or modification." Finding the term, she finds that there are less than two columns of entries to read.

Louise now finds sub-subheadings like "change of circumstances," under which are such useful entries as "arrears" (found in the "Divorce and Separation" article, §§741-745), "earning capacity or income potential," and "financial condition of parties."

Louise then flips to the subheading "Child Support" under the "Divorce and Separation" heading, and finds about three pages of entries. She can either look through each entry (three pages isn't too much information to read) or try to further fine-tune her search using other keywords.

Of course, it isn't always possible to fine-tune a search, especially as a beginning researcher, because often you won't know what topics you're looking for in the first place. If you recognize that you're not really certain what kind of information you need, prepare yourself to slog through many pages in the index and to write down anything that seems related to your topic. In Louise's case, however, she has been successful in fine tuning her search—the sub-subheading "amendment or modification" appears under the "Child Support" subheading, and she is directed to the article "Divorce and Separation," §§1078–1091, a readable number of sections. Louise is on her way.

CONTINUING THE SEARCH

Just because you have one article and a few section numbers written down doesn't mean you're ready to abandon the indexes and delve into an encyclopedia. Save yourself the frustration of taking the indexes off the shelf, finding what seems to be a relevant reference, returning them to the shelf, searching for one section in an article, realizing it has nothing to do with your question, and then having to go to the indexes again, and so on. Instead, keep jotting down articles and section numbers until you have at least five different groups of references to check. As you'll soon see, a large number of your references will turn out to be distressingly irrelevant to your question. Guard against having to go back to the index-searching step later by sticking with the indexes now, even after you generate a list of a few articles to refer to. Spend several hours or more with the indexes if you need to.

> **Helpful Hint**
>
> Most, if not all, of the volumes you'll refer to while researching include an explanation of how to use the particular reference. Typically, this explanation is found in a section entitled something like "To the Reader," "How to Use this Book," "Foreword to the Edition," or some such title. This explanation is a quick way to learn about how to use the volume and can refresh your memory whenever you've forgotten how to search the book. Additionally, some of the volumes you'll use contain tables of abbreviations, which explain what otherwise undecipherable groupings of letters means (like Adj J or Affi). Remember to use this explanation feature if you ever find yourself holding a volume in your hands and wondering what to do with it next.

CHECKING THE ARTICLES

When you have collected a list of several references, it's the moment of truth—time to check which references hold your answers. Find a volume on your list of references and turn to the section number you jotted down. Read the entire section. Hopefully, it will be related to your legal question, even if tangentially. If you can see no connection whatsoever between the section and your research question (this sometimes happens), but the article in general seems to be related to your legal problem, turn to the table of contents at the beginning of the particular article. Scan the table and see if any of it is related to your legal question. If the outline contains any parts that seem like they could answer your question, turn to the more detailed table of contents and scan the sections listed under that part. Are there any sections that seem relevant to your question? If so, jot down the section numbers and then turn back to the body of the article to read them.

Back to Louise: She has managed to find several sections that address her questions. Open up 24 Am. Jur. 2d, "Divorce and Separation," and turn to §§712 and 713. Section 712 is entitled "Changes in financial circumstances" and section 713 is entitled "—Of obligor spouse." (A dash before the title of a section means that the section is a subhead of the preceding section.)

To get some perspective, you can trace the work she's done by turning to the table of contents for the "Divorce and Separation" articles, where you'll find that § 712 falls under

VII. Spousal Support; Maintenance or Alimony and Other Allowances
- G. Permanent Alimony
  - 9. Modification as to Future Payments
    - b. Circumstances Affecting Right to Modification
      - § 712 Changes in financial circumstances.

So this section discusses spousal support. But what about child support? By looking through the sections she has copied down during her index search, Louise eventually finds this section: § 1085, entitled "Financial resources of obligor." Reading through the table of contents for the article again, you can see that the section falls under

XI. Support of Children
  H. Modification and Variance of Child Support Award or Decree
    b. Particular Changes
      § 1085 Financial resources of obligor.

It's always a good idea to orient yourself using the table of contents for the article you're reading, because sometimes the headings under which the section is found provides important clues to what the section discusses.

CHECKING THE SUPPLEMENTS AND USING THE NEW TOPIC SERVICE

Make sure you check the supplements, found at the back of the volume in a separate bound section, for any new sections or cases that might have been added since the volume was originally published. Because some of these volumes were last published in the 1970s, you can imagine how useless and outdated they would be if the publisher didn't print supplements. Usually, the supplements are found in a pocket in the back cover, called pocket parts (grab a volume and you'll see what we mean). But if the main volume hasn't been updated in a long time and lots of cases have cropped up in a particular area of the law, the volume's supplement might be found as a stand-alone paperback. When there are more than a couple hundred supplement pages and the supplement can no longer fit in the pocket part, the publisher will put a card in the pocket telling you that the supplement has been published as a stand-alone paperback. If the supplement stands alone, it will typically say on its spine the volume that it supplements (for example, Volume 65 of Am. Jur. 2d). On the library shelf, the supplement should be located right next to its parent volume, but sometimes we've noticed that in the library where we do research the supplements get misshelved. So, if there is no supplement tucked into the back of your volume, just take a glance in the general

Section 1085, the first page of which is shown here, proves to contain relevant information addressing Louise's research questions.

§ 1085 DIVORCE AND SEPARATION 24 Am Jur 2d

§ 1085. Financial resources of obligor.

The change of conditions which is most frequently presented to the courts as a basis for modifying a judgment for child support is a change in the ability of the responsible parent to make the payments. A material or substantial increase in the parent's income may justify an increase in child support payments;[77] a substantial decrease in income, on the contrary, may justify or require a reduction in the amount of payments for child support by the responsible parent.[78] Obviously, there is great difficulty in determining how much of a financial change is required in order to establish that the change is material;[79] but an order will not be upheld where it appears to have resulted

391 So 2d 810, petition dismd (Fla) 397 So 2d 777.

A motion to decrease child support would be denied and an order for support would, in fact, be increased, where there was ample evidence of changed conditions with regard to the child's financial needs. Smith v Smith (**Mo** App) 558 SW2d 785.

77. Nelson v Roberts, 216 **Ga** 741, 119 SE2d 545; Dillon v Dillon, 318 **Mich** 686, 29 NW2d 126; Demrick v Demrick, 214 **Mich** 295, 183 NW 29; Flowers v Flowers (**Mo** App) 622 SW2d 414; Jones v Jones, 173 **Neb** 880, 115 NW2d 462.

Annotation: 89 ALR2d 30, § 9.

Where the father's income had risen in two years following the divorce and a minor child's physical condition had worsened and generated additional medical expenses during same period, the court improperly denied the wife the opportunity to show a significant change of circumstances justifying an increase in child support. Bayuk v Bayuk, 79 **Ill** App 3d 877, 35 Ill Dec 159, 398 NE2d 1109.

On a mother's motion to increase child support, the increase was properly granted where the child had begun college, and where the father's income had increased substantially, notwithstanding the fact that the separation agreement approved by the court provided for the termination of child support when the child reached 18 years of age. Re Marriage of Goodrich (**Mo** App) 622 SW2d 411.

The increase in a divorce husband's income from $13,000 annually to $24,000 annually was sufficient to support an order increasing his child support payments from $125 per month to $300 per month. Holt v Holt **Tex** Civ App 5th Dist) 620 SW2d 650.

Where a father and his second wife had no children and the father's salary was $2,400 per month, an increase of six percent since the prior support order, and where the first wife had divorced her second husband since the prior support order and thus lost his contribution to the children's support, a finding of material and substantial change of conditions justifying an increase of child support was supported by factually sufficient evidence. Craig v Jess (**Tex** Civ App 10th Dist) 620 SW2d 221.

In a former wife's action for increased child support, the increase was properly denied where the incomes of both former spouses had increased, and where the former husband had undertaken the support obligations of his second wife's two children. Smith v Smith, 98 **NM** 468, 649 P2d 1381.

In a former wife's action for increased child support, the increase was properly awarded since a personal injury damage award to the former husband constituted a change of circumstances that justified the increase. Sommer v Sommer (App) 108 **Wis** 2d 586, 323 NW2d 144.

78. Fowler v Fowler, 159 **Fla** 100, 31 So 2d 162; Gesmacher v Gesmacher, 247 **Iowa** 836, 76 NW2d 790; Paul v Paul, 217 **Iowa** 977, 252 NW 114; Cupit v Brooks, 223 **Miss** 887, 79 So 2d 478; Nelson v Nelson, 225 **Or** 257, 357 P2d 536, 89 ALR2d 1.

Annotation: 89 ALR2d 39, § 14.

A reduction in alimony and child support payments from $2,500 to $100 per month was warranted by the former husband's loss of income and assets, even though the reduction was severe, where the corporation of which he had been president had failed and was in bankruptcy proceedings, he was presently unemployed, he had no assets other than $1,500 in jewelry, had received no income for three weeks, and had liabilities of $997,443.53. Deaton v Deaton (**La** App) 393 So 2d 408.

A sufficient change in circumstances to warrant modification of a child support order was shown by evidence that there had been a decrease in the father's income and that the mother received additional income from her recently acquired employment. Conway v Dana, 456 **Pa** 536, 318 A2d 324.

79. Keyser v Keyser, 193 **Iowa** 16, 186 NW 438.

In a former husband's action seeking reductions in child support and alimony, alimony was properly reduced where the husband's income from his farming operation ceased while he attended law school and where his only income was from his disability check and his veteran's educational benefits, although a reduction in child support was properly denied where the husband's college education and training as a helicopter pilot showed his ability to earn at least some additional income. Sansom v Sansom (**Ala** App) 409 So 2d 430.

1072

Figure 2

area where the supplement should be and see if you can find a paperback supplement (because they look very different from the hardback volumes, you shouldn't have to hunt too hard).

Whichever form the supplement comes in, check inside to see whether your article has new sections or cases added to it. The articles and sections you found in the hardbound volume will appear in the same order in the supplement. If no new cases that would impact the sections have come out since the volume was published and no new relevant statutes have been enacted, your sections might not even be included in the supplement. If that's the case, good for you! Nothing extra to jot down. Probably, though, there'll be a least some new information in the supplement relating to your article, even if it doesn't correspond to the particular sections you've found useful so far.

Another facet of Am. Jur. 2d that might be important for your search, especially if you're searching a cutting-edge legal issue, is the New Topic Service. The New Topic Service is a volume that contains topics that have not yet been integrated into the regular set. For instance, the Americans with Disabilities Act was in the New Topic Service right after it was passed in Congress. When the relevant Am. Jur. 2d volume was updated, the Americans with Disabilities article was added to the volume and taken out of the New Topic Service.

DON'T GIVE UP

Meanwhile, for the sizable number of you who still haven't found any material in the encyclopedias that seems even remotely connected to your research question, don't worry. That's why you have an entire list of articles and sections that you can still tackle. Just hang in there and repeat the process of grabbing books off the shelf, hunting through the articles on your list, returning the volumes to their shelves, and looking through other volumes. If worse comes to worse, you can always return to the general index search and start anew (see pages 56–61, which explains how to search the indexes). Don't be discouraged by your inability to find relevant information in the early stages because it is certainly not

Helpful Hint

When angry, count four; when very angry, swear.
—Mark Twain, Pudd'nhead Wilson, 1894

Section 1085, of 24 Am Jur 2d, Divorce and Separation is updated in the supplement to volume 24.

In determining father's child support obligation under formula established in Wisconsin Administrative Code for determining child support obligation of shared-time payer, trial court erred when it reduced father's support obligation by 50 percent to reflect 50 percent of time children would be placed with father as trial court overlooked fact that 30 percent of time children would be with father was already accounted for in percentage basis in formula thus trial court reduced father's obligation more than necessary to achieve its stated purpose. Prosser v Cook (1994, App) 185 Wis 2d 745, 519 NW2d 649.

In child support action, trial court erred in terminating father's obligation on ground that 17-year-old daughter who was high school senior, had refused to visit father and hence had emancipated herself from father was error since denial of visitation rights by either custodial parent or child does not constitute change in circumstances justifying reduction or termination of non-custodial parent's support obligation. Broyles v Broyles (1985, Wyo) 711 P2d 1119.

Court erred in increasing father's child support obligation where increase was premised solely on conclusion that it cost more to raise children as they grew older, where mother's modification action was heard 13 months after divorce and custody plan were granted and 14 months after mother instituted action, and where during that period father held three jobs, was sometimes unemployed, and eventually found apparently stable employment earning $275 per month less than at time of divorce. Barto v Barto (1993, La App 2d Cir) 618 So 2d 613.

§ 1085. Financial resources of obligor

Practice References:

27 Am Jur POF 3d 540, Loss of income due to incarceration as affecting child support obligation

Consideration of obligated spouse's earnings from overtime or "second job" held in addition to regular full-time employment in fixing alimony or child support awards. 17 ALR5th 143.

Case Authorities:

Divorced father's motion to decrease or terminate his child support obligation was properly denied by trial court where, though father's income had been substantially reduced due to his unemployment, father had sought work only as union pipe fitter, and there was nothing in record to indicate that he was unable to do other kinds of work. Patterson v Gartman (1983, Ala App) 439 So 2d 171.

Trial court erred in increasing child support payments, where, although father's income increased approximately 27 percent since time of divorce, there was no showing that child's needs had changed substantially. Cox v Cox (1991, Ala App) 591 So 2d 90.

In post-divorce proceeding by noncustodial mother seeking suspension or substantial reduction in her child support obligation due to fact that she had quit her job and was attending law school, court erred in terminating mother's child support obligation where mother had voluntarily quit her job and had deliberately chosen to financially discontinue her responsibilities to her children because she preferred to choose new, nonessential path as student; under circumstances, mother's ability to earn, as opposed to actual income, was appropriate consideration, there was no evidence to show that she was without ability to pay support, mother never requested that her obligation be terminated but only that it be suspended or reduced; there was evidence of increased needs of children, father testified that he was having difficulty meeting needs, and even though mother's legal education may have possibly provided financial benefit for children in future, she should not have been totally relieved of her responsibility to contribute to daily ongoing needs of children. Johnson v Johnson (1991, Ala App) 597 So 2d 699, later proceeding (Ala App) 1992 Ala Civ App LEXIS 76, reh overr, supp op (Ala App) 1992 Ala Civ App LEXIS 77.

Trial court's order denying father's motion to suspend $1,000 per month child support obligation during six-year period father was to serve in prison, on ground that father could use property and other assets to satisfy child support obligation, would be vacated and remanded for further hearing and formal findings where record showed that father had $31,000 pension fund but did not establish whether pension fund was currently available as source of child support, and where father should not be liable for child support while incarcerated absent affirmative showing that he had income or assets to make such payments. Clemans v Collins (1984, Alaska) 679 P2d 1041.

In proceeding by father seeking to reduce his child support obligation, court did not err in refusing to reduce obligation despite fact that father had taken job paying $4.21 per hour after losing job paying $26 per hour, where change in income was temporary condition in that it was related to temporary suspension of his driver's license, where mother was unable to meet expenses of children and had already paid more than half of child-related costs, and where father was soon to receive cash distribution from his pension fund. Patch v Patch (1988, Alaska) 760 P2d 526.

Court did not err in granting mother's post-divorce petition for increase in father's child support obligation where, based on father's spending habits which included new car purchase and gift of diamond ring for his girlfriend, court found that father had estimated income of at least $25,000. Irvin v Irvin (1994) 47 Ark App 48, 883 SW2d 862.

In proceeding by former wife seeking increase in husband's alimony and child support obligations based on increase in his income subsequent to dissolution, court properly denied increase where record amply showed that parties knew at time of dissolution that husband's income would be increasing due to his plan to take tenth and final exam to attain accreditation as actuary, and where increase in income therefore had been

Figure 3

uncommon for us (we've worked with legal research for years now and attended law school for three years as well!) to be in the same boat you are in—abandoning the first few leads and returning to the indexes.

MAKING A REFERENCE LIST

Tackling the cases

Although we'll discuss case citations more fully in Chapter 5, we'll turn to them briefly here so that you get some rudimentary knowledge of what a case cite looks like. Briefly, you can recognize cases in the encyclopedia footnotes because they will usually contain two names separated by a "v." (*Marbury v. Madison; Johnson v. Pacific Bell; Taylor v. Fortensky*) and they will be followed by a string of numbers, dates, and incomprehensible (for now) abbreviations: 138 P.2d 428 (disagreed with *Joe v. Moe*, 138 So. 2d 22); 52 F. 3d 967; 16 F.R.D. 82; 128 LEXIS 528, aff'd 122 S.W.2d 58, and so on. Sometimes cases contain only one name, like *In re T.A.C.P.*, or *Matter of Baby Jane Doe*, or *In re Application of Johnson.* If you see any references resembling the above, these are also valid court decisions you should take note of. When you start copying these citations into your notebook, be sure that you copy down *all* the numbers, dates, and names that follow the case name.

Once you find a section in one of the encyclopedias that seems to be related to your legal question, you'll notice that it contains extensive footnotes to cases and other resources. Even if your questions have all been miraculously answered by reading the section, you still have to research these cases in further detail for two reasons:

- to make sure that, yes, the case in fact does say what the text purports it to say; and
- to find out whether the case itself can refer you to even more cases that either agree with the reasoning in the encyclopedia or refute it. (You will want to know all sides of your issue to understand the strength of your own argument).

Before you start jotting down tons of case cites though, you'll have to make a judgment call. If you live in New York and the section you're reading (look at the supplement to see if there are any other cases that have been added to your section, by the way) contains 15 references to New York law and 7 references to cases decided within the Second Circuit Court of Appeals (where New York is located), you probably shouldn't worry about copying down cites to the Hawaii or Florida cases that are also mentioned. But, if the section only contains 6 references to cases and only one refers to your state or circuit, then it's probably best to copy down all the references and read what other states and circuits are saying about your issue.

Helpful Hint

Turn back to the chart in Chapter 1 to find out in which circuit you live. Write down the circuit and keep it on had to remind yourself which circuit court's decision might be of interest to your research.

Reading cases from other jurisdictions has two major advantages:

- reading other courts' analyses will familiarize you with other courts' reasoning on an issue; and
- those other courts might refer you to additional cases in your own state or circuit.

Courts often turn to other jurisdictions when analyzing an issue, especially if there is not yet a lot of case law on a particular topic in their own jurisdictions. In these cases, an Arkansas court, for example, might write something like "The concept of comparative negligence has been adopted in 22 other states, including New York, where the *Fezzlewick* case provides the seminal reasoning on the issue." Then the court will provide a cite for the case, and, if you live in New York and are researching comparative negligence, you've been led straight to an apparently very important case in your jurisdiction!

Such is the importance of checking out cases from other jurisdictions, especially if your research contains few (or no) references to cases in your own state or circuit.

Tackling all the other resources

You probably noticed that the footnotes you've been looking at contain references to other resources besides cases. References to practice guides, forms books, and other mysterious-looking volumes (American Law Reports, Proof of Facts, and various journals, to name just a few) abound. What do you do with these references?

As a general rule, ignore form books, practice guides, and specialized texts at the beginning of your research. Although valuable resources, their value depends on a basic knowledge of the background legal material—something you don't yet have. The exception to the rule pertains to those people who are interested in the writing of wills or other standard agreements. For these people, looking at forms for wills and other such transaction forms is really the whole purpose of their research. In these cases, going immediately to the forms books and the more specific state forms volumes, which are referred to in the state encyclopedias (discussed below), makes sense. All the rest of us can decide whether to look at these references later. The same approach should be taken with practice guides (see Chapter 10 for a list of form volumes and practice references). What use is it to read about tips for proving medical malpractice when you're still wondering what the elements of a medical malpractice claim are in the first place?

Instead of writing down the cites for these references, it's far better just to make a note on your pad to look back at the section at some future date in case you find that you're still interested in such details as sample form and legal practice-oriented information. Remember, for the present, you're trying to develop an understanding of the big picture.

STATE ENCYCLOPEDIAS

Keep in mind that not every state has a state encyclopedia (sometimes called state jurisprudences). If your state has no encyclopedia, you'll have to depend on one of the national encyclopedias for most of your research references. Here is a partial list of state jurisprudences:

California Jurisprudence 3d ed. (Bancroft-Whitney)
Encyclopedia of Georgia Law (The Harrison Co.)
Illinois Law and Practice Encyclopedia (West)
Illinois Jurisprudence (Lawyers Coop)
Maryland Law Encyclopedia (West)
Michigan Civil Jurisprudence (Lawyers Coop)
Michigan Law and Practice Encyclopedia (West)
New York Jurisprudence 2d (Lawyers Coop)

Ohio Jurisprudence 3d (Lawyers Coop)
Pennsylvania Law Encyclopedia (West)
Strong's North Carolina Index 4th (Lawyers Coop)
Summary of Mississippi Law (Lawyers Coop)
Texas Jurisprudence (Lawyers Coop/Bancroft-Whitney)

Even if your state has no legal encyclopedia, consider reading further for additional research examples.

Because we've already looked through the national encyclopedias (Am. Jur. 2d or C.J.S.), this next step won't be too unfamiliar. You'll follow the same steps you followed in looking through the national encyclopedia, only now you will (hopefully!) find even more detailed and state-specific references on your topic.

Before we get started with the state encyclopedias, we want to warn you about a jurisdictional matter. Chapter 1 contains a basic discussion of jurisdiction. As we mentioned there, it's a difficult concept even for professionals and academics to put their fingers on—more than one lawyer has tripped up when it came to understanding jurisdictional matters and thus ended up losing a case.

For our purposes, if your legal issue indisputably arose in one state (in other words, you were hit by a car in Kentucky or you live in Kentucky and got divorced [or will get divorced] in Kentucky or you were fired in Kentucky or breached a contract in Kentucky or are a landlord or tenant in Kentucky), you can be pretty sure that Kentucky law will govern your case.

Some of you might even be researching the issue of jurisdiction in itself. For instance, suppose you want to get divorced, but you lived in Washington, Georgia, and Maryland during your marriage. In which state do you petition for a divorce? Or suppose you already were divorced in Georgia, but now live in Colorado and want to petition the court to modify your alimony payments. Do you have to petition a Georgia court, or can you go to a Colorado court instead? Or suppose a company in Utah sold you a defective computer and refuses to refund your money. You live in Iowa. Can you sue the company in Iowa? (And we're not even addressing the question of whether a federal or state court hears the case!)

As you can see, there's an endless permutation of facts that can confuse the issue of jurisdiction. Because we are looking at state encyclopedias right now, simply go to your particular state's encyclopedia if all your facts involve one state. If you're not sure which court would have jurisdiction over your case, go to the state where you would like a court to hear your case. Then, look up the term "jurisdiction" in the general index (not the individual indexes at the end of each volume) and use your keywords to find your particular issue within the jurisdiction heading. Remember that this process can be as time-consuming as it was researching through national encyclopedias. Plug away until you find, say, divorce matters under the jurisdiction heading. Copy down the corresponding section numbers and read the section about jurisdiction in the appropriate article. If your particular jurisdiction question is not mentioned in the index, then discard the jurisdiction problem for now. It may have to wait to be resolved until later, as you read the cases you found.

Finally, if you're researching a legal topic simply because you want to get a general grasp of what most state or federal laws say, then don't get hung up on jurisdiction. Reading the discussion of your legal issue in a national encyclopedia might be good enough.

A brief look at federal versus state law

Before you start your state search, a cautionary word: Many legal problems have both federal and state aspects. For instance, a case of employment discrimination or housing discrimination involves both federal civil rights law and state civil rights law. Similarly, environmental protection laws or corporate securities laws exist both at the federal and state levels. Other legal problems involve only federal law, such as copyright protection and federal taxation. Finally, there are those legal problems that concern only state law, such as most criminal law, divorce law, and most tort law.

No matter what your legal question, though, you'll always be wise to start with the national encyclopedia (Am. Jur. 2d and C.J.S.). The national encyclopedias discuss both state and federal law (not just federal law, as you might have guessed).

For matters that only involve federal law, you can sometimes avoid looking through the state encyclopedias at all. At this stage though, it's best to look through your particular state's encyclopedia, no matter what issue you're researching. Even if your research tells you that the matter is governed solely by federal law, some of the state encyclopedias contain sections discussing federal law, as applied in your state. Therefore, searching through a state's jurisprudence can be valuable for any researcher, no matter what his or her topic is.

Case citations

To search the index of the state encyclopedia, follow the same steps as those involved in searching the index of the national encyclopedia (see pages 56–61). Copy down case citations from the appropriate sections and those sections' supplements. You can safely copy down all case citations you find in a state encyclopedia, because all cases referred to will probably have been decided in your particular state or by the Supreme Court, whose interpretations of the law apply to all states.

Let's return to Louise again. Because she lives in Florida now and was divorced there, she's decided that the Florida encyclopedia will be the most appropriate state encyclopedia for her needs. Looking through the *Florida Jurisprudence 2d* general index, she once again tries the topic "divorce." The only entry under the heading is "See index heading Dissolution of marriage." Turning to "Dissolution of marriage," she looks up the subheading "alimony." She finds the entry: "Alimony. See index heading Alimony."

She makes one last try and looks up "child support." Although she doesn't find that topic, she does find "Children: support of children. See index heading Support of Children."

Looking at the alimony issue, Louise turns to the "Alimony" heading and finds the subheading "Modification or termination." Confused by many of the entries, Louise chooses to copy down the general discussion entry, which refers the reader to Fam L (the Table of Abbreviations explains that Fam L stands for Family Law) §§ 722 et seq., §§ 1163 et seq.

Helpful Hint

The term *et seq.* means "and following," and can be read as referring the reader to the section named and the subsequent sections. For instance "§§ 722 et seq." actually means "§§ 722 and the following sections."

Note that Louise, whose issues include increasing alimony and child support and collecting past-due support payments, is now directed to an article entitled "Family Law." Even though she found relevant material in an article entitled "Divorce and Separation" when she used Am. Jur. 2d, this doesn't mean that all encyclopedias use the same titles to discuss the same topics.

Because Louise has been referred to an undisclosed number of sections (how can she be sure how many sections she has to check?), she should check the table of contents to see which sections she'd like to make use of. Section 722 falls under

VI. Allowance of Alimony
E. Termination or Modification of Alimony
2. Proceedings to Modify or Terminate
a. In General
§ 722 Generally; statutory authority to modify.

Skimming further through the contents, she see that under "2. Proceedings to Modify or Terminate" is part "b. Substantial Change in Circumstances as Grounds." Under this subpart, she finds the section: "§ 739 Income of obligor." Aha!

After making a note to check that section, she then turns to her other entry: "Section 1163 et seq." The table of contents reveal that this section falls under

X. Postjudgment Proceedings
B. Modification of Alimony, Child Custody and Visitation, and Child Support Awards
1. Generally
§ 1163. In general.

These sections look potentially interesting to her, so she makes a note to check some of the sections found under "B. Modification of Alimony, Child Custody and Visitation, and Child Support Awards." She also happens to glance at "Part C: Enforcement of Alimony, Child Custody, Visitation, Child Support Awards, and Orders for Attorney Fees," and decides to check these sections as well. Louise is once again on her way to finding the right material. Note that this time she had to look a little further afield from the references she wrote down to find the relevant sections. You should also be ready to skim some of the surrounding sections to see whether any of them might be of use to you.

References to other sources

As was the case for your research of the national encyclopedias, you'll ignore all references to forms and practice guides at this point. Once again, the exception is for those people who are specifically looking for forms, such as will forms or incorporation forms. For these researchers, the state-specific forms are even more valuable than the more generic national forms, because state forms are tailored to meet the demands of state law.

been said that inflation is only one factor to be considered and by itself is insufficient to establish a change of conditions sufficient to justify an increase in an award of alimony.[8] And it is erroneous for the trial court to simply assume that inflation has reduced a party's standard of living, without an explicit finding to that effect.[9]

§ 739. Income of obligor

A substantial change in the income of the obligated party will often constitute a substantial change in circumstances and justify an increase,[10] decrease, or termination[11] of alimony, but the change in income must have already occurred—a prospective change does not provide grounds for modification.[12] Similarly, the fact that

1214, later proceeding (Fla App D3) 527 So 2d 260, 13 FLW 1355 and (disapproved on other grounds by Bedell v Bedell (Fla) 583 So 2d 1005, 16 FLW S401).

Annotations: Change in financial condition or needs of husband or wife as ground for modification of decree for alimony or maintenance, 18 ALR2d 10 (§ 5).

8. Greene v Greene (1979, Fla App D3) 372 So 2d 189.

9. Waldman v Waldman (1988, Fla App D3) 520 So 2d 87, 13 FLW 463, review den (Fla) 531 So 2d 169.

10. The trial court erred in ordering an increase of only $100 per month where the fact that, inter alia, the husband had experienced an increase in net monthly income from $2,600 to $4,500 after the dissolution of marriage created an imbalance in livelihood of such magnitude as to result in inequity and to require, in the interests of justice, that the wife and the two remaining minor children be restored to a more reasonable approximation of the standard of living they had experienced during the marriage. Shrine v Shrine (1983, Fla App D1) 429 So 2d 765, appeal after remand (Fla App D1) 454 So 2d 26, review den (Fla) 461 So 2d 116.

11. Tompkins v Tompkins (1978, Fla App D1) 362 So 2d 689.

When an inability to pay support alimony arises and the inability to pay is not a result of intentional refusal to work or other willfully created inability, liability for such alimony should cease. Davis v Davis (1988, Fla App D5) 528 So 2d 34, 13 FLW 1380.

A divorced husband was entitled to have his alimony obligation terminated, where he had been forced to take an early retirement by his employer and was living on a modest pension, while his former wife had found employment and was in a superior financial position. Berryman v Berryman (1982, Fla App D3) 417 So 2d 1087.

12. Fleischer v Fleischer (1942) 149 Fla 621, 6 So 2d 836.

Only when he is in fact drafted into military service may the obligor apply for a reduction of alimony on the ground that his civilian pay has

Figure 4

AMERICAN LAW REPORTS

American Law Reports (ALR) contain articles ranging from 15 to over 200 pages (called annotations) and tend to concentrate on specific legal issues. Can homosexuals adopt their partner's biological children? Is a landlord liable for his or her tenant's lead paint poisoning? May a self-employed worker collect unemployment compensation after his or her business shuts down? Each ALR volume contains from 4 to 12 such annotations.

ALRs come in two types: federal and state. Topics that are completely controlled by federal law (such as, the Endangered Species Protection Act and the Workers Adjustment and Retraining Notification Act) can be found in the federal volumes, which look just like the ALR state volumes, except that state volumes use red detailing, and the federal volumes have blue detailing. The ALR state volumes cover matters that are controlled by state law (like criminal law, corporate law, landlord-tenant law, tort law, and so on), though these annotations also include references to federal courts, because federal courts often hear matters of state law.

Don't worry: It's not necessary for you to decide whether you need an ALR state or federal volume. Just look up your topic in the index, and if there is an annotation that discusses it, the multi-volume hardbound index will direct you either to ALR state or ALR federal, depending on which volume covers your topic. Although there are also handy one-volume paperbacks, called Quick Indexes, these are specific to either ALR state volumes or ALR federal volumes, and thus require that you know whether your topic deals with state or federal law.

When you look at the index and find some references to the ALR texts, you'll see references like 18 ALR3d 568, 26 ALR4th 33, 78 ALR2d 968, and 5 ALR5th 455. What do these numbers mean?

First, the ordinal numbers following the ALR (like the 5 in ALR5th) refer to the series. Because there are so many ALR volumes, the publishers have divided the volumes into series (no one even uses the first series anymore, so you won't find any references to plain old ALR in the indexes). ALR2d's were written before the ALR3d's, which were written before ALR4th's, which are older than ALR5th's. In fact, the most recent issue of ALR would be the ALR5th series. If you look at your library's collection of ALRs, you'll see the ALR2d, ALR3d, ALR4th, and ALR5th collections organized sequentially. When you're searching for an ALR, make sure you're looking at the right series.

As far as the numbers surrounding the ALR abbreviations, the system is straightforward. The number before the ALR refers to the volume number. The number which comes after the ALR (and series number) is the page number where the annotation is found. Thus, if you want 26 ALR5th 422, you must find the ALR5th series, find volume 26 (written on the spine of the book), and then open the book to page 422. Voila! You should be on the first page of the annotation for which you were looking.

Another type of reference you'll find in the ALR indexes is the ALR Fed (ALR Federal) reference. Just as you did with the ALR state volumes, make sure you're looking at a federal volume when the index directs you to ALR Fed. The volume number and page number system is the same as is used for the ALR state volumes. Pretty simple, huh?

As with the encyclopedias, remember to check the supplement, found in the back cover of the volumes, for any new case or laws that might be relevant for your purposes.

Helpful Hint

Remember that not all legal topics are covered in the ALR volumes. Unlike your excruciating search using the encyclopedias, if you can't find your topic in the ALR indexes after a few tries, don't sweat it. Move on to your next resource.

ALR annotations are written to be exhaustive of all the case law on any subject they cover. In other words, if any case that falls within the scope of a particular annotation topic is decided anywhere in the country, it should be referenced in that annotation. Although this is the theory, the updated supplements to the volumes of annotations are not always as exhaustive of the case law as the original annotation. This means that just because you happen to find an annotation that directly addresses your issue, don't assume that your search for cases is necessarily over, because cases that have been handed down since the volume was published may not have been included in the updated supplement.

One other note: Besides the paperback and hardback indexes, each annotation has an index. The individual indexes are found near the beginning of the annotation, however, not at the end of the volume. Also found near the beginning of each annotation is a table of states; under each state is a list of cases from that state that are contained in the article and the annotation section in which each case can be found. This table makes it easier for readers to gather all the cases from their state and read only the pertinent material.

Let's move back to Louise. She's searching through the ALR state Quick Index because she knows that divorce and alimony matters are matters of state law. (She could also search the hardback index if she wanted—certainly, this is the more cautious and safer approach to finding both state and federal ALR annotations).

The differences between encyclopedia and ALR indexes should be immediately clear to you. Although Louise found all the entries she needed in Am. Jur. 2d under the heading "Divorce and Separation," if she looks up "Divorce and Separation" in the ALR index, and then logically looks under the subheading "Alimony," the index says Alimony (this index). This means she should flip to the A's and look up the heading "Alimony" in the index. (See Figure 5).

There are less than two pages of entries under the heading "Alimony," so Louise decides not to narrow her search but to read all the entries. On the page reproduced here, she finds an entry under the subheading "Delinquent or overdue payments," which might be of interest. It reads "—laches or acquiescence as defense, so as to bar recovery of arrearages of permanent alimony or child support 5 ALR4th 1015." Although she doesn't yet know what laches means, she knows that she has acquiesced to her ex-husband not paying alimony and child support, so she copies down the reference 5 ALR4th 1015. This is good work on Louise's part, by the way, because she is anticipating that her ex-husband will defend his failure to pay support by saying that Louise acquiesced in his nonpayment. Any second-guessing you can do too might be helpful to your research.

As to the child support payments, Louise tries looking up "Children" under the "Divorce and Separation" heading. She finds "Custody and Support of Children (this index)." She flips to the heading "Custody and Support of Children." It would certainly be proper for her to look now under the subheading "change or modification" to search for relevant annotations.

But just to show you how useful it can be to read all the entries under a heading without prematurely narrowing your topic (reading all the entries under a heading is a good idea when the material is only a couple of pages long): If Louise insisted only on looking at the "Change or modification" subheading, she would have completely missed a potentially useful annotation. The annotation, "Divorce and separation: attributing undisclosed income to parent or spouse for purposes of making child or spousal support

ALR QUICK INDEX

For assistance using this Index, call 1-800-527-0430

36

Figure 5

award. 70 ALR4th 173" is found only under the subheading "Profits or income" and not under "Change or modification," as one might have suspected (or hoped). As you can see, there is an advantage to resisting the urge to narrow your search too much when looking through an index.

At this point, Louise has at least two or three annotations that she can check. When she does so, she should carefully read the "Scope" section, which is at the beginning of the body of the annotation, so that she can see whether the annotation's scope includes the issue that she is researching. You should read the "Scope" section too.

LOOSE-LEAF SERVICES

There are a bevy of references called loose-leaf services, which contain specialized information in certain legal concentrations. They are called loose-leaf because their pages are usually housed in three-ring binders and can be easily withdrawn or replaced with other pages as the law changes (or new pages can be added as new decisions are handed down by the courts); these resources are called services because those who buy them are actually subscribers who receive weekly, monthly, quarterly, or yearly updated pages with instructions as to which pages should be discarded and where any new pages should be placed. Loose-leaf services have the advantage of being easy to use, because the researcher doesn't have to flip constantly between a volume and the supplement to find changes in the law or new information.

Appendix 2 contains a catalog of some of the more important loose-leaf services. Skim the list and see if any of the titles of the services seem relevant to your needs. If so, check to see whether your library has copies of the particular service you want to search.

LAW REVIEWS AND JOURNALS

Law reviews and journal articles provide yet another source for learning about a topic, particularly those topics that are affected by rapid changes in the law (for example, computer espionage law or civil rights laws protecting homosexuals). Law reviews and journal articles also discuss more traditional areas of law and, though not exhaustive of all case law, provide a level of analysis that usually is not found in ALR annotations. Many of them argue one side of an issue and therefore can be helpful in marshaling arguments for why a line of cases or a statute should be changed or followed in any particular case. To find these resources, you may either use indexes or a computer system called Infotrac, found in many law libraries.

Remember your keywords? Dig them out because you can use them again in searching the indexes or Infotrac. The bound indexes come in two different editions: *Index to Legal Periodicals* and *Current Law Index*. The search method is the same one you used to search the encyclopedia indexes and the ALR indexes. Whichever bound index you choose, be sure to check the table of abbreviations found near the beginning of each index for the full names of the journals and law reviews.

The bound indexes are organized by date. The latest volume contains the most recent periodical articles and tends to be the most useful because legal periodicals aren't supplemented to reflect changes or new trends in the law.

If you want to avoid having to look through several indexes, use a computer that has Infotrac on it, if your library has one available. (You should be able to use it for free.) Instructions for using the program are provided on screen. The system allows you to type in your keywords. You are then electronically led to the portion of the index that matches the word you typed in, if there is such an entry. If not, type in other keywords. Frequently, the index that appears on screen after you type in your keyword will cross-reference other terms for you to try searching. As always, finding legal information is trial and error, with the rewards going to those who persevere and are not discouraged by a few blind alleys.

WHAT NOW?

By this time, you are somewhat familiar with several possible legal analyses of your problem. You also have a list of case citations. Believe it or not, you've taken a big step in your research by finding background material as well as case citations—in many ways, the hardest part of your research is over.

To orient yourself in the research process, the tasks that remain are: searching out more case citations; finding the cases in the library, reading them, and making sure they're still good law;

checking for any applicable statutes, ordinances, or regulations; and drawing conclusions from your research. To give you even more perspective, remember that you've already tackled several indexes, looked through the national encyclopedia and maybe even a state jurisprudence, familiarized yourself with one or several legal concentrations, perhaps found an ALR annotation, looked through some legal periodicals, and written down several case citations to start your case search with. Still, there's a lot more to explain—so, on to a more concentrated look at cases, which, together with the statutes, form the very backbone of the law.

CHAPTER HIGHLIGHTS

National legal encyclopedias

- Search the general indexes of a national encyclopedia, either Am. Jur. 2d or C.J.S., using your keywords and copy down several references
- Look up the references to see if they are useful
- Check the updated supplements for new cases and the New Topic Service for new encyclopedia articles not yet in the regular volumes
- Repeat the above steps until you find sufficient background material
- Make a reference list of any cases and other research resources as you go

State legal encyclopedias

- Search your state's legal encyclopedia (if there is one), starting with the general index and using your keywords
- Use the same method outlined for the national legal encyclopedias when searching the state encyclopedias

American Law Reports (ALRs)

- Use the keyword/index searching method to find out whether there are any relevant ALR articles

- If you find a relevant article, check the volume supplements for newer material and cases
- Write down all relevant cases and other resources you find in the article, and add to your reference list

Loose-leaf services

- Look in Appendix 2, containing a partial list of loose-leaf services, for relevant resources
- Check with your law librarian, or check the law library's card catalog, for other loose-leaf services that may be helpful
- Use your keywords to search the loose-leaf indexes
- Copy down relevant cases and resources, and add to your reference list

Law reviews and journals

- Find an indexing service for the law reviews and journals—three main ones are available:

  – Infotrac (computer index available at most law libraries)
  – *Index to Legal Periodicals* (bound)
  – *Current Law Index* (bound)

- Using your keywords, search the index
- After reading or skimming an article, add any relevant cases to your reference list
- Take note of any new trends or persuasive arguments in the law

CHAPTER 5

READING A CASE

[The doctrine of the law] is to be traced in the main through a series of cases; and much the shortest and best, if not the only way of mastering the doctrine effectually is by studying the cases in which it is embodied.

—Christopher C. Langdell,
A Selection of Cases on the Law of Contracts (1871)

THE POWER OF CASES

Although many may curse him, Christopher C. Langdell, the inventor of the case method used by most American law schools to teach its students—the method of case reading and interrogation used by law professors and made famous in the book and film *The Paper Chase* and the book *One L*—is probably correct. Reading a series of cases is essential to understanding and applying the evolving doctrine of American law, even when you're dealing with civil law. This may seem daunting or boring or downright unnecessary. After all, aren't words words? Don't they mean exactly what they say? In the Land of the Law, however, the answer is yes, no, and maybe.

Actually, giving such an ambiguous answer is a bit unfair because it implies that lawyers, legislators, and judges are trying to confuse things for their own purposes. OK, sometimes they are, but the need to interpret the words that make up our laws doesn't just come from a desire to muddy the waters; it comes from the inadequacy of words themselves. Don't believe us? Try this. Imagine explaining what an apple tastes like to a person who has never tasted one. You may be able to come up with what you think is a good description or you may not, but the bottom line is it's not the same as eating an apple, and we don't have the resources to give everybody an apple or to fly in the legislators who wrote the laws or the judges who wrote the opinions to tell us in person what they meant. So, we're stuck with words—with the laws and the cases that interpret them. Let's learn how to read them.

THE BASICS

What is a case?

Before we can start to read cases, we have to agree on what we're talking about. A *case* can mean many things because the term is used to identify the legal action brought by you or against you as a whole, but it is also used as a shorthand way of referring to certain portions of the entire process. What we mean when we say that you will have to read a case is that you will have to find and read an opinion handed down by a court.

LAW FACT

Another phrase that is often used is "state a case" such as in "the plaintiff failed to state a case." When used in this manner "case" means legal theory.

These opinions are usually found in what are called case reporters, or merely reporters. (For a list of available reporters see Appendix 3.) Once you have a citation in hand, it will lead you to the text of the case.

Helpful Hint

Not all judicial opinions are published in reporters; nevertheless, they may appear elsewhere, such as through on-line legal services like LEXIS and Westlaw (see Chapter 8 for an explanation of how these computer services work). These opinions are called, logically enough, unpublished opinions, and it will say at the beginning of the case that it was not deemed suitable for publication. Your use of these opinions should generally be avoided; however, if there is no other opinion available to back-up your argument, you may attempt to use an unpublished opinion. Be warned, though, there are usually fairly strict rules, also listed at the beginning of the case, that you will have to follow before the court will let you use an unpublished opinion.

How to read a case citation

To teach you how to read a case, we're first going to introduce you to Bob. Bob was once a famous reporter with the *Washington Post* but has since given up that sort of hustle and bustle for a quieter life in rural Pennsylvania. He's now the editor of a local newspaper, but he hasn't quite shaken off his big city reporter zeal and is thinking about filing a suit against the local township because it won't give him access to records that he thinks should be made public. Namely, he wants to see a copy of an agreement that settled a suit brought by an individual against the township who claimed that the local police had been routinely harassing him.

Bob thinks he has a right to see the settlement agreement, but the township disagrees. Luckily for Bob he has a secret source deep inside the town council that has given him the citation to a case that says he is right, but Bob is a reporter, not a lawyer, and he doesn't understand how to read the citation so that he can find the case. Let's look at Bob's citation and see what it says:

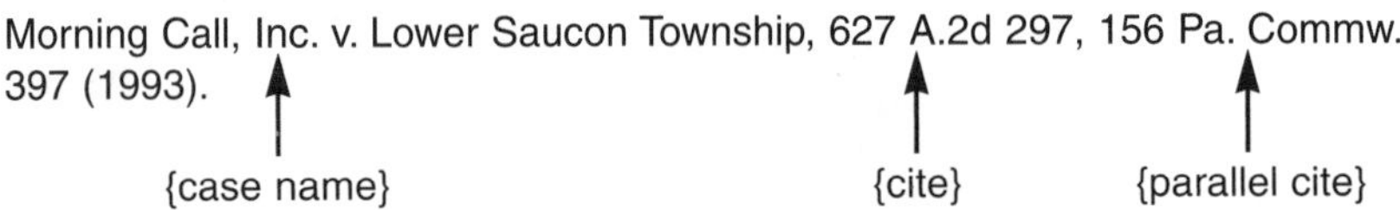

It looks like a code, and it is a code of sorts because a case citation such as this is an abbreviated way of telling you not only the name of the case, but where to find the case, which court decided it, and when the decision was handed down—all of which can be important information for reasons of stare decisis, or for determining just how persuasive this case will be in Bob's situation (remember stare decisis and that stuff in Chapter 1). In this example, the name of the case (Morning Call, Inc. v. Lower Saucon Township) is listed first, followed by the volume number of the reporter (627), the name of the reporter (A.2d, which stands for *Atlantic Reporter, Second Series*), and finally, the page number (297).

The other cite, known as a parallel cite, refers to the exact same decision printed in a different reporter, but its abbreviations are organized in the same way: the volume number of the reporter (156), followed by the name of the reporter (Pa. Commw., which stands for *Pennsylvania Commonwealth Court Reports*), the page number (397), and the year that the decision was handed down (1993). The case name is left off of the second cite for the obvious reason that it would be needlessly repetitive. For the same reason, the date that the decision was handed down is left off of the first cite and only appears at the end of the second.

If you don't know what the abbreviations for the reporters stand for (and why should

Helpful Hint

It may seem tedious at first, but make sure that you write down the entire citation, including the parallel cites. It will save you time in the long run. We've learned through our own impatience early in our careers that you'll invariably need that date you left off because you thought it was unimportant or the parallel cite that seemed redundant at the time, which means that you have to waste time running back to the library and looking it up again.

you if you're not a lawyer), don't worry. For the most part you can check the book in which you found the citation and it will have a table of abbreviations telling you what they mean. Moreover, there are a number of books that the librarian can direct you to that list numerous abbreviations, such as D. M. Beiber's *Dictionary of Legal Abbreviations Used in American Law Books* or the *Legal Citation Directory* by M. D. Powers. Most law dictionaries will also contain a list of common abbreviations.

Again it may seem that lawyers and judges are trying to make things hard for laypeople by using all these arcane abbreviations, but there is a less fiendish reason for this:

Trees.

There are only so many trees on Earth out of which to make paper, and if lawyers, judges, and publishers were required to print the full name of every reporter in every citation, briefs, decisions, and law books would be so long that the paper used would denude the Earth of trees, which would destroy life as we know it. So you see how important it is to use abbreviations.

Still this doesn't explain why there are parallel citations. Shouldn't citing to one reporter with the text of the case be enough? It can be, but often it isn't. There are basically two reasons for this:

- because it's helpful and
- because the rules say you have to.

When you go to the library you'll probably notice that there are a lot of lawyers there, which means there is a good chance that someone else may be using the volume you need. If you have another citation to the same case, you can continue your work by locating the case in the other volume, or you might be able to find the case under one citation and not the other because the library that you are using doesn't have both sets of reporters. That's why parallel cites are helpful. They may also be necessary because court rules in your jurisdiction may require citation to the official reporter, even though most lawyers and judges use the unofficial reporters to do their research. Let's look back at the full citation that Bob was using before.

In this instance, the citation to the unofficial, commercially produced regional reporter *Atlantic Reporter, Second Series* is listed first, and the official state reporter *Pennsylvania*

Commonwealth Court Reports is second. Official reporters were begun by various states back in the 1800s, but because of the mass of cases decided and the glacial speed and irregularity of their publication, commercial publishers soon found a market for unofficial reporters. Out of habit and for accuracy's sake, some courts still require that citation to cases be to the official reporter. Some jurisdictions, however, as a cost-saving measure, or because the volume of cases handed down has never warranted a separate reporter, have made the regional reporter "official" and no longer require a parallel state reporter cite. Furthermore, the commercial reporters will have the official cite listed at the beginning of the case, if it is available at the time of publication; however, because the official reporters frequently come out later than the unofficial reporters, sometimes the official cite will be missing.

Helpful Hint

Look to the court rules for your jurisdiction to find out whether you will have to cite to an official reporter when submitting a brief or other supporting documents to the court. It's often considered good form to follow the citation method laid out in *A Uniform System of Citation*, published by the Harvard Law Review Association, a handy little volume known in the profession as the Bluebook because of its distinctive blue cover. Another popular form is detailed in *The University of Chicago Manual of Legal Citation*, sometimes called the Maroon book.

Enough of that. Now that we understand Bob's citation, let's find the volume it's in, take a look at the actual case, and learn how to read it.

Where does the opinion start, or what's all that stuff at the beginning of the case?

Bob has read the citation according to the method above. He found the unofficial reporter volume on the shelf, opened to the proper page, and is now greeted with what appears in Figure 6. He's ready to read the opinion, but is this it? Actually no, but he shouldn't skip this stuff. It's important. In fact, these features are what make the commercial reporters more useful and popular than their official kin. This stuff at the beginning of the printed case, if properly used, will help Bob read the case, understand it, and find what he needs from the case quickly (a good idea when he may have to read many cases), or it will help him determine whether the case is on point or relevant at all.

LAW FACT

On point is a phrase often used by lawyers to mean a case that treats the issue that you are concerned with in your case. It is similar to another often used phrase *on all fours*, which refers to a case where the facts and issues are so similar to yours that its holding should control the outcome of your case. Think of a case that is on all fours as a sturdy table with all four of its legs planted firmly on the ground; it is one that can clearly hold up your case.

Let's look at how a case is laid out in an unofficial reporter (see Figures 6 & 7). Starting from the top, it can be broken down in the following way:

a. Running head
b. Official citation
c. Complete title
d. Court
e. Date of decision: Argued/decided
f. Synopsis
g. Headnotes
h. Attorneys
i. Names of panel
j. Name of judge
k. Text of the opinion

Let's take these elements one at a time.

A. Running head

This line at the top of the case, above the rest of the text, is called the running head. It contains the short name of the case and its unofficial citation. The publisher places the running head at the top of all pages throughout the case so that you will always know what case your are reading, just in case you get sidetracked or forget. Bob is probably thinking that this would never happen to him but let us tell you after you've read about 20 cases on the same issue, they can tend to blend together.

B. Official citation

The official citation will appear above the complete title of the case, if one is available. In the case that Bob chose, apparently the official cite had not been designated at the time the volume of the *Atlantic Reporter, Second Series* went to press. As discussed

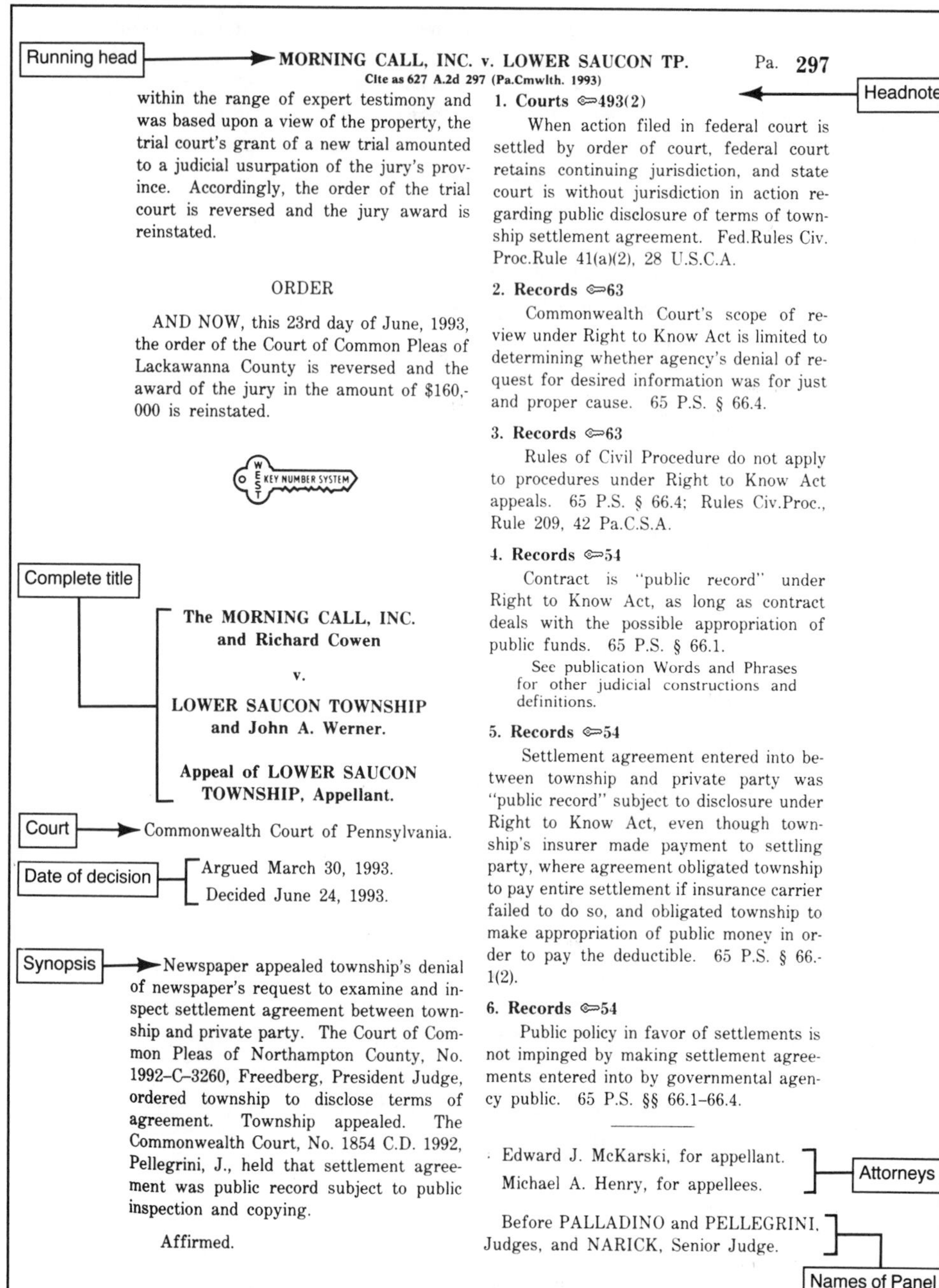

Reprinted with permission from 627 A.2d, Copyright © by West Publishing Company.

Figure 6

298 Pa. 627 ATLANTIC REPORTER, 2d SERIES

PELLEGRINI, Judge.

Lower Saucon Township (Township) appeals an order of the Northhampton County Court of Common Pleas (trial court) requiring the Township to disclose the terms of a settlement agreement between itself and John Werner (Werner) to The Morning Call pursuant to the Right to Know Act, Act of June 21, 1957, P.L. 390, *as amended*, 65 P.S. §§ 66.1–66.4.

On February 14, 1991, Werner filed a federal civil rights lawsuit in the United States District Court for the Eastern District of Pennsylvania [1] against the Township, alleging his civil rights were violated by Township police officers. The Township reached an out-of-court settlement (Settlement Agreement) with Werner in which he was compensated by the Township's Comprehensive Law Enforcement Liability Insurance policy issued by Scottsdale Insurance Company (insurance carrier).[2] The Settlement Agreement provided that none of the parties were to disclose its terms. Because the Township had a Five Thousand Dollar ($5,000) deductible, it was required to pay that portion of the award. However, it did not pay that amount directly to Werner, but to its insurance carrier.

[1] The Morning Call, a newspaper of general circulation in Northhampton County, requested the Township make the Settlement Agreement available for inspection as a "public record" under Sections 1(2) and 2 of the Pennsylvania Right to Know Act.[3] Based upon the non-disclosure clause in the Settlement Agreement, the Township refused to allow it to be inspected or copied.[4] The Morning Call filed an appeal [5] with the trial court, seeking an order requiring the Township to disclose the terms of the Settlement Agreement and joined Werner as a party. Both the Township and Werner opposed the request, asserting that the Settlement Agreement did not fall within the definition of a "public record" as defined in the Right to Know Act.[6]

[2] The trial court granted The Morning Call's appeal, holding that the Township's Settlement Agreement with Werner was a public record both because it created a

1. *John A. Werner v. Lower Saucon Township, Brian F. Paulson and Stephen Lindstedt*, No. 91–0313 (E.D.Pa. filed February 14, 1991).

2. Scottsdale Insurance was not joined as a party in this appeal and no allegation is being made that it is a necessary party. The insurance policy between the Township and Scottsdale is not part of the record. We do not address whether a settlement agreement entered into by an insurance carrier to cover a claim made under a policy that does not require a government agency's consent and to disburse any funds is a "public record".

3. Section 1 of the Right to Know Act, 65 P.S. § 66.1(2), defines "public record" as follows:

> Any ... contract dealing with the receipt or disbursement of funds by an agency ... and any minute, order or decision by an agency fixing the personal or property rights, privileges, immunities, duties or obligations of any person....

Section 2 of the Right to Know Act, 65 P.S. § 66.2, provides:

> Every public record of an agency shall, at reasonable times, be open for examination and inspection by any citizen of the Commonwealth of Pennsylvania.

4. Because there was no court order approving the settlement, the federal action was apparently settled pursuant to Fed.R.Civ.P. 41(a)(1) which provides:

> (a) Voluntary Dismissal: Effect Thereof.
> (1) By Plaintiff; By Stipulation. Subject to the provisions of Rule 23(e), of Rule 66, and of any statute of the United States, an action may be dismissed by the Plaintiff without order of court ... (ii) by filing a stipulation of dismissal signed by all parties who have appeared in the action. Unless otherwise stated in the notice of dismissal or stipulation, the dismissal is without prejudice....

When a lawsuit is dismissed pursuant to this subsection, the federal district court does not retain jurisdiction over the settlement agreement. If, however, this matter had been settled by order of court in accordance with Fed. R.Civ.P. 41(a)(2), which provides for settlements with court approval, the federal district court would have retained continuing jurisdiction; correspondingly, the trial court and this court would be without jurisdiction to hear this matter. *See Smith v. Phillips*, 881 F.2d 902, 904 (10th Cir.1989); *Hinsdale v. Farmers National Bank and Trust Company*, 823 F.2d 993, 996 n. 1 (6th Cir.1987).

5. Section 4 of the Right to Know Act, 65 P.S. § 66.4.

6. Werner did not appeal from the trial court's decision.

Figure 7

previously, you may need the official citation if you are going to cite to a case in documents filed with the court.

C. COMPLETE TITLE

Up to now, we've been referring to this case by a shortened title. Obviously this is done for convenience sake, but a short title may not always be specific enough to distinguish a case. Can you imagine how many criminal cases there must be that are referred to in short form as, say, *State v. Smith* or *Commonwealth v. Jones*? So here is the full name of the case, with all of the parties, set out (full titles can sometimes be long and strange).*

D. COURT

At this point, the case will list the full title of the court that decided the case—essential information for purposes of determining precedential value and applying stare decisis.

E. DATE OF DECISION: ARGUED/DECIDED

Here, the case lists the date on which it was argued and the date on which the decision was handed down by the court—again essential information for the same reasons that the court name is important.

F. SYNOPSIS

This is the first element that you will come to that actually begins to explain what the court says in this opinion. The synopsis tells the reader in one succinct paragraph the essential facts of the case, and the decisions of any of the lower court opinions that led to the case's present stance. It will give the resolution of the case in this instance and the action taken by the court. Some reporters also have an official as well as a commercial synopsis. Just by reading the synopsis you may be able to determine quickly whether you should read the entire opinion, because it may not even be on point.

---

*One of the longer and stranger titles that we've ever run across appeared in a case that involved the Marine Mammal Protection Act, where owners of a fishing boat challenged a regulation that required that they allow observers on to their boats before they would be granted fishing permits. The full title was: John R. Balelo, Andrew Catagnola, Leo Correia, Manuel S. Jorge, Bryan R. Madruga, Harold Medina, John A. Silva, Ralph F. Silva, Jr., John B. Zolezzi, Jr., Plaintiffs-Appellees v. Malcom Baldridge, Secretary of Commerce of the United States, Richard A. Frank, Administrator, National Oceanic and Atmospheric Administration and Terry Leitzell, Assistant Administrator for Fisheries, National Marine Fisheries Service, Defendant-Appellants. United States of America, Plaintiff v. 50,178 dollars and 80 cents, The Monetary Value of 57 Tons of Tuna, Defendant.

LAW FACT

In the case of the *United States Reports*, the official reporter for the U.S. Supreme Court, this synopsis is called a syllabus.

G. Headnotes

Headnotes are helpful because they summarize in one sentence the issues and rules of law that appear in a case. They are numbered and laid out in the order that they appear in the case. So, once you have found the headnote that discusses your issue, all you have to do to find that issue in the case's text is to find the corresponding number of the headnote bolded and bracketed in the text of the opinion. Another useful aspect of the headnotes is their classification by topic, such as Records, and (in the case of the West reporters) keynumber. These topics and keynumbers (the numbers following the little graphic of a key) give you access to digests that collect and organize by topic and keynumber headnotes from other cases on the same or similar issues. But more about digests in the next chapter on "Locating the Case You Need."

Helpful Hint

Because the headnotes and synopses are prepared by editors employed by the publishers of the commercial reporters, they are the property of the individual publishing company. What this means is you can't lift material directly from the headnotes or synopses and use it in a paper or brief without plagiarizing or infringing the company's copyright in the material, and there is little need to do so. The actual text of the opinions themselves are in the public domain, which means that it belongs to you as much as anyone, and you can quote from it freely.

The synopses and headnotes are created by lawyer-editors, so it's a good idea to make the most of them. It's like having private counsel sitting right at your elbow helping you to find your way through the maze of the opinion. Nevertheless, be warned that you can't always rely on the summary or headnotes to be accurate. Editors (despite the godlike esteem in which they are held by their lawyer-colleagues) are human, and thus fallible, and on occasion mistakes may creep in undetected. Furthermore, determining what issues are addressed and how the court resolved them is a matter of interpretation. Therefore, there may be legitimate disagreement between professionals as to what is correct, but for the most part, the summary and headnotes that you run across will be right far more often than not.

H. Attorneys

Directly after the headnotes, the names of the counsel representing the parties are usually listed, often with the name of the city and state where they practice (although not in Bob's example), so that you can contact them if you are looking for a lawyer who has dealt with your particular issue before.

I. Names of the panel

In appellate cases like Bob's, frequently the names of the judges on the panel that heard the case will be listed.

J. Name of judge

After the names of the panel, the case will then list the name of the judge who wrote the decision.

K. Text of the opinion

Last but not least, there is the text of the opinion itself. We'll discuss what Bob should look for in the opinion at length in the next section.

Reading the text of the opinion

Bob has read through the preliminary material up to this point, has a pretty good idea that this case is on point, and is ready to get into the meat of the opinion, but he doesn't know what to look for. Let's take him through it step-by-step.

A legal opinion ordinarily contains the following elements:

a. Procedure
b. Facts
c. Issues
d. Holding
e. Reasoning
f. Court Action

Let's look at each of these individually.

A. Procedure

Procedure refers to the legal mechanisms that the parties use to reach the stage of the case that we are reading. In other words, procedure reflects the legal maneuverings made by each party so that the case ended up here before this court. Just for argument's sake, think of going to court as a game, like a board game. In such a circumstance procedure would not deal with whether a person took your money or didn't, bought a piece of property or didn't. That would be an argument over *substantive law*. Procedure would be the rules that came printed on the lid of the box. So, if you had a conflict over procedure, it would have something to do with whether your opponent rolled the dice too many times, or whether he or she went out of turn.

In the sample case that Bob chose, the procedural aspects are sprinkled throughout the first four paragraphs of the case and are also addressed in footnotes 4, 7, and 8. For instance, in the first paragraph, the commonwealth court notes that the township is appealing the order of a lower court. In footnote 4, the commonwealth court concludes that the settlement at the heart of the case must have been reached under Federal Rule of Civil Procedure 41 (a) (1), otherwise the state courts would not have jurisdiction. In footnote 7, the commonwealth court recognizes its limited scope of review, and in footnote 8, it points out that the Federal Rules of Civil Procedure do not apply to procedures under the Right to Know Act.

Sometimes courts will deal perfunctorily with the rulings below, and make note of the rule that gives the appellate court the power and jurisdiction to hear a case. If there isn't any real procedural argument between the parties, this is usually how the procedural posture is dealt with, but this isn't always the situation. In Bob's case, almost half of the opinion deals with procedure, and some cases go into long arguments over whether an issue is procedural or substantive. Now Bob might be thinking, "This is a whole lot of fighting about nothing." Such arguments might appear to be too esoteric, but whether an issue is procedural or substantive can impact the rights involved. For instance, you've probably heard of due process or *due process of law*. It's a right guaranteed by the U.S. Constitution, and there is a difference recognized by the courts between substantive and

Helpful Hint

You may notice some unfamiliar words or phrases right from the beginning when you start reading your first cases. Often some of the procedural terms can be confusing because they are old, specific to the practice of law, and are based on court rules. They're not the sort of thing that comes up in your normal dinner conversation: "By the way, Betty, I hear that case was brought in assumpsit." Therefore, it might be a good idea to keep a law dictionary at hand when you first start reading cases. We still refer to ours. No one can keep all of this stuff in his or her head.

procedural due process. Substantive due process, as opposed to the procedural due process that we have been discussing, has to do with whether or not a law passed by Congress is a legitimate exercise of Congress' power.

LAW FACT

Due process of law is recognized in the Fifth Amendment of the U.S. Constitution, which applies to actions of the federal government, and in the Fourteenth Amendment of the U.S. Constitution, which protects the infringement of the right by the states.

B. Facts

Most cases will have, as here, a paragraph or more detailing the essential facts of the case. Essential facts are those events or circumstances that have an impact on the outcome of the case. Facts help put problems in perspective and are important for Bob so that he can match the facts of his proposed case with the facts in the case that he is reading, for the purpose of calling on precedent or stare decisis to support his argument. They are also important in helping him determine the facts that are different from the facts in his situation, so that he can distinguish his case from the precedent. Sometimes the facts will appear, as in this example, at the beginning of the case; other times they will be spread throughout, related by the court as they become necessary to the discussion of individual issues.

As with procedure, facts will occasionally be dealt with in only a cursory manner. Sometimes, for example, where the court is dealing primarily with a *question of law*—that is, when the court is trying to decide whether a certain common-law principle or civil law is applicable or not—there will be few, if any, facts related because there are few facts that are essential to the outcome of the issue being discussed.

In Bob's chosen case, the court talks about how an individual named Werner filed a civil rights lawsuit against the township, and was paid off by the township's insurance policy in an out-of-court settlement. The settlement agreement said that no one could tell anyone what its terms were. The township had to pay the $5,000 deductible as part of the award, but it paid it to the insurance carrier and not Werner. The local newspaper wanted to see the settlement because it claimed that it was a "public record" under the Pennsylvania Right to Know Act, but the township refused, and the lawsuit was brought. The trial court found in favor of the newspaper.

C. ISSUE

An *issue* is a question. It is the legal problem that brought the parties to court and what the court is trying to solve. Every case will have at least one issue; sometimes there will be several. Not infrequently there are subissues or preliminary issues that must be resolved before the larger issue on which the case is based can be determined.

LAW FACT

Issue, although not used in this sense here, can also refer to the descendants of an individual. The term often crops up in cases involving estates.

In the sample case, the court does not clearly state the issues that it is going to resolve, but they can be discerned by looking at the holding and other conclusions and how the court lays out the arguments. The commonwealth court defines the issues here by telling us what the township, the party that is pursuing the appeal, is arguing. Here then the argument, and therefore the issue that the commonwealth court is being asked to decide, is whether the trial court was correct or not in holding that the settlement agreement was a public record that could be inspected by the newspaper.

D. HOLDING

The *holding* of a case is the legal conclusion that a court reaches. As there can be several issues in a case, there can be several holdings.

Not every legal observation made by a court is considered a holding. Courts make many other statements in the process of resolving the issues before it. These other statements, even when phrased in the manner of a conclusion may be merely *dicta*, statements that may be interesting and even helpful, but are not essential to the determination of the case.

An example of dictum in the sample case can be found in footnote 4 where the commonwealth court comes to the conclusion that the settlement of the first case brought in federal court was reached under Federal Rule of Civil Procedure 41 (a) (1). It is dictum because it appears that there is no argument, and therefore no issue, as to what Federal Rule of Civil Procedure that case was decided under, but the commonwealth court decides to address it because it could jeopardize its jurisdiction.

As to the holding in the sample case, the court clearly states it on page 301 where it says, "Because it (the settlement) obligates the Township to disburse public funds to satisfy an obligation, the Settlement Agreement is a public record and subject to public inspection and copying." What is holding and what is dictum is sometimes muddled, and in fact, there are occasions where the dicta of a case can have a greater impact than the holding. Strictly speaking, however, you should remember that only a holding can be of precedential value. It would be a mistake to argue to a court that it is bound by the dicta of a prior case.

E. Reasoning

There is a lot of dicta in the reasoning of any case. The reasoning is the process or steps that the court uses to show how it reached its conclusion and to emphasize why it is correct. Courts may support their decision through any number of ways: reasons of history, reasons of social policy, by looking at the plain meaning of words, by employing long-standing rules on how to interpret the language of statutes—called canons of construction. But the technique that is probably most often employed is reasoning by analogy. It's important to understand this technique because it is probably the technique that you will use to convince the court that your position is correct.

In reasoning by analogy, a court looks for a past case that had the same or similar fact situation or issue as the case it is presently attempting to decide. Then they look to see what the court in that case decided and how the court decided it. Then it uses the rules and methods from that case to decide the case at hand. Frequently, however, there is no one case that a court can look to for complete guidance. A court will then look at a number of cases and will try to blend them to form a new rule that can be applied in its new situation. Think of the court as a composer who is looking for just the right note, but all the single notes that the composer tries just don't work. By playing a number of notes together, harmonizing them, the composer comes up with a new sound; he or she hopes, the correct one. Legal reasoning can be like that, like music, a mixture of science and art.

In the sample case, the reasoning of the court starts with the paragraph that begins with **[4]**, and continues until the holding sentence. In footnote 10, the newspaper tries to use the classic reasoning by analogy to persuade the court that settlement agreements are public records, but the court doesn't buy it this time. Instead, the court uses the plain meaning of the words of the statute to reach its holding.

F. COURT ACTION

Finally, at the end of the opinion there is usually a sentence or two, that states succinctly, sometimes in confusing legalese, what action the court is taking in the case. In Bob's chosen case the court action is listed under a title called Order.

That's the end of the case, and if you and Bob read it thoroughly (maybe even more than once because these things are hard to understand in the beginning—hey, sometimes they're hard to understand for us even now) then you should've gotten a lot out of it. If you find that a case that you've read is on point for your issue or issues, now you'll want to take some notes on the case.

Taking notes on relevant cases

The best way to organize your note taking is by using the elements of the case to which we've already introduced you:

a. Procedure
b. Facts
c. Issue
d. Holding
e. Reasoning

Keep your notes brief on each of these elements. You may want to eliminate some elements, such as procedure or court action, entirely if they don't have anything to do with your issue. For instance, you wouldn't want to waste your time writing down a complete procedural history of a case if the issue that you are researching for your own potential

Helpful Hint

One other way to get a lot out of the cases that you read is to keep a pad and pencil or pen handy at all times. This way you can write down the names of cases, statutes, regulations, and the like that the court mentions during its analysis. This is one of the simplest and most common techniques for compiling a list of cases and civil law for you to read, analogize, and use in your own arguments.

lawsuit doesn't have anything to do with procedure. The idea is that you want to keep your notes complete but brief—in fact, that's what these things are called, case briefs.

You could save some time by merely photocopying cases and highlighting the relevant elements of the case on the copies, but we think that actually going through the trouble to write things down is, in and of itself, helpful. Sometimes you may feel as though you understand a case until you actually try to organize your thoughts on paper, and then you realize that you have to go back and read the case again because you don't quite get what the court was trying to say. Remember, if you decide to go to court you're going to have to understand the cases that you rely on as precedent.

CHAPTER HIGHLIGHTS

Cases and how to find them

- Cases are legal opinions handed down by courts
- Cases are gathered together in volumes called case reporters
- Cases can be found in case reporters by using case citations such as in the following example:

Morning Call, Inc. v. Lower Saucon Township, 627 A.2d 297, 156 Pa. Commw. 397 (1993).

{case name} {cite} {parallel cite}

How to read a case citation

- The case name is the abbreviated form of the names of the parties involved in the cases (e.g., Morning Call, Inc. v. Lower Saucon Township)
- The cite lists the volume number (e.g., 627), the abbreviated name of the case reporter (e.g., A.2d), and the page number (e.g., 297) where the case can be found
- Parallel cites are notations to other reporters where the same case can be found (e.g., 156 Pa. Commw. 397)
- Usually, case citations also contain some reference to the date on which the case was decided (e.g., 1993)

Understanding what a case looks like

➤ Cases in unofficial reporters are usually printed containing eleven elements

- A running head at the top of each page with the unofficial cite
- An official citation to the case—if one is available
- A complete title, including all the parties involved
- The court that decided the case
- The date on which the case was argued and decided
- A synopsis of the case
- The headnotes, prepared by lawyer-editors, of the legal issues discussed in the case
- The names of the attorneys who argued the case
- The names of the judges who heard the case
- The name of the judge who wrote the opinion
- The text of the opinion

How to read a case

➤ Begin by reading the synopsis and headnotes to gain a preliminary understanding of what the case discusses before attempting to read the text

➤ To understand the text of a legal opinion, while reading, identify the following six elements:

- Procedure—the legal mechanisms used by the parties to bring the case before the court
- Facts—events or circumstances that have an impact on the outcome of the case
- Issue—the legal problem that brought the parties to the court
- Holding—the court's answer to the issue
- Reasoning—the process or steps that the court uses to show how it reached its holding
- Court action—what the court will do to enforce its holding

CHAPTER 6

LOCATING THE CASE YOU NEED

The ordinary man of business cares little for a "beautiful" case. He wishes it settled somehow on the most favorable terms he can obtain.

—W. G. Miller, The Data of Jurisprudence (1903)

ONE GOOD CASE OR MANY

It's not that people don't care about justice. We all want justice to be done. It's simply that we have trouble conceiving of a scenario in which justice does not match the outcome that we desire. Miller is probably correct. When our interests are on the line, we don't care whether the opinion that we find is a model of judicial clarity, or that its logic or scope takes our breath away. It does not have to be sublime. It does not have to be "beautiful." When we are wrestling with the law, we don't care about beauty. We care about answers, and we care most about the answers that are most advantageous to us. How are we going to find them?

We've read that many judges and justices hate to write opinions. It may be true (considering the wordiness of many opinions, this might be hard to believe), and it may simply be that the litigious nature of our society and our common law heritage require that opinions be written, but no matter the cause or desire behind it all, there certainly are a lot of opinions that have been written. Which may be good, because this increases the chances that we will find an opinion that is almost exactly on point and says what we want. On the other hand, it may turn out that there is no such opinion and the excess of case law will simply be something that we will have to wade through, only to have to turn around and construct an analogy from a case that we hope is leading and persuasive.

This dilemma, whether to use leading cases or to attempt to find a case that is exactly on point, was at the heart of a rivalry in the American legal publishing industry for a number of years. It was West Publishing Company that championed the idea of publishing as many opinions as it feasibly could to give lawyers and other litigants the option of choosing from many and the most up-to-date cases when building their own arguments. Lawyers Cooperative Publishing and a number of allied publishers, on the other hand, promoted the idea of publishing only the important cases in the field and then creating annotations that clarified the status of the law in other jurisdictions. These two systems did not turn out to be as incompatible as at first they might have seemed, and in fact today are ordinarily used jointly by most researchers.*

USING CASES FOUND IN BACKGROUND SOURCES

The annotation system just discussed, although originally used to help lawyers clarify the law in their jurisdictions, and still valuable in this respect, has evolved into a case-finding tool. The series of short case abstracts on a single issue of law that make up the *American Law Reports* (ALR) and *ALR Federal* annotations are used nowadays as case finders similar to digests (more on these later). A researcher using annotations will make a list of the cases that she reads about in the case abstracts and will then use this list as a springboard for the in-depth search that will, hopefully, unearth that prized controlling case that says that she wins.

Essentially, this is how all background sources discussed in Chapter 4—Am. Jur. 2d, C.J.S., state encyclopedias, law reviews, monographs and treatises, legal dictionaries, Restatements of the Law, and loose-leaf services—act as case finders. While reading these books to get a firm grounding in the area of law that your legal problem fits into, if you've been following our hints, you will have already gathered a perhaps sizable list of cases from which to start your search.

> **Helpful Hint**
>
> You can also use annotated codes as case finders if you know that a particular statute is involved in your issue. For more information on using annotated codes, see Chapter 7 on finding civil law.

USING DIGESTS AND SHEPARD'S

At this point it is a good idea to give a brief description of the two basic sets of books that you are likely to use, other than your

*As it turns out, these systems will be even more compatible than ever because the parent company that owns Lawyers Cooperative Publishing recently bought the West Publishing Company.

background sources and annotated codes, to find cases. These sets include the following:

- digests, and
- *Shepard's Citations.*

Digests

Digests are books that collect summaries, usually one sentence long, of points of law from cases and then arrange them by topics. For example, a digest might classify case summaries under a heading such as "Corporations" or "Animals" or "Destruction of Property." The list of topics under which the case summaries are classified are extensive, so that the digests can be used almost like indexes, but the case summaries give a far more detailed picture of the law under that topic than any index entry ever could. In this way, the digests are designed to direct you to just the case or cases that you want.

There are many different digests. The *ALRs* have accompanying digests, as do most specialized reporters, in one form or another, such as *Americans with Disabilities Decisions*, the *Media Law Reporter*, *Wage and Hour Cases*, and the like. The most pervasive and commonly used digests, though, are the West digests organized under the key number system.

LAW FACT

Digests are not unique to the American legal system. The British began compiling something similar to our modern digests as early as 1490.

West's digests are organized and published by region and state, by federal and by U.S. Supreme Court cases, and in a comprehensive system, called the American Digest System, which collects all of the case summaries that appear in the other West digests.

West's Digests

Regional Digests	Atlantic, North Western, Pacific, South Eastern
State Digests	All states are covered by the state digest system except for Delaware (covered in the Atlantic Digest), Nevada (covered in the Pacific Digest), and Utah (covered in the Pacific Digest)
Federal Digests	Federal Digest (covers all cases decided before 1939), Modern Federal Practice

	Digest (1939-1960), Federal Practice Digest 2d (1961-1975), Federal Practice Digest 3d (1976-1988), Federal Practice Digest 4th (1989 to the present)
Supreme Court Digest	Digests all U.S. Supreme Court opinions from 1790 to the present
American Digest System	Century Digest (covers cases decided from 1658-1896), First through Tenth Decennial Digests (1897-1991), General Digest 8th (1991 to the present)

Shepard's Citations

Probably the strangest looking books you'll run across in your first attempt at legal research, but also among the most indispensable, are the volumes known as *Shepard's Citations*.* *Shepard's Citations* are one of the most indispensable of all legal publications because they are the most common form of case updating, in other words checking a case to make sure that the law it expresses is still valid. In fact, Shepard's citators are so widely used that the term Shepardizing has practically become synonymous with the process of checking the validity of cases (more on this and other case updating tools later in the chapter). Shepard's citators are organized by statutes, by regulations, by court rules, by topics (such as Bankruptcy and Medical Malpractice), by law reviews, and by Restatements of the Law, but the most commonly used form of citator is the case citator. Shepard's case law citators are organized by U.S. Supreme Court cases, federal cases, regional cases, and state cases.

LAW FACT

Shepard's is the name of a company, and not merely the general term for validating cases, in much the same way that Xerox is the name of a company and not the general term for making a photocopy. In fact, Shepard's claims a trademark in the term Shepardizing. Companies are very touchy about protecting their trademarks and trade names. Did you know that "aspirin" was the brand name of a product that we now think of generically as aspirin, and "thermos" is the name of a company that produces what were originally known as vacuum flasks?

*So we don't scare you, we aren't going to show an illustration of a page of *Shepard's Citations* at this point, but for those of you who can't wait, see Figure 13 in the section on Updating with Shepard's.

LAW FACT

Shepard's state citators may also cover state statutes, local ordinances, and attorney general opinions.

Shepard's Case Citators

United States Citations	Covers decisions of the U.S. Supreme Court
Federal Citations	Covers decisions of the U.S. Courts of Appeal, U.S. District Courts, and U.S. Claims Court
Regional Citations	Covers decisions published in West's Regional Reporters (Atlantic, North Eastern, North Western, Pacific, South Eastern, South Western, Southern)
State Citations	Covers decisions from each of the 50 states, Puerto Rico, and the District of Columbia

Finding cases by name

Now that you've been introduced to the digests and *Shepard's Citations*, let's introduce you to our new fictitious researcher, Henry. Henry marched to his own drummer, one might say. He lived in the woods away from everybody else in town, not because he didn't like people but because he didn't like the idea of spending all of his time working for someone else, living quietly and desperately, when he could simplify his life by fending for himself. There's nothing wrong with this, but Henry had another idea that the government didn't take kindly to: He didn't want to pay his taxes. So, naturally he was arrested and put on trial. Although Henry was a free spirit and an individualist, he wanted a lawyer to defend him against the charges. When he asked for one to be appointed to him because he couldn't pay for one, the judge refused. Henry had to conduct his own defense, and he did a good job of it, but unfortunately now he's doing time in the penitentiary. Henry thinks that this was unjust, and he wants out. One of the other inmates told him about a case, *Gideon v. Wainwright*, which might help, but neither of them knows where to find it because they don't have its citation. Henry is worried and thinks that he'll never find the answer to his problem, but he shouldn't worry. There are ways to find a case when you only know the case name and not the rest of the citation.

DIGESTS

Almost all digests, including West's digests, have tables of case names. These tables are compiled with the names in alphabetical order, using the name of the case as it would appear in the running head (in other words, the case name will be abbreviated if it is long, with several plaintiffs or defendants.) The cases are usually alphabetized by the plaintiff or prosecuting party's name, but sometimes digests also include a separate table collecting and alphabetizing the cases by the defendants' names. These defendant name tables can come in handy if, as is often the case, you write the case name down incorrectly, the parties names were switched in order on appeal, or you can only vaguely remember the name of the case. Occasionally, we have run across this vague name problem where someone we were working for would ask us to find a case by saying, "I know there is a case out there called, I think, Gideon versus somebody or somebody versus Gideon. It has to do with a defendant's right to counsel."

Helpful Hint

Plaintiff's names are generally listed first in court cases and in court dockets because the plaintiff is the party who instigated the action. Sometimes, however, when a defendant appeals a decision, the defendant's name will then be listed as the first name in the case because the defendant is the *appellant*, the party who instigated the action in the appeals court.

LAW FACT

West's regional digests do not include tables of case names listed by defendants.

This last example indicates another interesting way of finding cases in digests. It is by using Popular Name tables. Popular names are just that, names that well-known cases go by (or at least cases that are well known by lawyers). Many older cases went by a popular name that described the thrust of the case, such as the War Time Profits Case or the Milk Price Control Case. Most of these cases were U.S. Supreme Court cases, and many of the decisions of that highest court are still referred to by popular names. Nowadays, the popular name usually just consists of one of the names of the parties involved, such as the Miranda Decision or the Gideon Case.

It is best to start searches by case name with the digests that are most specifically related to your case. So, if you know which

> **Helpful Hint**
>
> West has phased out the use of popular name tables in its digests, but the tables that exist, usually found at the front of the table of cases in the old decennials, can still be used to find older cases. Shepard's, however, still publishes the set Shepard's Acts and Cases by Popular Names: Federal and State.

jurisdiction the case was decided in, state or federal, start in those digests. If you know in what year your case was decided, then that can clue you in as to which edition of the digest you should search first, such as *Federal Practice Digest 3d* or the *Seventh Decennial Digest.* If you know that your case is a U.S. Supreme Court case then start with the Supreme Court digest. In other words, try to save yourself some time and book work at this point if you can, but don't be discouraged if at first you can't find your case in these digests of more narrow scope, you can always expand your search and make it more general if need be.

Once you've found that one case in the digest, it is easy to note what topic and key number (when using West digests) or what section or subsection the case is listed under, and then you can use this information to find other cases like it in the digests. In Henry's example, he can find *Gideon v. Wainwright* in the *Seventh Decennial Digest* because, say, he knows that it was decided sometime in the late 1960s. By searching the Table of Cases he finds out that its citation is 83 S. Ct. 792 (see Figure 8).

SHEPARD'S CITATIONS

It is also possible to find a case when you only have the name by using *Shepard's Citations.* As was already mentioned in the helpful hint in the preceding section, Shepard's puts out a set of books entitled *Shepard's Acts and Cases by Popular Names: Federal and State.* As you may have guessed from the title, however, this set is fairly broad in scope, and consequently the coverage of cases by name is not very thorough. It is more useful for finding statutes by popular name because referring to statutes by popular name (such as WARN, the Workers Adjustment and Retraining Notification Act) is still a common practice nowadays (You can see why. Many of these statutes can be a real mouthful.)

OTHER SOURCES

There are other ways to find cases by name, but we'll only touch on them here. Almost every reporter has a table of the cases that it contains listed by name, either at the front or back of the volume.

GIBSON

References are to Digest Topics and Key Numbers

Gibson v. Robinson, TexCivApp, 299 SW2d 777, ref n r e—Bills & N 518 (1), 525.

Gibson v. Scheidt, NC, 130 SE2d 679 —Autos 136, 144, 144.1(1), 144.2(1).

Gibson v. South Broadmoor Service Co, LaApp, 168 So2d 869—Mast & S 30(3), 79.

Gibson v. State, CalApp, 7 CalRptr 315—App & E 1064(1); Autos 246 (60); Death 84, 95(1), 99(4); Trial 241.

Gibson v. State, CalApp, 25 CalRptr 284—App & E 110, 181, 1033(5), 1097(1); Autos 163(1), 245(19, 50); High 168; Neglig 3; States 112; Trial 267(1); Witn 388(7).

Gibson v. State, FlaApp, 173 So2d 766—Const Law 263; Crim Law 223, 273, 997(3), 998(19), 1026.

Gibson v. State, FlaApp, 180 So2d 685 —Crim Law 394.6(1).

Gibson v. State, Md, 209 A2d 242— Crim Law 260(11); Mal Mis 9.

Gibson v. State, OklCr, 328 P2d 718 —Crim Law 1141(1), 1186(1); Embez 5, 20, 32, 35; Ind & Inf 110(4); Larc 3(2), 15(1).

Gibson v. State, Tenn, 362 SW2d 470 —Rape 51(1).

Gibson v. State, TexCivApp, 288 SW2d 577, error dism—App & E 1177(6); Plead 110.

Gibson v. State, TexCrApp, 290 SW2d 899—Crim Law 1090(1).

Gibson v. State, TexCrApp, 357 SW 2d 569—Crim Law 911, 939(1), 945 (1), 1134(4), 1156(1), 1192.

Gibson v. Thomas, Ky, 307 SW2d 779 —App & E 882(17).

Gibson v. Thompson, USTex, 78 SCt 2—Mast & S 276(6).

Gibson v. Thrifty Drug Co, CalApp, 343 P2d 610—Costs 3, 32(1), 146, 169, 175.

Gibson v. Todd Shipyard Corp, NJ SuperAD, 138 A2d 543—Work Comp 549, 573, 1969.

Gibson v. Todd Shipyard Corp, NJCo, 132 A2d 337, aff 138 A2d 543—Work Comp 549, 1488, 1492, 1540.

Gibson v. Town of Danville, Ind, 170 NE2d 444—App & E 706(2); Mun Corp 491.

Gibson v. Turner, Tex, 294 SW2d 781—Covenants 47, 102(1); Mines 73, 79(1, 3).

Gibson v. U S, CADC, 268 F2d 586— Crim Law 447, 1134(3); Evid 397 (2), 433(6).

Gibson v. U S, CAVa, 244 F2d 32— Crim Law 995(4); Escape 9; Ind & Inf 110(14).

Gibson v. U S, DCArk, 163 FSupp 385 —Autos 244(10, 34); Damag 95, 113; Neglig 101, 135(9).

Gibson v. Watson, TexCivApp, 315 SW2d 48, ref n r e—Deeds 93, 95, 98, 114(1); Mines 55(2, 4, 5).

Gibson v. Winterset Community School Dist, Iowa, 138 NW2d 112— Admin Law 328; Mand 27, 28, 71, 72, 74(2); Schools 97(4); Statut 227.

Gibson v. Wright, FlaApp, 179 So2d 245—Bound 25, 33, 37(3); Quiet T 10(2).

Gibson v. Zoning Bd of Adjustment 13 D & C2d 203, 44 DelCo 251— Mun Corp 621.2, 621.17, 621.35, 621.- 57.

Gibson Art Co v. Oxford 216 Ga 389, 116 SE2d 299, foll'g Owens-Illinois Glass Co v. Oxford, 216 Ga 316, 116 SE2d 293.

Gibson Auto Co v. Finnegan 217 Wis 401, 259 NW 420—Trade Reg 866.

Gibson City v. McClellan, IllApp, 209 NE2d 363—Crim Law 1024(2, 4).

Gibson, Com ex rel v. Maroney 29 FayLJ 21. See Com ex rel Gibson v. Maroney.

Gibson Distilling Co v. Netter 62 Pa Super 136—Trade Reg 648, 703.

Gibson General Hospital, State ex rel, v. Warrick Circuit Court, Ind, 214 NE2d 655. See State ex rel Gibson General Hospital v. Warrick Circuit Court.

Gibson, Inc v. Omaha Coffee Co, Neb, 133 NW2d 462. See Frank H Gibson, Inc v. Omaha Coffee Co.

Gibson, Inc v. Omaha Coffee Co, Neb, 137 NW2d 701. See Frank H Gibson, Inc v. Omaha Coffee Co.

Gibson, People ex rel, v. Peller, Ill App, 181 NE2d 376. See People ex rel Gibson v. Peller.

Gibson Pool Co v. Glens Falls Ins Co, SC, 128 SE2d 157. See Gibson v. Glens Falls Ins Co.

Gibson's Discount Center v. Dickens, Miss, 183 So2d 480. See West Bros of Pascagoula, Miss, Inc v. Dickens.

Gibson's Estate, In re, CalApp, 35 Cal Rptr 103—Ex & Ad 17(1), 18; Infants 4.

Gibson's Estate, In re, CalApp, 43 CalRptr 302—Ex & Ad 20(10, 12), 111(1), 500.

Gibson's Estate, In re, Sur, 164 NYS 2d 626—Wills 449, 547, 629, 630(10).

Gibson's Estate, In re, Sur, 164 NYS 2d 630—Judgm 570(5).

Gibson's Estate, In re, Sur, 169 NY S2d 918—Wills 707(2).

Gibson's Estate, In re, Sur, 242 NYS 2d 994—Courts 29; Ex & Ad 518(2, 3, 4), 519(2).

Gibson's Estate, In re, Sur, 261 NYS2d 550—Ex & Ad 93(1, 2), 96, 122(1); Trusts 217(3); Wills 18.

Gibson's Estate, In re, Wis, 96 NW 2d 859—Compromise 15(1); Divorce 2, 62(1), 354, 358, 359(2), 386(2); Estop 95; Ex & Ad 70; Insurance 583(1); Judgm 299(1), 304, 307, 326.

Gibson, State ex rel and to Use of, v. Missouri Bd of Chiropractic Examiners, MoApp, 365 SW2d 773. See State ex rel and to Use of Gibson v. Missouri Bd of Chiropractic Examiners.

Gibson-Stewart Co v. Wm Bros Boiler & Mfg Co, CAOhio, 264 F2d 776, cert den 79 SCt 1448—Pat 26(1¼), 312(1⅛, 3), 324(5⅝), 328.

Gibson's Tri-State Wholesale, Inc v. Scottish Union & Nat Ins Co, La App, 149 So2d 123, writ refused 150 So2d 590—Insurance 335(2, 3).

Gibson's Will, In re, Sur, 212 NYS2d 335—Bast 6; Evid 383(4); Marriage 3, 13, 20(1, 2), 50(1, 4).

Gibson's Will, In re, Sur, 224 NYS2d 169—Evid 76; Wills 277, 302(5), 303(3).

Gichner v. Insurance Companies of North America, DCMunApp, 180 A 2d 842—Courts 444.6; U S 67(12).

Giddens v. Isbrandtsen Co, CAVa, 355 F2d 125—Adm 34.1; Ship 84(1), 86(1, 2⅜).

Giddens v. Moore, TexCivApp, 348 SW 2d 404—Plead 52(2); Ven & Pur 18(1, 3), 334(5).

Giddings v. Wyman, IllApp, 177 NE2d 641—Damag 127, 131(6); New Tr 75(1); Trial 139(1), 140(1).

Gideon, Application of, CalApp, 320 P2d 599, cert den Gideon v. Gideon 78 SCt 561—Divorce 269(1); Judgm 524.

Gideon v. Gideon, CalApp, 303 P2d 619, vac 310 P2d 90.

Gideon v. Gideon, CalApp, 310 P2d 90 —Divorce 221, 226, 229.

Gideon v. Gideon, CalApp, 314 P2d 1011—App & E 994(3), 1010(1), 1012 (1); Divorce 46, 124, 130, 150(2), 184(6), 223, 302; Evid 150.

Gideon v. Superior Court In and For Los Angeles County, CalApp, 297 P 2d 84—Divorce 269(1), 311; Prohib 11; Trial 400(1).

Gideon v. Tuscbay Properties, Inc, CAFla, 314 F2d 445—Fed Civ Proc 673; High 68, 159(2).

Gideon v. Wainwright, USFla, 83 S Ct 792, on remand 153 So2d 299— Const Law 268(1), 268.2(3); Courts 397½.

Gideon v. Wainwright, Fla, 153 So2d 299—Courts 400.

Gidge v. Security Realty Co, Mass, 199 NE2d 518—App & E 1057(1); Land & Ten 168(1); Neglig 67.

Gidley v. Gladden, DCOr, 237 FSupp 477—Hab Corp 45.3(1, 3).

Gidley v. Industrial Commission, Mo App, 356 SW2d 550—Social S 650.

Gidlow, Application of, Cust & Pat App, 345 F2d 196—Pat 66(1.15, 1.24), 101(5).

Gidney v. Gidney, Sup, 242 NYS2d 924—Divorce 104, 352(3); Plead 276.

Gidney v. Sterling, DCArk, 202 FSupp 344—Hab Corp 41, 45(1), 45.3(1); Mental H 37.

Gidney v. Wayne Oakland Bank, CA Mich, 252 F2d 537. See National Bank of Detroit v. Wayne Oakland Bank.

Gidney Auto Sales v. Cutchins, Fla App, 97 So2d 145—Witn 379(10); Work Comp 235, 1434, 1939.

Gidwitz v. Lanzit Corrugated Box Co, Ill, 170 NE2d 131—Corp 180, 281, 312(1), 592, 612, 614(5).

Giebelman v. Vap, Neb, 126 NW2d 673—App & E 1066; Autos 208; Neglig 122(3); Trial 139(1), 142, 252(7).

Giegerich, In re, Sup, 198 NYS2d 585 —Parent & C 2(2, 3.7).

Giegerick's Adoption, In re, Sur, 199 NYS2d 535—Adop 7.

Giegling v. Helmbold, Mich, 98 NW 2d 536—Ease 2; Judgm 665, 707, 715(1), 735.

Giello v. James A. Freaney, Inc, Mass, 150 NE2d 921. See Barresy v. James A. Freaney, Inc.

Gielski v. State, CtCl, 155 NYS2d 863—Courts 26; Health 6; Phys 14 (4); States 112, 184.9, 184.25.

Gielskie v. State, AD3d, 200 NYS2d 691, order settled 205 NYS2d 1003, aff 216 NYS2d 85, 175 NE2d 455— Phys 14(2); States 112.

Gielskie v. State, CtCl, 191 NYS2d 436, motion den 194 NYS2d 445, rev 200 NYS2d 691, order settled 205 NYS2d 1003, aff 216 NYS2d 85, 175 NE2d 455—Damag 132(3); Drug 8, 9; States 112.

Giemza v. Allied Am Mut Fire Ins Co, Wis, 103 NW2d 538—App & E 1177(6), 1178(6); Autos 168(10), 224(1, 8), 247; New Tr 41(1), 60; Plead 237(2); Trial 350(6, 7), 352 (5).

Giemza v. Allied American Mut Fire Ins Co, Wis, 106 NW2d 609—Costs 251; Statut 223.2(24).

Gier v. Clark, Mo, 300 SW2d 519— App & E 78(1), 105, 110, 151(2); New Tr 164.

Gier v. Gier, Colo, 339 P2d 677— Divorce 286.

Gierczic v. Gierczic, LaApp, 145 So2d 362—App & E 99.

Gierczic v. Gierczic, LaApp, 150 So 2d 84, writ refused 151 So2d 692— App & E 73(2), 78(1).

Gierczic v. Gierczic, TexCivApp, 382 SW2d 495—Divorce 312.1.

Gierhart v. State, Ind, 186 NE2d 680 —App & E 781(4), 792.

Giering v. Lemoine, LaApp, 106 So 2d 534—Phys 24(1, 3).

Gierkont v. Gierkont, NJSuperAD, 134 A2d 10—App & E 757(1); Paupers 37(1, .2).

Gierman v. Toman, NJSuperL, 185 A2d 241—Damag 181; Discov 31, 41; False Imp 12; Mal Pros 68.

Gies v. Boehm, Wyo, 329 P2d 807— Evid 49; Trial 62(3); Waters 224, 225.

Gies v. Fischer, Fla, 146 So2d 361 —Estop 62(1); Nav Wat 38.

Giese v. Mountain States Tel & Tel Co, NM, 376 P2d 24—Judgm 185 (2); Mun Corp 806(3), 821(18); Neglig 1, 10, 32(1), 136(9).

Giese v. Smith, Kan, 408 P2d 687— Courts 89; Wills 435, 439, 441, 442, 470, 597(1), 601(1), 629.

Gieseke v. Doyel, MoApp, 290 SW2d 189—Covenants 49.

Gieseke v. Hardware Dealers Mut Fire Ins Co, IllApp, 195 NE2d 32— App & E 242(2), 1010(1); Insurance 92.1; Princ & A 136(1), 190 (1); Witn 139(1).

Gieseke v. Hardware Dealers Mut Fire Ins Co, IllApp, 208 NE2d 900—App & E 1180(1), 1190, 1198, 1203(1), 1210(1); Execution 8; Witn 139 (1), 141.

Figure 8

These, of course, are only useful for finding a case by name if you already happen to know the jurisdiction in which it was argued and the date that the decision was handed down. If you know this much information, though, you could probably find it more quickly by using one of the digest case name tables.

Naturally, one of the best and most efficient ways of finding a case by name only is through a computer search in one of the on-line legal databases available, like LEXIS and Westlaw. Word, or in this instance name, searching is one of the major breakthroughs of computer research. You don't have to figure out how an indexer or editor may have classified the case or information that you want. You can search directly using your desired terms. The problem with using these commercial legal databases (you knew there was a catch didn't you, or we would have allotted more space in this chapter to the subject of case name computer searching) is that they tend to be rather expensive. In many law firms associates aren't even allowed to search these systems because of the cost (sometimes they just let the paralegals do it because they have more experience). And, unless you work for a law firm, library, or government agency, you probably don't have access to them. Even if you do have access through your employer, the employer might not take kindly to you doing your personal legal research on company time and at company expense (shame, shame, who would even think of doing that). If you have to know now and you just can't wait to find out how to do computer legal research, then turn to Chapter 8 where we open that can of worms. For now, like most novices though, we think you and Henry are probably better off sticking to the books.

Finding more cases with the digests

In the preceding sections we mentioned digests and how their case summaries are arranged by topic. Either with or without one relevant case in hand, you can use this careful arrangement to help you find cases that address your issue. Let's start with a discussion of how you can access the digests when you already have one case.

THE WEST KEY NUMBER SYSTEM

In this section, we are going to concentrate on how to use West key numbers to teach you and Henry the basics of accessing digests. We're going to do this because the West case reporter system is the most extensive reporter system available, covering every jurisdiction in the United States, and the basics of how to access the digests by topic numbers is essentially the same for all digests. The major difference is that West puts a little graphic of a key next to their topic subheadings and other publishers don't. This is not to say that West and other publishers divide the law into the same topics and subheadings, although there may be some overlap. What we mean is that almost all digests use a topic and subheading breakdown for their structure, with the topics given short names, like "Search and Seizure," combined with short subheading numbers for greater specificity.

To start, let's look at Henry's sample case, *Gideon v. Wainwright* (see Figure 9). The number starting on the left with the period behind it is the number of the headnote. For instance, in Figure 9, the arrow is pointing to the number 3. This indicates that this is the third headnote in the opinion, and if Henry glanced through the opinion he would be able to find the paragraph from which this headnote was derived (in this case, it is on page 795 in the opinion). The topic in this example is "Constitutional Law." Topics in the West digests are arranged alphabetically. Which means that if Henry wanted to find other cases in the West digest system that deal with this same topic, he would look for this topic in the digest. He could find "Constitutional Law" in the digest between the topics "Conspiracy" and "Consumer Credit." The topic in the headnote is followed by a graphic of a key and the number that follows the key is the key number, in this instance 268. The key number is the subtopic classification of this particular issue in the digest. This is important because Henry probably wouldn't want to have to wade through every case under the broad topic "Constitutional Law," when he could save time and hone in on the particular issue that he wants to research: Whether the right to assistance of counsel in the Sixth Amendment of the U.S. Constitution must also be followed by the states in the state courts.

Now, let's go to the *Seventh Decennial Digest* (because that is the digest that contains the year that Henry's case was decided) and take a look under this topic and key number to see what other cases we can find that deal with this same issue. As Henry and you can immediately see (Figure 10) there is a problem here. There should be a topic and number directly corresponding with the one in the headnote, and our headnote should be classified under it. But let's make the most of this snafu.

Headnote #3

792 83 SUPREME COURT REPORTER 372 U.S. 335

372 U.S. 335
Clarence Earl GIDEON, Petitioner,
v.
Louie L. WAINWRIGHT, Director, Division of Corrections.
No. 155.
Argued Jan. 15, 1963.
Decided March 18, 1963.

The petitioner brought habeas corpus proceedings against the Director of the Division of Corrections. The Florida Supreme Court, 135 So.2d 746, denied all relief, and the petitioner brought certiorari. The United States Supreme Court, Mr. Justice Black, held that the Sixth Amendment to the federal Constitution providing that in all criminal prosecutions the accused shall enjoy right to assistance of counsel for his defense is made obligatory on the states by the Fourteenth Amendment, and that an indigent defendant in a criminal prosecution in a state court has the right to have counsel appointed for him.

Judgment reversed and cause remanded to Florida Supreme Court for further action.

1. Courts ⚷397½

United States Supreme Court granted certiorari to review judgment of Florida Supreme Court denying habeas corpus on ground that indigent defendant in criminal prosecution in state court has no right to have counsel appointed for him, in view of fact that problem of defendant's federal constitutional right to counsel in state court has been continuing source of controversy and litigation in both state and federal courts. U.S.C.A.Const Amends. 6, 14.

2. Constitutional Law ⚷268

Where provision of Bill of Rights of federal Constitution is fundamental and essential to fair trial, it is made obligatory on states by Fourteenth Amendment. U.S.C.A.Const. Amends. 6, 14.

3. Constitutional Law ⚷268

Sixth Amendment to federal Constitution providing that in all criminal prosecutions the accused shall enjoy right to assistance of counsel for his defense is made obligatory on the states by the Fourteenth Amendment, and indigent defendant in criminal prosecution in state court has right to have counsel appointed for him. Betts v. Brady, 316 U.S. 455, 62 S.Ct. 1252, overruled. U.S.C.A.Const. Amends, 6, 14.

Abe Fortas, Washington, D. C., for petitioner.

Bruce R. Jacob, Tallahassee, Fla., for respondent.

J. Lee Rankin, New York City, for American Civil Liberties Union, amicus curiæ, by special leave of Court.

George D. Mentz, Montgomery, Ala., for State of Alabama, amicus curiæ.

336

Mr. Justice BLACK delivered the opinion of the Court.

[1] Petitioner was charged in a Florida state court with having broken and entered a poolroom with intent to commit a misdemeanor. This offense is a felony under

337

Florida law. Appearing in court without funds and without a lawyer, petitioner asked the court to appoint counsel for him, whereupon the following colloquy took place:

> "The COURT: Mr. Gideon, I am sorry, but I cannot appoint Counsel to represent you in this case. Under the laws of the State of Florida, the only time the Court can appoint Counsel to represent a Defendant is when that person is charged with a capital offense. I am sorry, but I will have to deny your request to appoint Counsel to defend you in this case.
>
> "The DEFENDANT: The United States Supreme Court says I am entitled to be represented by Counsel."

Put to trial before a jury, Gideon conducted his defense about as well as could

Figure 9

CONSTITUTIONAL LAW

XI. DUE PROCESS OF LAW—Continued.

🔑264. —— Summary trial and conviction.
265. —— Indictment or information.
266. —— Rules of evidence.
267. —— Right to trial by jury.
268. —— Course and conduct of trial.
(1). In general.
(2). Particular cases and problems.
(3). —— Time of trial in general; opportunity to obtain counsel and prepare.
(4). —— Undue delay; right to speedy trial.
(5). —— Disclosure to defendant.
(6). —— Presence of accused and counsel; public trial and confrontation.
(7). —— Bias and prejudice generally; improper publicity and disclosing of other offenses.
(8). —— Qualification, actions and comments of judge, jury or prosecutor.
268.1. —— Assistance of Counsel.
(1). In general.
(2). Necessity in general.
(3). Stage of proceedings.
(4). Offer of counsel or notice of right.
(5). Choice of counsel; necessity of request and waiver.
(6). Adequacy and effectiveness of representation.
268.2. —— Disadvantaged persons, counsel and trial.
(1). In general.
(2). Incompetents or psychopaths; determination of sanity.
(3). Indigents; transcript and financial aid.
(4). Infants.
269. —— New trial.
270. —— Judgment and sentence.
271. —— Appeal or error.
272. —— Execution of sentence.
273. Contempt proceedings.
274. Deprivation of personal rights in general.
275. Deprivation of liberty as to occupation or employment.
(1). In general.
(2). Regulation of employment of labor.
276. Deprivation of liberty to contract.
277. Property and rights therein protected.
(1). In general.
(2). Public office.
278. Deprivation of property in general.
(1). In general.
(2). Creation, alteration, and regulation of municipalities.
(3). Municipal interference with franchise.
(4). Health regulations.
(5). Administration on estates of absentees or persons presumed to be dead.

Figure 10

The headnote from Henry's case was designated as Constitutional Law 268, but when we look under this topic and key number we see that 268 has grown to include 268(1)-(8) as well as 268.1(1)-(6) and 268.2(1)-(4). So where is Henry's headnote for *Gideon v. Wainwright* and others like it? The best way to find it at this point is to break down the elements of the headnote and figure out where the editors would put it. Henry's headnote is concerned with three basic elements (1) the right to assistance of counsel; (2) indigent defendants—in other words, defendants who are poor; and (3) the application of the Sixth Amendment to the states through the Fourteenth Amendment. Looking at the table of contents for this new range of key numbers under the topic Constitutional Law, we see several likely key numbers we could check here, but the one that seems to encompass most of the elements of Henry's headnote is 268.2—Disadvantaged person, counsel and trial (3) Indigents; transcript and financial aid. And there, the second headnote under the new key number, is his headnote (see Figure 11) (following a headnote that doesn't even appear at the beginning of *Gideon v. Wainwright*—editors will play with your head sometimes). Now that we've found it though, Henry can use this same topic and key number to search other West digests covering earlier years, later years, or specific jurisdictions to find more cases dealing with this issue.

Remember—a digest is sort of like an elaborate index. Well, it also suffers from the same classification problems that indexes do. Editors, like all lawyers reading a case, may see the issues in a slightly different way, and so they may classify the issue that you are concerned with under different topics and key numbers. In fact, some headnotes in other cases are already classified by the editor as falling under two or more classifications. What this means is that you will probably have to search more than one topic and key number when doing your research, even if you have only one legal issue that you are concerned with.

TOPIC APPROACH

Sometimes, of course, you may have no case in hand to help you access the digest through the headnotes, although this should be unlikely if you've done the background searching recommended in Chapter 4. Digests are still helpful though, and in fact many lawyers, because they already know the background of the law out of which their client's issues arise, will start their research here.

Sup. 1942. The provisions of the Desmond Act prescribing procedure for trying an issue of present insanity of a person accused of crime, which provide a judicial examination with an opportunity for defendant to be heard are not unconstitutional as denying defendant "due process of law". Code Cr.Proc. §§ 658 to 662–d, 870, as added by Laws 1939, c. 861, § 2; Penal Law, § 724; U.S.C.A.Const. Amend. 14.—People ex rel. Klesitz v. Mills, 37 N.Y.S.2d 185, 179 Misc. 58.

Sup. 1943. The provisions of statute prescribing procedure for trying an issue of present insanity of a person accused of a felony or misdemeanor, which provide a judicial examination with an opportunity for defendant to be heard, are not unconstitutional as denying accused "due process of law". Code Cr. Proc. § 662 as amended by Laws 1942, c. 284, § 1, §§ 662–a, 662–b as added and renumbered by Laws 1942, c. 284, §§ 2, 3; Code Cr. Proc. § 870 subd. 1, St.1939, c. 861, § 2.—People ex rel. Anderson v. Superintendent of Creedmoor State Hospital, 40 N.Y.S.2d 84.

N.J.Co. Where 18 year old boy who was of defective intelligence who could not read, and who was not represented by an attorney entered non vult pleas to 14 separate charges of breaking, entering, and larceny, and court imposed on five of the charges separate consecutive sentences and suspended sentences on the remaining charges, and he served the equivalent of one maximum term as reduced by work credits, county court in habeas corpus proceeding would order him discharged from imprisonment under the four remaining sentences imposed on pleas of non vult, on ground that sentencing court had no jurisdiction to impose them because of denial of due process, and would order him remanded to custody of sheriff to be dealt with according to law. R.S. 2:190–3, 30:4–92; R.S. 2:190–3, 30:4–92, N.J.S.A.; Const.1844, art. I, par. 8; U.S.C.A.Const. Amend. 14.—Ex parte Carter, 82 A.2d 652, 14 N.J.Super. 591.

Okl. Provisions of Mental Health Law authorizing temporary commitment of accused to a state mental hospital for observation, by necessary implication, provide for a hearing with the accused being given notice and an opportunity to be heard, and hence statute does not deprive an individual of his liberty without "due process of law" in violation of state Constitution. 43A O.S.Supp. § 60; O.S. 1951 Const. art. 2, § 7.—In re Lutker, 274 P.2d 786.

Due process of law entitled one accused of crime to notice and an opportunity to be heard before entry of order pursuant to Mental Health Law committing him to state mental hospital for observation. 43A O.S.Supp. § 60; O.S.1951 Const. art. 2, § 7.—Id.

Where district court without notice to accused or opportunity to be heard committed him to state mental hospital for observation upon oral motion of county attorney stating that sanity of accused was in question, accused was deprived of his liberty without due process of law in violation of state Constitution, and order of commitment should be vacated and accused remanded to custody of sheriff. 43A O.S.Supp. § 60; O.S.1951 Const. art. 2, § 7.—Id.

Pa. Where prisoner was confined to jail which had superintendent and an experienced physician, but neither moved to have prisoner committed as an insane person, and although prisoner once had been committed to an insane asylum as presently insane he had later been discharged as sane, and at time of murder trial prisoner's counsel made no request for appointment of psychiatrist, but court appointed qualified psychiatrist to examine prisoner and psychiatrist testified that prisoner was not psychotic when he shot and killed deceased and had completely recovered from mental illness, there was no denial of due process of law in placing defendant on trial without further investigation of his mental state.—Com. ex rel. Smith v. Ashe, 71 A.2d 107, certiorari denied 71 S.Ct. 40, 340 U.S. 812, 95 L.Ed. 597.

In murder prosecution, that defendant's attorney was not furnished through the court with psychiatrist to testify on behalf of defendant was not a denial of due process.—Id.

In habeas corpus proceeding, evidence did not establish that defendant was insane when he committed murder charged or when he pleaded guilty or at time he was sentenced to death or that defendant was denied due process of law.—Id.

S.C. Where insanity is interposed as defense in criminal prosecution, compulsory examination of accused by experts for purpose of determining his mental condition and testifying in regard thereto does not violate either constitutional privilege of accused of not being compelled to be witness against himself or constitutional guaranty of due process of law. Code 1942, § 6239; Const. art. 1, § 17.—State v. Myers, 67 S.E.2d 506.

Wash. 1941. If one accused of crime and put on his trial is insane at time of trial his constitutional rights are violated, and if found guilty and sentence executed he would be deprived of life or liberty without "due process of law." Rem.Rev.Stat. § 2175.—State v. Davis, 108 P.2d 641, 6 Wash.2d 696.

Wash. The presumption of continuance of unsound mental condition of one previously adjudged to be insane requires appointment of attorney as next friend and counsel prior to arraignment for criminal charge, in order that such step in criminal procedure can be made with due process of law.—Kenstrip v. Cranor, 235 P.2d 467.

An adjudication of the issue of defendant's insanity prior to trial is not necessary to satisfy due process, but defendant is afforded his day in court by determination by jury of issue of insanity as separate issue in principal trial.—Id.

Wash. The presumption of continuance of unsound mental condition of one previously adjudged to be insane requires appointment of attorney as next friend and counsel prior to arraignment on criminal charge, in order that such step in criminal procedure can be made with due process of law.—Varner v. Cranor, 259 P.2d 417.

Wash. 1964. A defendant convicted of first degree murder was not denied any Fourteenth Amendment rights as result of trial court's denial of irresistible impulse or other variations thereof, either as a defense to the charges of which defendant was convicted, or in regard to application of the death penalty. U.S.C.A.Const. Amend. 14.—White v. Rhay, 390 P.2d 535.

Wyo. Facts that defendant who pleaded insanity was subjected to mental examination by State's physicians and to electroencephalogram test and that physicians who examined him and person who made such electroencephalogram test testified for State did not deny defendant due process of law or result in his being compelled to testify against himself or in his being subjected to unlawful search and seizure. W.C.S.1945, § 10–903.—State v. 298 P.2d 349, rehearing denied 300 P.2d 567.

⚷268.2(3). Indigents; transcript and financial aid

U.S.Fla. 1963. State court's refusal to appoint counsel, upon request, for an indigent accused of non-capital felony, violated due process clause. U.S.C.A.Const. Amend. 14.—Gideon v. Wainwright, 83 S.Ct. 792, 372 U.S. 335, 9 L.Ed.2d 799, 93 A.L.R.2d 733, on remand 153 So.2d 299. ⟵

Sixth Amendment to federal Constitution providing that in all criminal prosecutions the accused shall enjoy right to assistance of counsel for his defense is made obligatory on the states by the Fourteenth Amendment, and indigent defendant in criminal prosecution in state court has right to have counsel appointed for him. Betts v. Brady, 316 U.S. 455, 62 S. Ct. 1252, overruled. U.S.C.A.Const. Amends. 6, 14.—Id. ⟵

U.S.Ill. The right to counsel of indigent accused may, under relevant circumstances, be part of the due process which the Fourteenth Amendment guarantees. U.S.C.A.Const. Amend. 14.—Loftus v. People of State of Ill., 68 S.Ct. 1212, 334 U.S. 804, 92 L.Ed. 1737.

U.S.Md. 1942. Where circuit court of Carroll county, Md., refused request of accused, indicted for robbery, for appointment of counsel on ground that it was not practice in Carroll county to appoint counsel for indigent defendants save in prosecution for murder and rape, accused was man of ordinary intelligence and ability to take care of his own interests on trial of narrow issue presented by alibi defense and accused was not wholly unfamiliar with criminal procedure and examined witnesses to prove his defense, conviction and sentence was not deprivation of liberty of accused without "due process of law" in violation of Fourteenth Amendment. Declaration of Rights Md. art. 21; U.S.C.A.Const. Amend. 14.—Betts v. Brady, 62 S.Ct. 1252, 316 U.S. 455, 86 L.Ed. 1595.

C.A.Ill. The concept of due process in the Fourteenth Amendment does not require the states to furnish counsel to an indigent defendant in every case, so that in a noncapital conviction, there is no fundamental right to counsel, except where special circumstances are such that without counsel, defendant cannot enjoy a fair, adequate hearing. U.S.C. A.Const. Amend. 14.—Wiggins v. Ragen, 238 F.2d 309.

C.A.Mass. The due process clause of the 14th Amendment does not in all non-capital cases inflexibly require a state to supply counsel to an indigent accused, in contrast with mandate of Sixth Amendment, under which counsel must be furnished to an indigent defendant prosecuted in federal court in every case, whatever the circumstances. U.S.C.A. Const. Amends. 6, 14.—Buchanan v. O'Brien, 181 F.2d 601.

C.A.N.M. 1965. Due process requires appointment of counsel to represent indigent defendant in state criminal trial. U.S.C.A.Const. Amend. 14.—Peters v. Cox, 341 F.2d 575.

C.C.A.Pa. Where indigent defendant was held in custody, appointment of counsel for him, only one minute before case went on trial was insufficient and deprived defendant of due process. U.S.C.A.Const. Amend. 5.—U. S. v. Helwig, 159 F.2d 616.

C.A.Pa. 1964. Conviction of indigent defendant who, after his request for appointment of counsel was refused, entered guilty plea to two separate counts of robbery, resulted from fundamentally unfair procedure violative of due process. U.S.C.A.Const. Amend. 14.—U. S. ex rel. Craig v. Myers, 329 F.2d 856.

C.A.Tex. 1964. Right of indigent state prisoner to counsel rests on Sixth Amendment and its inclusion in due process clause of Fourteenth Amendment. U.S.C.A.Const. Amend. 14.—Lyles v. Beto, 329 F.2d 332.

For subsequent case history information, see Table of Cases

Figure 11

If you don't have a case to give you a key number, one way of searching the digests is to use the topic approach.

West divides the law into basic categories:

1. Contracts
2. Crimes
3. Government
4. Persons
5. Property
6. Remedies
7. Torts

LAW FACT

In the legal world when someone mentions *remedies* what he or she means is the money award that the plaintiff wants to receive or other sort of actions that the plaintiff wants the court to take in his or her favor.

Helpful Hint

As you saw in our example with Henry, above, digest topics are not carved in stone. As the law changes, the classifications sometimes also change, with new topics being added and old, out-of-date, topics being retired. You may, therefore, want to keep alert to such changes. Sometimes you may start searching the digests under one key number only to have that number disappear. This could be because the legal issue that it covered was reassigned to a new number. The digest will usually keep you apprised of such developments through tables and notations in the text that describe the changes, but when you are embroiled in a search it can be easy to miss.

These categories are then further divided into topics, which are still further divided into legal issues that are assigned key numbers.

You can search with the topic approach by using the background material and initial brainstorming that you used to define your legal issue, as discussed in Chapter 3. Use your keywords to try to match your legal issue with one or more of the digest topics. These topics can usually be found at the front of each digest volume. For instance, returning to Henry's constitutional right to counsel problem, we can find an appropriate topic in two ways. We can classify this problem first under one of the seven legal categories provided by West, which are located at the front of the Descriptive Word Index. In this case, "Government" would probably be a good guess because only government action is covered by the Constitution, and then we can look for a specific topic, or we can go directly to the list of topics and look for a topic which might be a likely candidate to search. In Henry's case, either method would probably lead to the topic "Constitutional Law." Then, once having found the topic in the digest, by skimming the contents at the beginning of the text of that topic, we can narrow down to the key numbers that would make the most sense to search.

THE DESCRIPTIVE WORD INDEX

Another method of accessing the digests when you don't have a specific case to go on, is by using the Descriptive Word Index that goes along with each set of volumes. This can be a good place for the lawyer and nonlawyer alike to begin a digest search because you don't have to necessarily know what legal category your issue falls under. All you need is a word or short phrase that encompasses your issue, albeit a word or phrase that the indexer thought was important enough and descriptive enough to include in the index.

To access the Descriptive Word Index we should use the categories outlined in Chapter 3 and brainstorm. Using the keywords that we come up with, we can start looking in the Descriptive Word Index with Henry. As you can see in Figure 12, the pages of the index have general headings, like **ASSIGNMENTS** or **ASSUMED OR FICTITIOUS NAMES**, bolded and in capital letters, with more specific subheadings in capitals, and even more descriptive issues followed by key number notations as to where these issues can be found in the digest volumes. For instance, in the page reproduced, you see that there is a heading for **ASSISTANCE OF COUNSEL**, and under this there is a specific issue, criminal trial, due process of law, and after this issue the index says, in an abbreviation, that the issue is addressed in the volume containing the key numbers Const Law 268 (as we already know, this is the key number that we want). The volumes are set up in ranges, like encyclopedias. So, don't worry if you don't see the title you are

> **Helpful Hint**
>
> Before spending too much time skimming the key numbers, it is a good idea to read the "Subjects Included" and the "Subjects Excluded" paragraphs at the beginning of the topic. Although it may sound to you as though the topic you've picked is right on target, the editors may have designated your problem differently. For instance, if you were having trouble about racial discrimination, even though this is covered by the Fourteenth Amendment to the U.S. Constitution, issues relating to this problem might be found under the topic "Civil Rights" and not under "Constitutional Law."

> **Helpful Hint**
>
> As we've mentioned before with reading cases, it might be a good idea to keep a law dictionary at hand when doing your initial digest search because some of the digest topics, like "Detinue," are legal terms of art, and are probably not immediately recognizable.

ASSIGNMENTS

35-7th D—112

ASSIGNMENTS—Cont'd

Prisoner of moneys to third parties, commitment to prison for contempt, determination of validity of assignment. **Prisons 4**

Privilege tax. **Tax 117**

Receivables as security, action on account, assignor's right. **Assign 117**

Record of assignment—

Account—

Assign 46

Fraud Conv 136, 242(1)

Redemption rights, support liens. **Divorce 256**

Reformation—

Royalty leasehold interest. **Ref of Inst 25**

Remainder in trust, foreign state, usury. **Usury 2(3)**

Conflict of laws. **Courts 359**

Remainders—

Security for notes. **Remaind 14**

Rental agreements, assignments as not releasing guarantor. **Guar 53(2)**

Reservoir, etc., effect as notice. **Waters 243**

Right to receive money due or to become due. **Assign 10**

Secured transactions, see this index **Secured Transactions**

Security—

Assignment as—

Receivables, assignor's action on account. **Assign 117**

Shares in corporation, inclusion of shares in assets of decedent's estate—

Corp 125

Ex & Ad 55

Statutory provisions—

Trust beneficiary's assignment of income interest. **Trusts 130**

Stay of proceedings until completion of examination of assignor's officers. **Action 68**

Subrogation, nature of equitable assignment. **Subrog 1**

Tax lien of United States, attachment of interest in assigned claim—

Assign 46

Interest 1717, 1721

Tax lien on payment of amount due. **Tax 514**

Tax liens—

Subjects of, chose in action. **Int Rev 1719.2**

Television station license, federal communications commission's findings, evidence. **Tel 410**

Title insurance companies, drafting, unauthorized practice of law. **Corp 377½**

Tort actions for personal injury. **Assign 24(2)**

Torts, liability of members. **Assoc 16**

Trading With the Enemy Act. **War 12**

Trusts—

Beneficiary's right to income. **Trusts 147(1), 148**

Jurisdiction to determine validity and priority of assignments against judgment. **Trusts 298**

Vacation pay accrued, employee's rights. **Assign 16**

Vendor and purchaser, lien in favor of purchaser's assignee for amount of down payment and expenses of examination of title. **Ven & Pur 337**

Wages, cancellation, hearing. **Can of Inst 49**

War risk insurance, enforcement. **Armed S 78**

Warranties, conditional sales. **Sales 475**

Well drilling contractor. taxes and penalties is not entitled to preference over assignees. **Int Rev 1719.3**

Workmen's Compensation, see this index **Workmen's Compensation**

ASSIGNMENTS FOR BENEFIT OF CREDITORS

Administration of assigned estate, discretion of trustee. **Assign f B C 35**

Attorneys—

Fees and expenses—

Allowance on assignee's accounting or settlement. **Assign f BC 399, 400**

ASSIGNMENTS FOR BENEFIT OF CREDITORS—Cont'd

Attorneys—Cont'd

Assignee of corporate assignor. **Corp 550(10)**

Preference over tax claims, services for debtor benefiting creditors—

Assign f B C 318

Corp 550(9)

Insolv 185, 188

Bankruptcy—

Act of bankruptcy, assignment for creditors—

Estoppel or forfeiture of right to file petition in bankruptcy. **Bankr 76(3)**

Effect of Federal Bankruptcy Act on Virgin Islands code provision. **Bankr 9(2, 3)**

Powers and duties. **Bankr 115**

Regulation of assignments by state statute notwithstanding Federal Bankruptcy Act. **Bankr 9(2)**

Statute, suspension by bankruptcy act. **Bankr 9(2)**

Time for filing of petition. **Bankr 79**

Claims—

Presentation, proof and payment—

Taxes, priority. **Assign f B C 308(1)**

United States, priority. **U S 76**

Constitutional and statutory provisions, power of state to regulate by statute notwithstanding Federal Bankruptcy Act. **Bankr 9(2)**

Conveyances—

Failure to file deed of assignment. **Assign f BC 170**

Trust property or trust fund. **Assign f B C 176(2)**

Corporations, estoppel of wife who joined in assignment to deny corporate existence of assignee. **Corp 34(3)**

Debt consolidating agencies. **Assign f B C 23**

Deed, recording, necessity against subsequent judgment creditor without notice. **Assign f B C 330**

Discharge of assignor, suspension of Virgin Islands Code provision by Federal Bankruptcy Act. **Bankr 9(2)**

Estoppel, inconsistency of conduct and claims. **Estop 63**

Foreign sovereign's consent to motion in assignment proceeding. **Intern Law 10.32**

Insurance—

Assignee's right to proceeds of insurance carried by assignor. **Assign f BC 176(1)**

Insured's assignment of assets as transferring policy to assignee. **Assign f B C 174**

Reference to determine proceeds allocable to assignee. **Refer 7(1)**

Landlord and tenant—

Right of recovery by tenant's assignee of security deposited. **Land & Ten 184(1)**

Set-off against tenant's assignee. **Assign f B C 186**

Mechanics' liens—

Dismissal of lien foreclosure action on ground of failure to timely file claim with assignee. **Mech Liens 284**

Pre-existing debt, sale or security of debtors' property subject to execution or creditor's claim. **Assign f B C 12(3)**

Preferences—

Attorney's fees—

Support of proceedings, priority over federal tax claim. **Corp 550(9)**

Fringe benefit payments. **Assign f B C 308(2)**

Medical benefits, trust fund payments. **Assign f B C 308(2)**

Retirement benefits, trust fund payments. **Assign f B C 308(2)**

Welfare benefits, trust fund benefits. **Assign f B C 308(2)**

Public employee's future wages. **Assign f B C 34**

ASSIGNMENTS FOR BENEFIT OF CREDITORS—Cont'd

Rights, creditors, corporation's assignment. **Corp 550(9)**

Trusts, property held in, assignor's title or possession. **Assign f B C 176(2)**

ASSIMILATIVE CRIMES ACT

Disorderly conduct, application to federal reservations. **Arrest 63(4)**

State law against drunk driving, application to federal roads. **Crim Law 16**

United States marshal's arrest, disorderly conduct under state law. **Arrest 63(4)**

ASSISTANCE OF COUNSEL

Criminal trial, due process of law. **Const Law 268**

Preliminary hearing, failure to appoint as not denying due process—

Const Law 268

Hab Corp 59

ASSISTANCE, WRIT OF

Appealable decisions, quashal order. **Courts 405(12.14)**

ASSOCIATION FOR ADVANCEMENT OF RACIAL GROUP

Contempt—

Certiorari review. **Contempt 67**

Noncompliance with order to produce books, documents, etc. **Discov 25**

Discovery—

Failure to answer or make disclosure. **Discov 25**

Production and inspection of writings, etc. **Discov 23**

Privilege as to production of document. **Witn 298**

ASSOCIATIONS AND SOCIETIES

Actions—

Unincorporated associations, actions against. **Assoc 2**

Actions by or against associations, defenses, coverture, wife's action against husband's association. **Hus & W 205(2)**

Admission tax—

Exempt performances. **Int Rev 1112**

Aged persons, name, splinter group using. **Clubs 3**

Airlines' mutual aid association, foreign unauthorized insurers, application of law. **Insurance 26**

Architects' society, class action, unlawful practices. **Decl Judgm 305**

Assets—

Members' interest. **Assoc 15(2)**

Attorney's action against association to recover compensation, questions of law or fact. **Atty & C 167(2)**

Automobiles—

Casualty insurance, writing. **Insurance 6**

Baseball, workmen's compensation liability, player's death, traveling to join club. **Work Comp 201**

Board of trade—

Incorporation by legislature, status. **Exchanges 1**

Bowlers—

Expulsion of member. **Assoc 10**

Exhaustion of association remedies before suit. **Assoc 20(1)**

By-laws—

Contract among association members. **Assoc 14**

Cemetery associations—

Impairment of obligation of association's contract by statute. **Const Law 154(1)**

Plots, proceeds from sales, deposits in maintenance funds, constitutionality. **Const Law 154(2)**

Unemployment compensation laws, exemption. **Tax 111.23**

Citizenship, diversity jurisdiction cases. **Courts 315**

Constitutional and statutory provisions, uniformity. **Statut 72**

Ordinance compelling membership disclosure, interference with freedom of association. **Const Law 46(1)**

Figure 12

searching for on the spine of one of the volumes. Just determine where the title would fall if it was alphabetized in the ranges that appear on the spines of the books. For instance, the topic and key number Constitutional Law 268 would be found in the *Seventh Decennial Digest* in the volume containing the ranges Common Lands to Contracts 235.

Once you've found your key numbers, you can start reading the little digest paragraphs to determine which cases are relevant or helpful in addressing your problem, and then you can add them to your list for a later, in-depth reading.

> **Helpful Hint:**
>
> Some of the abbreviations for the topics, like: "Assign f BC," can be a little cryptic. The Descriptive Word Index, however, has a list of the abbreviations in the front of the book. In this case, Assign f BC means Assignment for Benefit of Creditors.

Henry's complaining that this is very labor-intensive. We know, we know, it can be tedious, it can be dull. Hey, we've done digest searches that started in the digests that contained cases from the late 1800s and then followed the search all the way to the present. Unfortunately, this is how legal research is done.

Finding cases while updating

Remember those pocket parts we talked about in Chapter 4? Well, they're back again. The more recent volumes of the digests have them. These pocket parts, and the other updating systems that we will soon discuss, exist because of the doctrine of stare decisis and precedent that we talked about in Chapter 1. They are necessary because the common law, with new cases always being decided, is more like a growing plant that is being pruned and shaped (and some people would say fertilized) continuously, than like a statue, which is essentially static, unchanging, except that it gets a little dirtier over time. So, check the pocket parts! They may be able to tell you if one of the cases that you would like to rely on has been challenged, overruled, or limited in its application.

Still, we've found that pocket parts just aren't as complete as we'd like them to be. For some reason, they tend to miss important cases. They aren't exhaustive. What does come close to being exhaustive in updating cases is *Shepard's Citations*. And as you will see, not only can you use Shepard's for your essential updating, you can use it as a case finder too.

UPDATING WITH SHEPARD'S

You can't access Shepard's citators through a descriptive word index or through a topical approach the way you can with digests. To access Shepard's you need at least one case in hand. That's because Shepard's was born as a case-updating service, and has become a case-finding tool only by logical extension.

We've already given you and Henry a brief introduction to Shepard's in this chapter so that you could find the index of popular case names. Now let's take a closer look at this series by walking through the updating of a case. This is the best way to introduce you to all of the aspects of Shepardizing. We'll update the case that Henry was working with before, *Gideon v. Wainwright.*

The first thing that Henry should check when grabbing the *Shepard's* volumes is that he has the volumes appropriate to his case, and that he has all of the volumes that he will need. He has to find the *Shepard's Citations* appropriate for the reporter that he found the case in, whether state, region, or federal. In this instance, he will want the Shepard's that covers the *Supreme Court Reporter.* Next, he'll have to make sure that he has the volumes of this set that are related to the volume number of the reporter in which he found the case; this information will be printed on the cover and spine of the volume. For example, for *Gideon v. Wainwright* 83 S. Ct. 792 he will want the citators that cover volume 83 of the *Supreme Court Reporter.*

We should note at this point that there are softcover books that are issued regularly by Shepard's to update the updating system (we told you the law was ever changing). You have to make sure that your research is as up-to-date as possible, so when updating a case, check that you have all of the volumes that have been published up to the present date. On the front cover of the paperbacks, at the top, the month and year that the supplement contains is listed. Make sure that you have the most recent month because you are going to have to follow your search all the way up to the present day (or as close as possible). If you do not, or if you are not sure (perhaps because the month just changed and you're not sure whether the new supplement has been

Helpful Hint

When you are using a regional or state *Shepard's Citations* volume it may not be so easy to turn right to the section of the Shepard's that is appropriate for your reporter. When you have trouble finding the proper section, look in the front of the *Shepard's Citations* volume that you are using and there will be a table of contents of the reporters that the volume covers and where that coverage begins.

issued) then ask a librarian if the volumes that you found on the shelf are the latest.

> **Helpful Hint**
>
> Parallel cites can be important in brief writing for when a court insists that you give the official cite or you want to see the editorial treatment of the case in other reporters.

Now, in Henry's case, he'll start his search by looking in the dark red hardcover volume, number 3.4, and will turn to the pages that contain the information regarding his reporter number. He can tell when he is looking at the right pages because the reporter number will be in the upper left- or right-hand corner of the page, in this example 83, and the name, *Supreme Court Reporter*, will appear as a heading at the top of the page (see Figure 13). He can find his specific citation in the Shepard's citator by looking for the page number that he wants, page 792, in the columns following the volume number of his reporter. The page numbers are in bold with dashes on either side (see Figure 13) and the case name appears under this page number.

Now that he's found his place in the Shepard's citator, Henry is met with column after column of letters and numbers following the citation. These letters and numbers are merely abbreviations, and they aren't too difficult to understand.

Shepard's Citations does not use Bluebook or Maroon book abbreviations. It uses its own, even more compact, but similar system of abbreviation. There is a list of these abbreviations printed in the front of every *Shepard's Citations* volume. In Henry's case, the reporter that he is using, the *Supreme Court Reporter* is abbreviated as SC. The second thing he notices at the beginning of the column with his case are abbreviations in parentheses. These are parallel cites of *Gideon v. Wainwright*, the exact same case, same text that is reported in different reporters. There are frequently parallel cites like this for two reasons:

- The text of cases themselves are in the public domain, in other words they belong to everyone, and so anyone can make a buck by creating a reporter and printing these cases, and
- Some states and the federal government in some instances have "official" noncommercial reporters, like the *United States Reports*.

The next series of citations that Henry sees are the citations that concern the history and further treatment of Henry's case. A little explanation here is in order. If a case, any case, mentions the

Wyo
803P2d80
850P2d598
59Cor777
62Geo1111
74McL260
60MnL717
74MnL446
48NYL602
126PaL759
77VaL470
55Æ21072s
66Æ3958n
87Æ3259n
27Æ4629n

—789—

General Drivers Warehousemen and Helpers Local Union No. 89 v Riss and Company Inc. 1963

(372US517)
(9LE918)
s 83SC31
s 298F2d341
84SC[4]372
38FRD90
Cir. 1
458F2d[2]591
458F2d[3]592
560F2d[4]1048
699F2d560
908F2d1044
f 240FS[4]429
d 327FS[2]1180
331FS[4]266
574FS[4]454
Cir. 2
377F2d[2]715
441F2d[4]601
491F2d[4]190
547F2d[2]201
574F2d[2]725
858F2d[2]831
912F2d[2]612
299FS[3]890
365FS[2]316
377FS[2]1213
384FS[4]186
451FS[4]769
549FS[2]437
594FS[2]671
622FS[2]568
647FS[1]798
Cir. 3
396F2d[4]37
428F2d[4]506
457F2d[4]611
475F2d[2]435
518F2d[4]1124
f 561F2d[4]1096
f 561F2d[3]1097
574F2d[4]786
591F2d[4]216
666F2d[4]809
666F2d[3]810
670F2d[4]405
703F2d[2]69
900F2d[4]613
217FS[4]164
217FS[4]626
224FS[4]740
226FS[4]798
228FS[4]425
f 230FS[4]386
231FS[4]716
234FS[4]567
234FS[4]905
246FS[4]64
300FS[4]647
332FS[4]377
343FS[4]1131
344FS[2]291
356FS[3]725
368FS[4]1162
375FS[4]660
419FS[2]54
430FS[4]1259
447FS[2]390
f 448FS[4]1352
463FS[2]57
476FS[4]168
486FS[3]704
532FS30
555FS[2]815
Cir. 4
468F2d[4]197
490F2d[4]1268
f 242FS[4]424
307FS[2]323
307FS[4]323
353FS[2]871
f 353FS[3]871
353FS[4]872
365FS[3]167
387FS[4]601
506FS1350
529FS[2]420
630FS[2]1213
Cir. 5
328F2d[4]95
362F2d[4]417
374F2d[2]935
557F2d[4]524
625F2d[2]42
e 218FS[4]417
288FS[4]877
d 348FS[2]1153
400FS[2]14
490FS[2]414
Cir. 6
707F2d[2]256
707F2d[4]256
j 958F2d1354
233FS[4]645
251FS[4]653
275FS[4]485
302FS[4]927
310FS[4]611
407FS[2]1221
460FS[2]1210
460FS[4]1211
465FS[4]437
490FS[4]466
493FS[2]149
f 501FS[2]104
701FS601
Cir. 7
337F2d[2]438
752F2d[2]1225
215FS[4]614
e 235FS[4]186
405FS[4]984
411FS[2]1282
541FS1336
638FS[4]180
Cir. 8
365F2d[4]658
544F2d[2]340
615F2d[4]1202
621F2d[4]299
792F2d[2]98
860F2d[1]300
233FS[4]533
244FS[4]90
335FS[2]990
335FS[3]990
335FS[4]990
f 374FS[2]422
614FS[4]876
759FS1420
812FS[2]953
Cir. 9
327F2d[4]444
422F2d[2]113
422F2d[4]113
446F2d[2]214
614F2d[2]1215
679F2d[4]1286
708F2d[4]490
756F2d[2]744
768F2d[2]1118
768F2d[4]1119
828F2d[2]1375
859F2d[4]760
946F2d[2]724
227FS11
273FS[2]549
278FS[2]759
278FS[4]764
304FS[4]1324
755FS933
Cir. 10
574F2d[4]502
589F2d[2]504
443FS[2]3
502FS[4]1296
670FS[2]919
Cir. DC
478F2d[4]991
603F2d[4]1021
722F2d830
Alk
602P2d432
Calif
226CA2d261
96CA3d757
128CA3d1036
38CaR31
158CaR82
181CaR18
Ky
398SW237
Md
83MdA114
573A2d844
Mass
6MaA443
376NE893
Mich
397Mch597
424Mch93
424Mch108
427Mch435
427Mch443
130McA378
248NW531
343NW560
378NW473
378NW480
398NW337
398NW341
Mo
384SW534
589SW645
N J
40NJ89
104NJS279
198NJS527
255NJS142
190A2d840
228A2d332
249A2d638
487A2d1264
604A2d673
N M
93NM531
602P2d628
N Y
32NY130
67NYM852
296NE248
325NYS2d13
343NYS2d349
61CaL692
66Cor246
17Æ2614s

—792—

Gideon v Wainwright 1963

(372US335)
(9LE799)
(93Æ2733)
s 82SC1259
s 135So2d746
s 153So2d299
101LE1020n
102LE1052n
j 83SC[3]819
j 83SC[3]866
83SC[3]1103
83SC[3]1104
83SC[3]1105
83SC[3]1106
83SC[3]1107
83SC[3]1391
f 83SC[3]1419
f 83SC[3]1540
j 83SC1646
f 83SC1688
f 83SC1875
f 83SC1878
f 83SC1879
f 83SC1880
f 83SC1881
f 83SC1882
f 83SC1884
f 83SC1887
f 83SC1891
f 84SC[3]80
f 84SC[3]81
j 84SC[3]81
f 84SC[3]137
f 84SC[3]151
f 84SC[3]152
f 84SC274
84SC702
84SC[3]1117
84SC1141
84SC[3]1202
84SC[3]1491
84SC[3]1497
j 84SC[3]1503
j 84SC[3]1509
84SC[3]1759
j 84SC[3]1767
j 84SC[3]1797
j 84SC[3]1921
j 84SC[3]1925
85SC[3]218
j 85SC[3]766
85SC943
85SC[3]1066
85SC[3]1072
85SC[3]1378
85SC[3]1489
85SC[3]1633
85SC[3]1641
85SC[3]1663
j 85SC[3]1677
85SC[3]1684
j 85SC[3]1704
85SC[3]1737
j 86SC270
86SC[3]465
86SC[3]1122
86SC[3]1477
86SC[3]1627
j 86SC[3]1648
j 86SC1658
86SC1778
87SC[3]208
j 87SC[3]526
87SC547
j 87SC633
87SC[3]653
j 87SC663
j 87SC666
87SC[3]828
87SC[3]837
j 87SC[3]842
87SC[3]993
87SC[3]1198
f 87SC[3]1399
87SC[3]1448
j 87SC[3]1467
87SC[3]1922
87SC1925
87SC[3]1956
j 87SC[3]1963
87SC[3]1970
j 87SC[3]1973
j 87SC[3]2000
88SC[3]214
88SC[3]256
88SC[3]261
j 88SC[3]325
88SC[3]1447
88SC[3]1455
j 88SC[3]1464
88SC[2]1922
88SC[3]1922
j 88SC[2]2096
j 88SC[3]2096
89SC[3]33
89SC[3]36
89SC[3]578
89SC1034
j 89SC[2]1044
j 89SC[3]1044
j 89SC1050
89SC[2]2063
89SC[3]2075
j 90SC477
j 90SC[3]1026
j 90SC[2]1082
90SC[3]1449
90SC[3]1469
j 90SC[2]1922
j 90SC[3]1922
j 90SC[2]2008
j 90SC2012
91SC[2]267
j 91SC[2]793
j 91SC984
91SC[3]1090
91SC1153
j 91SC[3]1180
j 91SC[3]1481
j 91SC1492
91SC1590
91SC[3]1626
j 92SC[3]436
j 92SC514
92SC591
92SC[3]592
j 92SC594
92SC[3]760
92SC[3]918
j 92SC921
92SC[3]1016
j 92SC[3]1020
j 92SC[3]1025

Continued

Figure 13

case that you are updating, ideally, this fact is noted by the editors of Shepard's and the cases are listed, chronologically from oldest to most recent, in the *Shepard's Citations* volume. Not every mention of the case that you are updating will affect your case, however. Sometimes a case is merely cited in passing or in a string of citations as authority to back up what a court is saying. Nevertheless, sometimes what another court says will have an effect on your case, and this situation is noted by a letter preceding the cite. Looking at Henry's case for example, you may notice the "f" in front of the citation 83SC^{3}1419 (see Fig. 13). This means that this new case followed the rule handed down by the court in Henry's case. We know this because there is a list of abbreviations in the front of every *Shepard's Citations* that explains the meaning of these history abbreviations (later actions involving the case that you are updating) and treatment abbreviations (cases that are not direct extensions of the case that you are updating, but may have a bearing on the validity of the case). (For our own explanations of what these abbreviations mean, see Appendix 5.)

There are two other important things to notice while we are looking at the citation to 83SC^{3}1419. First, this citation, unlike citations in Bluebook or Maroon book format, does not direct you to the first page of the case, but rather it directs you to the page of the new case where your case is cited, page 1419. Furthermore, the little superscript^3 following the SC (which again, stands for *Supreme Court Reporter*) tells us that the rule of law that is in headnote number three in Henry's case is the particular rule of law that the court in the new case applied. As you can imagine, having this information can really speed up research in finding cases that address the exact issue you are interested in rather than having to track down a case and read it only to find out that the new case certainly discusses your case, but is concerned with another issue, one entirely unrelated to the issue you want to see discussed.

Helpful Hint

It is always best to check for yourself, however, whether your case and issue are in fact discussed in the cited case. Again, editors are human or sometimes typographical errors creep in. We've run across citations in Shepard's that didn't exactly match the page number cited, discussed an issue that was different from the one in the headnote, or didn't even mention the case we were researching. It's always best to double-check for yourself before you rely on anything.

So, as a case finder, you and Henry can see that each of the cases cited in Shepard's may then cite to other cases, all of which can also be Shepardized so that each case multiplies itself, the way one seed grows a plant with more seeds, each of which grows more plants with still more seeds, and so on. In this way you can collect a vast number of cases from which to choose.

A few more features you may notice as you are flipping through the list of citations to see if your case was overturned, reversed, or limited in some way is that *Shepard's Citations* breaks down its list of citations by jurisdiction (First Circuit, Second Circuit, and so on) or by state (Maryland, North Carolina, Pennsylvania, and so on). So, if you want to focus on how a particular jurisdiction has treated your case, you can do so. And, as an added bonus to your research, *Shepard's Citations* also give citations to secondary sources of law, not just primary sources. These are listed after the case law in the series of citations and frequently they consist of articles in law reviews, journals, and annotations (ALR in its various series, and *ALR Federal*). If you missed these sources during your background search, this is a good place to pick them up because they can also be used as case finders.

Before ending this discussion, although we know we've said it before, we want to be absolutely clear about one thing:

You must check all, repeat, ALL of the *Shepard's Citations* volumes that relate to your reported case in the series (here we used the *Supreme Court Reporter* series) in which you have chosen to do your research. You can't just check the hardbound volumes or the paperback supplements. CHECK THEM ALL FROM THE TIME YOUR CASE WAS DECIDED UP TO THE MOST RECENT SUPPLEMENT TO MAKE SURE YOUR CASE IS VALID!

Sorry about that. We don't like to be so heavy handed, but this is really important. We've heard many a lawyer being embarrassed by his or her opponent and scolded by the judge for failing to update a case that the lawyer relied on. Worse than the embarrassment, though, you are wasting the court's time, and you could be fined for doing so.

Computerized updating

We'll just touch on this here to let you know that these services are available (we will discuss these in-depth in Chapter 8). You can run searches and update cases on-line. You can search Shepard's or Insta-Cite on the Westlaw database or Auto-Cite on the LEXIS database to update the cases that you want to rely on. All of these services are good, but with some holes, like any case-updating service. In fact, if truth be told, we really like using these computerized updating systems. They save time in the long run. Unfortunately, they suffer from the same problems that we mentioned when we discussed finding cases by name on these computer databases: They are really expensive to use, and you may not have access to them. You'll probably end up using the books, but we just wanted to let you know that they're out there.

CHAPTER HIGHLIGHTS

While doing preliminary research, make lists of cases cited in the following resources:

- *American Law Reports* (*ALR*) and *ALR federal*
- National and state legal encyclopedias
- Law reviews
- Monographs and treatises
- Legal dictionaries
- Restatements of law
- Loose-leaf services
- Annotated codes

Finding a case if you only know the name but not the cite

- Search tables of case names, compiled by plaintiff, prosecuting party, or defendant, or popular name tables in digests.
  - Start the search with the digest that is most specifically related to the case you are seeking by jurisdiction, court, or date—if this information is known
  - If lacking specific information concerning the case you are researching, start the search in general digests
  - After finding the case in the table, write down the case cite and where it can be located in the digest

- Search *Shepard's Acts and Cases by Popular Names: Federal and State*
- Search tables of cases in reporters
- Perform case name searches on electronic databases such as LEXIS and Westlaw

Finding more cases once you have one case cite

- Once you find the case in the digest or reporter, note the topic and key number, section or subsection under which the issue you are interested in is catalogued
- Search this topic and key number, section or subsection in other digests from the same publisher to gather more relevant case citations

Finding cases in digests using the topic approach

- Use the topic approach where you don't have a case to give you a key number, section or subsection to access the digest
- Create a list of terms to search by using the background materials and brainstorming that you used to define your legal issue
  - Use terms developed from brainstorming to try to match your legal issue with one or more of the digest topics
  - Digest topics can usually be found at the front of each digest volume
- Skim the contents, which are located at the beginning of the text of that topic, to narrow the search to specific key numbers, sections or subsections

Finding cases in the digests using the Descriptive Word Index

- Use the Descriptive Word Index where you don't have a case to give you a key number, section or subsection to access the digest

- ➤ Create a list of terms to search by using the background materials and brainstorming that you used to define your legal issue

Read the cases found in the digest search, and note other relevant cases cited by the courts for further research

Finding cases while updating

- ➤ Check the pocket parts of the digests under the key number, sections or subsection chosen to find more cases
- ➤ Shepardize the cases that you have found in background and digest searches using Shepard's case citators
  - – Find the volumes of Shepard's that cover the case you are updating and the reporter in which it was found—including all of the updates to these volumes
  - – Locate the case your are updating by its cite in the list of cases in the relevant Shepard's volumes
  - – Note the cases that cite to the case you are researching, especially those preceded by history and treatment abbreviations
  - – Research any new cases that appear relevant, especially if they appear to reverse, overturn, or limit the application of the case you are updating

Use computer query searches, names searches, and updating services to find more cases

CHAPTER 7

DETERMINING WHETHER YOUR ISSUE IS AFFECTED BY CIVIL LAW

No man's life, liberty, or property are safe while the Legislature is in session.

—Gideon J. Tucker (1866)
Final Accounting in the Estate of A. B. Tucker (N.Y. Surr.) 247.

THE VORTEX

This is an old saw that was trotted out frequently by our law professors to instill in us the virtue of updating the statutes that we were working with. This, like case updating, is essential. The legislature is always tinkering away with the law, adding to it, cutting it, or getting rid of it entirely. We're not too sure, however, that that is what Tucker meant. He probably was pointing out another problem with legislatures, and that is, as Madison, Hamilton, and Jay point out in the *Federalist Papers*, that the legislature if not checked has a tendency to suck all of the other powers of government into its vortex.

This may explain the scope of the civil law. As was pointed out in Chapter 1, even though this is a common-law country, the civil law, enacted by legislative and administrative bodies, is becoming more and more pervasive. What this esoteric discussion of law and legislature means to you is that there is probably a pretty good chance that some statute, regulation, or ordinance impacts on your legal problem—and if one of them does you'll want to know how you can find it and whether it's still valid before you rely on it.

HOW LEGISLATURES WORK

How do legislatures work? Money, favors, the old-boy network, posturing for the press and the voters, political blackmail, and dirty tricks—this may all be true, but it's not what we mean here. We mean ideally how do legislatures work. What are the mechanics of how an idea in the head of a legislator or the president becomes a law?

Legislatures in the United States are generally made up of two houses or chambers, hence they are called bicameral. We didn't come up with this system. It, like much of our legal structure, was based on the English model, although in England they have a House of Commons, which used to be made up of common people, and a House of Lords, which used to be reserved for nobles. Our nation's founders liked this style of legislature, but because we had a certain disdain for nobles—we had after all just dumped a king to gain our independence—we decided to create a House of Representatives, which would be more closely tied to the common people, and a Senate, which would act as a body of elder statesmen.

A short trip through the legislative process

Now that you've got a little historical background, let's use the federal legislature, it's similar to most state legislatures, as a model to demonstrate how a new law is created. This information will be important later if you want to track the development of a law which might affect you, to construct a legislative history (an important way to demonstrate how a law should be interpreted), and to let you know where in the legislative process the documents that you will be looking at occur so that you can put them in context.

When a member of Congress wants to create a new law, say to protect workers from being laid off without enough notice so that they can get retraining somewhere or try to find a new job, the member will draft a model of the law, which is called a *bill*, and will introduce the bill into the chamber, either the House of Representatives or the Senate, of which he or she is a member.

LAW FACT

In the law, a bill can also mean that slip of paper that you get when someone does work for you, the tally that is produced to show you what you have to pay for goods that you want to buy, or money itself.

After the bill is introduced, it is assigned to a legislative committee that handles the subject matter of that bill for either the House or the Senate. In the example that we are using, such a bill, if introduced by a member of the House of Representatives might be directed to the House committee that handles issues of labor relations between companies and their employees. It is the committee's job to weigh the pros and cons of the bill. To do this it will conduct discussions between its members and will usually hold hearings where outside experts and other members of the public opposing or supporting the bill will be asked to speak. At this point the bill may be changed to "improve" it, or it may die because it is not acted upon or because it is seen as not being appropriate legislation at this time.

LAW FACT

A law can be introduced, and frequently is introduced, by more than one member of Congress. In fact, sometimes bills that attempt to create a law regulating the same subject matter are introduced by different members in both the House of Representatives and the Senate.

If the bill makes it out of committee, it will then go to the floor of the introducing member's chamber where it will be debated, perhaps amended, and voted on. It is possible, again, at this time that the bill will be defeated or will die because the Speaker of the House or the Majority Leader of the Senate will not let it be voted upon or because a minority is able to put up a filibuster, a series of long speeches, which procedurally tie up the floor (at least in the Senate this can happen, in the House the rules of procedure are much stricter), so that the bill cannot be voted upon. If the bill is voted upon and approved by the chamber, it will be sent to the other chamber. For instance, if the bill was introduced in the House and was passed, it would move on to the Senate.

This new chamber will then direct the bill, as before, to the committee of that chamber that handles such issues, and it will, as before, hold discussions between its members and hold hearings where outside experts and other members of the public opposing or supporting the bill will be asked to speak. Again, at this point the bill may be changed to "improve" it, or it may die because it is not acted upon or because it is seen as not being appropriate legislation at this time.

If the bill makes it out of committee, it will then go to the floor of this chamber where it will be debated, perhaps amended, and voted on. It is possible, again, at this time that the bill will be defeated or will die because the majority party will not let it be voted upon or because a minority is able to engage in a filibuster so that the bill cannot be voted upon. If the bill is voted upon and approved by this chamber without amendment, it goes to the president. If, as is more likely, the bill was changed by this chamber before it was approved, it will go to a joint committee of the two chambers, called a conference committee, that will reconcile the differences in the two bills. The reconciled bill is then sent to the president.

The president acts at this point something like a super legislator. He can say yea or nay to a bill and determine whether it will become a law at this point. He cannot, however, add anything to it before signing, or change it in any way.

LAW FACT

Even though the president is always saying that he is going to introduce legislation to promote this or remedy that, he actually can't introduce any bill into Congress but must get a member of Congress to introduce it for him. This is not to say that the president doesn't have a great deal of influence as to what new laws are enacted, but technically at least, every new piece of legislation is created by Congress and merely approved or disapproved by the president.

If the president signs the bill, it becomes a law. On the other hand, the president can reject the bill outright by exercising his veto power—refusing to sign a bill and sending it back to Congress with a list of objections—or he can use what is called the pocket veto. A pocket veto takes place when the president refuses to take any action on the bill within ten days of receiving it, and Congress is not in session. If the president vetoes the bill, it does not become law. If Congress is in session, however, the bill is returned. The bill then has to pass both chambers again, this time by a two-thirds majority, to override the presidential veto and become law. If the president refuses to sign a bill within ten days, but Congress is in session, then the bill becomes a law anyway without having to be approved by a two-thirds majority in both houses of Congress.

LAW FACT

The president is granted the veto power by Article I, section 7 of the U.S. Constitution.

HOW STATUTES ARE PUBLISHED

It's all well and good to know how a bill becomes a law, but of course, you are interested in finding the law that affects you. To do this you will have to know how statutes passed by the U.S. Congress are published in this country. (For a list of state statutory publications, see Appendix 4 in the back of this book.)

As federal statutes are passed, they are published in three different forms:

- as slip laws,
- as session laws, and
- in the *United States Code.*

Slip laws

Slip law is a fairly descriptive term. It indicates the first official publication of a law passed by Congress. When a statute is passed by Congress, it is printed and distributed in a small pamphlet or slip (well, not always so small, statutes can sometimes be hundreds of pages long). Slip laws are important for keeping you abreast of the latest laws coming out of Congress, but otherwise, they don't really give you all that much information that cannot be obtained more easily, elsewhere. For example, the slip law will give you the Public Law (Pub. L.) number, such as Pub. L. 100-379. What this means is that this statute was the 379th law passed by the one-hundredth Congress. The slip law will also give you the number of the bill that was passed that became this law; the date that the law was passed; the short title of the law; where the law will be published in the *United States Code*, such as 29 U.S.C. §2101; it will indicate where the law will be published in the session laws, such as 102 Stat. 890; a short list of citations to the legislative history of the bill; and the text of the law itself. All of this information, however, can also be obtained in the session laws.

Session laws

Because slip laws are issued piece meal, they are hard to keep organized, to keep together, and to use. Luckily for researchers, a more wieldy publication is available for the official session laws. Like slip law, session law is a rather descriptive term. Session laws are all the laws passed during a certain session of Congress, gathered together, and published with that reference.

The official publication of the session laws of Congress is called *Statutes at Large*. *Statutes at Large* contains the official text of the law. That is, if you want to quote a particular passage of the law and make sure that you have it absolutely correct, you would want to quote from and cite to the *Statutes at Large*. In court, the other government publications of the law, the slip laws, and the *United States Code* (more on that one in the next section) are merely evidence of what the law says; they are not the law itself. Like the slip laws, the session laws will give you the Public Law number, such as Pub. L. 100-379: the number of the bill passed that became this law; the date that the law was passed; the short title of the law, the *Statutes at Large* citation, such as 102 Stat. 890; a short set of citations to the legislative history of the law; the text of the law itself; and the *United States Code* citation of the law (see Figures 14 & 15).

Helpful Hint

In reality, most people probably don't need to bother with the session laws. They would be far more likely to check the law in the *United States Code* or in one of the commercial publications of the United States Code. Nevertheless, if your life, liberty, or property is on the line, it is probably best to get everything exactly right and to check *Statutes at Large* to make sure that the language of the law that you are relying on, or fighting against, is correct.

The *United States Code*

The *United States Code* (U.S.C.) contains the text of all the laws passed by Congress, conveniently separated into 50 different titles. Unfortunately, the U.S.C. is only recompiled every six years, with supplements added annually to keep track of changes in the law, or so they are promised. In reality, the supplements to the U.S.C. may not appear on your library shelf for much longer than that. Such tardiness is a problem with all of the editions of the law published by the government and is partially the reason why more researchers work with the commercial statutory publications than with the ones published by the government.

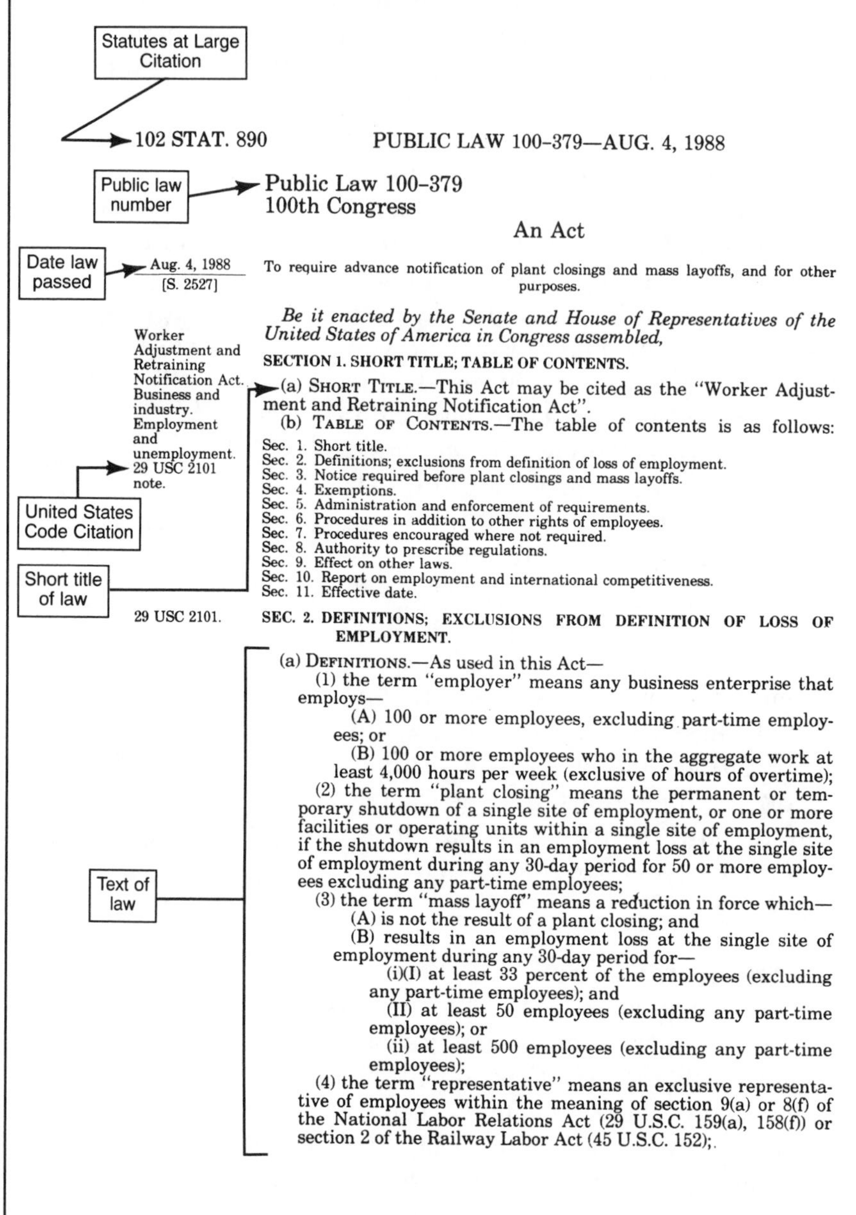

102 STAT. 890 PUBLIC LAW 100-379—AUG. 4, 1988

Public Law 100-379
100th Congress

An Act

Aug. 4, 1988
[S. 2527]

To require advance notification of plant closings and mass layoffs, and for other purposes.

Be it enacted by the Senate and House of Representatives of the United States of America in Congress assembled,

Worker Adjustment and Retraining Notification Act.
Business and industry.
Employment and unemployment.
29 USC 2101 note.

SECTION 1. SHORT TITLE; TABLE OF CONTENTS.

(a) SHORT TITLE.—This Act may be cited as the "Worker Adjustment and Retraining Notification Act".

(b) TABLE OF CONTENTS.—The table of contents is as follows:

Sec. 1. Short title.
Sec. 2. Definitions; exclusions from definition of loss of employment.
Sec. 3. Notice required before plant closings and mass layoffs.
Sec. 4. Exemptions.
Sec. 5. Administration and enforcement of requirements.
Sec. 6. Procedures in addition to other rights of employees.
Sec. 7. Procedures encouraged where not required.
Sec. 8. Authority to prescribe regulations.
Sec. 9. Effect on other laws.
Sec. 10. Report on employment and international competitiveness.
Sec. 11. Effective date.

29 USC 2101.

SEC. 2. DEFINITIONS; EXCLUSIONS FROM DEFINITION OF LOSS OF EMPLOYMENT.

(a) DEFINITIONS.—As used in this Act—

(1) the term "employer" means any business enterprise that employs—

(A) 100 or more employees, excluding part-time employees; or

(B) 100 or more employees who in the aggregate work at least 4,000 hours per week (exclusive of hours of overtime);

(2) the term "plant closing" means the permanent or temporary shutdown of a single site of employment, or one or more facilities or operating units within a single site of employment, if the shutdown results in an employment loss at the single site of employment during any 30-day period for 50 or more employees excluding any part-time employees;

(3) the term "mass layoff" means a reduction in force which—

(A) is not the result of a plant closing; and

(B) results in an employment loss at the single site of employment during any 30-day period for—

(i)(I) at least 33 percent of the employees (excluding any part-time employees); and

(II) at least 50 employees (excluding any part-time employees); or

(ii) at least 500 employees (excluding any part-time employees);

(4) the term "representative" means an exclusive representative of employees within the meaning of section 9(a) or 8(f) of the National Labor Relations Act (29 U.S.C. 159(a), 158(f)) or section 2 of the Railway Labor Act (45 U.S.C. 152);

Figure 14

PUBLIC LAW 100-379—AUG. 4, 1988 102 STAT. 895

SEC. 11. EFFECTIVE DATE. 29 USC 2101 note.

This Act shall take effect on the date which is 6 months after the date of enactment of this Act, except that the authority of the Secretary of Labor under section 8 is effective upon enactment.

[Note by the Office of the Federal Register: The foregoing Act, having been presented to the President of the United States on Friday, July 22, 1988, and not having been returned by him to the House of Congress in which it originated within the time prescribed by the Constitution of the United States, has become law without his signature on August 4, 1988.]

LEGISLATIVE HISTORY—S. 2527:

CONGRESSIONAL RECORD, Vol. 134 (1988):
June 22-24, 27-29, July 6, considered and passed Senate.
July 13, considered and passed House.
WEEKLY COMPILATION OF PRESIDENTIAL DOCUMENTS, Vol. 24 (1988):
Aug. 2, Presidential statement.

Legislative history of law

Figure 15

TITLES OF THE UNITED STATES CODE

1. General Provisions
2. The Congress
3. The President
4. Flag and Seal, Seat of Government, and the States
5. Government Organization and Employees
6. Surety Bonds—Repealed
7. Agriculture
8. Aliens and Nationality
9. Arbitration
10. Armed Forces
11. Bankruptcy
12. Banks and Banking
13. Census
14. Coast Guard
15. Commerce and Trade
16. Conservation
17. Copyrights
18. Crimes and Criminal Procedure
19. Customs Duties
20. Education
21. Food and Drugs
22. Foreign Relations and Intercourse
23. Highways
24. Hospital and Asylums
25. Indians
26. Internal Revenue Code
27. Intoxicating Liquors
28. Judiciary and Judicial Procedure
29. Labor
30. Mineral Lands and Mining
31. Money and Finance
32. National Guard
33. Navigation and Navigable Waters
34. Navy—Eliminated
35. Patents
36. Patriotic Societies and Observances
37. Pay and Allowances of the Uniformed Services
38. Veterans' Benefits
39. Postal Service
40. Public Buildings, Property, and Works
41. Public Contracts
42. The Public Health and Welfare
43. Public Lands
44. Public Printing and Documents
45. Railroads
46. Shipping
47. Telegraphs, Telephones, and Radiotelegraphs
48. Territories and Insular Possessions
49. Transportation
50. War and National Defense

Commercial publications of federal laws

There are four basic commercial publications that legal researchers use in lieu of the statutory materials printed by the federal government:

- *United States Code Congressional and Administrative News* (U.S.C.C.A.N.)
- *United States Code Annotated* (U.S.C.A.)
- *United States Code Service* (U.S.C.S.)
- *U.S.C.S. Advance Sheets*

U.S.C.C.A.N. and *U.S.C.S. Advance Sheets* publish the *Statutes at Large*, and U.S.C.A. and U.S.C.S. publish the United States Code but with useful added features. Not only does U.S.C.C.A.N. print the text of the law and the citations to the legislative history, it also includes selected legislative history materials, such as portions of the *Congressional Record* (where the floor debates are recorded) and some of the committee reports. *U.S.C.S. Advance Sheets* also contain the text of the session laws, but do not include any legislative history materials. On the other hand, they do include a current awareness commentary, which explains the meaning and applicability of new laws that are contained in each issue.

LAW FACT

Committee reports are given greater deference, that is are looked at more favorably, by courts when they are trying to determine the meaning of a law than other legislative history materials. This is because it is assumed that the committee members work more closely on the laws to which they are assigned than do other members of Congress and therefore that they understand the intent and meaning of the terms of the legislation better.

Both U.S.C.A. and U.S.C.S. are organized around the 50 titles of the United States Code, but they also include citations to cases and casenotes, one-sentence blurbs extracted from cases (much like headnotes), which give the researcher information about how the courts have dealt with particular issues. They have a section that provides the history of the statute, including the date on which the law became effective; the Public Law and *Statutes at Large*

Helpful Hint

U.S.C.S. Advance Sheets has a toll-free number that you can call so that you can get the latest information regarding statutory developments. Such information can be helpful because the publication only comes out about once a month.

citations; and some mention of secondary materials, such as law review articles, encyclopedia articles, loose-leaf services, annotations, and the like, which are related to the subject of the law. In addition, they may give citations to the regulations that have been created to help interpret and administer the law, if such exist.

FINDING A STATUTE THAT AFFECTS YOUR CASE

Now that you've been exposed to the federal legislative process and the federal statutory publications that come out of that process, let's walk through a sample problem so that you can learn how to find a statute that affects your case.

For our search we're going to introduce you to Norma Rae. Norma Rae went to work one day only to find out when she got there that everybody in her textile plant, over 100 full-time employees, had been laid off. Management claimed that they had lost a big contract and that because of this the plant was no longer viable. Norma Rae was upset (wouldn't you be?), and she thought that it was wrong that they all were laid off without notice, and figured that there must be a statute out there to back her up. Let's tag along with her as she goes about her search.

When you already know that one exists

If she had done the background research on her issue that we suggest throughout this book, read some encyclopedia articles, annotations, loose-leaf publications, and the like, found some cases and read them, she probably would have already discovered whether a statute is involved in her issue. In fact while doing her preliminary research, she discovered that there is a law that addresses her problem, a statute called (W.A.R.N.) the Worker Adjustment and Retraining Notification Act. As with that pesky case in the last chapter though, she forgot to write down the citation that would let her know where W.A.R.N. is located in the *United States Code* or one of its commercial kin.

Don't fear, she won't be punished for not remembering the citation—although it certainly

Helpful Hint

An act, as it is used here, is just another term for statute, which we also sometimes call a law. Having so many synonyms sounds a little confusing, but you can usually figure out if act means statute or law means statute by looking at the context in which the word is used.

would make life easier if she had. There are indexes that can tell us how to find a statute when we only know the name. In fact, in U.S.C.S. there is an index with something called a Popular Name Table. For our purposes we are going to want to find the volume called Tables, and among the tables will be a particular section called Popular Names.

Helpful Hint

You can also find an act's cite using only the name by looking in *Shepard's Acts and Cases by Popular Names: Federal and State*

If we look in the table of contents at the front of the book, we will see a notation for "Table of Acts by Popular Names" and the page on which it starts. Turn to that page. As you and Norma Rae can see, the table is organized alphabetically, so look in the W area and find Worker Adjustment and Retraining Notification Act. There is just one entry in the main volume and it says, August 4, 1988, Pub. L. 100–379, 29 U.S.C.S. §§ 2101 et seq. (see Figure 16) Let's take this apart and see what it means.

The first part of the entry is, of course, a date. This date is the date the Act was passed, the next number, the Pub. L. number we already know, because we discussed it above in the section on slip laws, is the Public Law number; and the last part of the entry is the interesting one for us here—it indicates that this Act can be found at Title 29 in U.S.C.S., starting with § 2101 and continuing on from there. That little § is a section mark, and two of them together means that there is more than one section involved in this Act.

The next step, as you and Norma Rae may have guessed, is to find 29 U.S.C.S. §§ 2101 et seq. To do that, we must go back to the U.S.C.S. set and look for Title 29. There is more than one volume under this title, which makes sense because it covers Labor. Among the volumes of Title 29 we'll have to find the one that covers § 2101. The sections are in numerical order from the smallest to the largest. There is one that says §§ 1201-end. This means that this volume covers Title 29 from § 1201 all the way through the rest of Title 29, so because 2101 is bigger than 1201, and there are no more volumes after this one, then we've found the volume that we are looking for.

As we flip through the volume, you and Norma Rae will notice that on the top, outside corner of each page is an abbreviation telling you that you are in 29 U.S.C.S., and following that it will say what section starts or ends on each page. Remember, this title is set up like all the titles, running from the section with the smallest

POPULAR NAMES

Wood Residue Utilization Act of 1980
Dec. 19, 1980, P. L. 96-554, 16 USCS § 1600 note.

Woodrow Wilson Memorial Act of 1968
Oct 24, 1968, P. L. 90-637, 82 Stat 1356, 20 USCS §§ 80e–80j.
May 26, 1978, P. L. 95-286, 20 USCS §§ 80g-1 et seq.
April 9, 1990, P.L. 101-268, 20 USCS § 80f.

Wool and Woolens Act (Tariff)
March 2, 1867, ch 197, 14 Stat 559.

Wool Products Labeling Act of 1939
Oct 14, 1940, ch 871, 54 Stat 1128, 15 USCS §§ 68–68j.
May 5, 1980, P. L. 96-242, 15 USCS §§ 68, 68 note, 68b.

Worker Adjustment and Retraining Notification Act
Aug. 4, 1988, P. L. 100-379, 29 USCS §§ 2101 et seq.

Work Hours Act of 1962
Aug 13, 1962, P. L. 87-581, 76 Stat 357, 28 USCS § 1499; 40 USCS §§ 327–332.

Work Relief Act
See EMERGENCY RELIEF APPROPRIATION ACTS

Work Relief and Public Works Appropriation Act of 1938
June 21, 1938, ch 554, 52 Stat 809.
June 27, 1942, ch 450, 56 Stat 392.
June 26, 1943, ch 145, 57 Stat 180.

Workmen's Compensation Acts
May 30, 1908, ch 236, 35 Stat 556.
Sept 7, 1916, ch 458, 39 Stat 742 (See 5 USCS §§ 8101 et seq.).
April 11, 1940, ch 79, 54 Stat 105.
July 18, 1940, ch 633, 54 Stat 762.

World War Adjusted Compensation Act
May 19, 1924, ch 157, 43 Stat 121.

World War Pension Act
July 19, 1939, ch 331, 53 Stat 1068.

World War Veterans' Act, 1924
June 7, 1924, ch 320, 43 Stat 607.
June 1, 1937, ch 285, 50 Stat 241.
Oct 17, 1940, ch 893, 54 Stat 1193.
March 23, 1943, ch 19, 57 Stat 41.
Aug 1, 1946, ch 728, 60 Stat 789.
April 15, 1947, ch 34, 61 Stat 39.
Aug 2, 1951, ch 286, 65 Stat 151.
July 12, 1952, ch 703, 66 Stat 595.
July 23, 1953, ch 240, 67 Stat 186.
March 16, 1954, ch 97, 68 Stat 28.
July 26, 1955, ch 389, 69 Stat 380.
Aug 1, 1956, ch 837, 70 Stat 883.
June 17, 1957, P. L. 85-56, 71 Stat 158.

World's Fair Act
April 29, 1939, ch 106, 53 Stat 625.

Wright Brothers Day Act
Dec 17, 1963, P. L. 88-209, 77 Stat 402, 36 USCS § 169.

Wunderlich Act
May 11, 1954, ch 199, 68 Stat 81, 41 USCS §§ 321, 322.
May 11, 1954, P. L. 83-356, 41 USCS §§ 321 et seq.

Wyoming Land Act
May 29, 1908, ch 220, 35 Stat 465, 43 USCS §§ 82, 224.

Wyoming Wilderness Act of 1984
Oct. 30, 1984, P. L. 98-550.

Y

Yacht Tax Acts
Aug 5, 1909, ch 6, 36 Stat 112.
Feb 24, 1919, ch 18, 40 Stat 1129.
Nov 23, 1921, ch 136, 42 Stat 297.

Yellowstone National Park Protection Act
May 7, 1894, ch 72, 28 Stat 73, 16 USCS §§ 24-31.

Young Adult Act
Aug 25, 1958, P. L. 85-752, 72 Stat 846, 18 USCS § 4209.

Young Astronaut Program Medal Act
May 12, 1986, P. L. 99-295, 31 USCS § 5111 nt.
Dec. 24, 1987, P. L. 100-210, 31 USCS § 5111 nt.
Sept. 20, 1988, P. L. 100-437, 31 USCS § 5111 nt.

Youth Employment and Demonstration Projects Act of 1977
Aug. 5, 1977, P. L. 95-93, 29 USCS §§ 801 note, 802 et seq.

Youth Employment Demonstration Amendments of 1981
June 16, 1981, P. L. 97-14, 29 USCS § 801 note.

Ysleta Del Sur Pueblo and Alabama and Coushatta Indian Tribes of Texas Restoration Act
Aug. 18, 1987, P. L. 100-89, 25 USCS §§ 731, 731 nt., 732-737, 1300g-1300g-7.

Yugoslav Emergency Relief Assistance Act of 1950
Dec 29, 1950, ch 1182, 64 Stat 1122.

Z

Zuni-Cibola National Historical Park Establishment Act of 1988
Oct. 31, 1988, P. L. 100-567, 16 USCS prec. § 410pp, § 410pp nt.
June 27, 1990, P. L. 101-313, 16 USCS § 410pp.

764

Figure 16

number to the section with the largest number, so we'll have to keep flipping through the pages until we reach § 2101. This is the beginning of the act that we want. Now let's take a break while we explain how to find a statute that involves our issue if we don't know that it exists.

When you don't know whether or not one exists

There may be times that you suspect that a statute exists that may affect your issue, but you're not sure and you haven't run across any in your preliminary research. On the other hand, you may not have done any preliminary research, but you want to start looking immediately for a statute related to your issue. We do not recommend this method of finding statutes. It's too easy to miss something this way because you have to deal with the vagaries of subject indexes and the resulting frustration of not being able to find a citation to something where you think it ought to be, but if you insist, we'll pretend that Norma Rae didn't bother to check the background materials.

There are two basic methods we can use to access the commercial versions of the United States Code in such situations: a topic approach and a descriptive word approach.

THE TOPIC APPROACH

The topics that we will be trying to classify our problem under this time will be those 50 Titles of the *United States Code* (see page 134). The commercial versions of the United States Code follow the same breakdown. Again, we'll be using U.S.C.S.

There are a few titles that just from the names look like they might possibly be repositories for a law dealing with a notice requirement during layoffs, such as "Commerce and Trade" (Norma Rae's employer is involved in such, and the law may have something to do with how layoffs affect commerce), "Public Health and Welfare" (welfare is a rather broad term, and massive layoffs could effect the "welfare" of the nation), and Labor. Of these three, the best bet is Labor because this title usually deals with laws that regulate the problems between workers and their employers. As you and Norma Rae can see already, this is a tenuous approach to the law, and it's best to know something about the titles of U.S.C.S. before beginning such a search.

At this point we will have to find the Labor title on the shelf, and search the table of contents at the beginning of that title to see if the name of an act jumps out at us as being related to our problem. This may be possible because the titles of acts are often rather descriptive, but sometimes the descriptions themselves are merely confusing. We're not sure that anyone would recognize the issue we are dealing with in the name of the act. What does Worker Adjustment and Retraining Notification Act mean anyway? A more descriptive name might be something like Worker Notification During Plant Closing and Layoff Act, but then it wouldn't have that acronym W.A.R.N. (Come to think of it, doesn't W.A.R.N. sound like an organization that James Bond would have fought against?) If during this search you did happen to see it, you'd see that it is located at 29 U.S.C.S. §§ 2101 et seq.

DESCRIPTIVE WORD APPROACH

Another approach to finding statutes in the U.S.C.S. or other commercially produced codes is by the descriptive word method. We come up with the keywords that we will search by using the categories outlined in Chapter 3 and by brainstorming—asking ourselves the basic questions about Norma Rae's issue of who, what, why, where, how, and when.

This questioning might produce key words like employer, employee, layoff, notice, work, and synonyms of such words as management, worker, termination, warning, and labor. As we look up these words and combinations of them, what we find is a number of cross-references to topics that we hadn't thought of, particularly like "Unemployment" and under this term we find "Layoffs, generally, 29 § 2101, 2102," and as you already know, that's what we want (see Figure 17).

Determining whether or not the statute you've found controls your issue

Now that we've found our statute, whether we knew it existed in the first place or not, we'll want to try to determine which section of the statute, if any, applies to Norma Rae's issue. To find the sections that we will want to look at, let's look at the contents at the beginning of the act (see Figure 18).

Acts typically, as here, start with a definition section because some of the important terms in the act may be used in a specialized way. For example, it is apparent from the definition of employer that W.A.R.N. does not include every employer who might fall under the dictionary definition of employer. When W.A.R.N. talks

GENERAL INDEX

For Assistance Using this Index, Call 1-800-527-0430 661

Figure 17

CHAPTER 23. WORKER ADJUSTMENT AND RETRAINING NOTIFICATION

---

§ 2101. Definitions; exclusions from definition of loss of employment

(a) Definitions. As used in this Act [29 USCS §§ 2101 et seq.]—

(1) the term "employer" means any business enterprise that employs—

(A) 100 or more employees, excluding part-time employees; or

(B) 100 or more employees who in the aggregate work at least 4,000 hours per week (exclusive of hours of overtime);

(2) the term "plant closing" means the permanent or temporary shutdown of a single site of employment, or one or more facilities or operating units within a single site of employment, if the shutdown results in an employment loss at the single site of employment during any 30-day period for 50 or more employees excluding any part-time employees;

(3) the term "mass layoff" means a reduction in force which—

(A) is not the result of a plant closing; and

(B) results in an employment loss at the single site of employment during any 30-day period for—

(i)(I) at least 33 percent of the employees (excluding any part-time employees); and

(II) at least 50 employees (excluding any part-time employees); or

593

Figure 18

about employers it means only those employers who employ a certain number of workers or a certain number of workers for a specific amount of time.

Helpful Hint

It is a good idea to at least scan the definition section of an act that you are working with, even before you read the section that you believe directly affects you, so that you will at least be aware that certain terms that you read in your section, even seemingly mundane terms like "employer" may have a special meaning.

Another typical and important section also stands out when we look at it, that is § 2104 on the "Administration and Enforcement" requirements. Such sections as these are important because they may tell Norma Rae what sort of remedy she can seek from her employer, or whether she personally can even bring a suit under this act. Sometimes Congress passes laws to help individuals, but does not want everyone harmed in violation of the law to have the right to bring a suit. This may happen because Congress thinks that too many people might flood the courts with suits or that the agency that administers the act is better qualified because of the technical nature of the law to bring the suit.

OK, we've read the definitional section, § 2101. We've already determined from it that Norma Rae's company fits the definition of employer used in the act because it employs more than 100 full-time workers (see § 2101 [a] [1] [A]) and that a plant closing occurred because all the workers at one site were let go (see § 2101 [a] [2]). We've also read § 2104 and it looks like she can in fact bring a suit under W.A.R.N. Now we'll want to get into the substance of her issue: Was it OK under this law for her company to let her go without notice? Well, let's see.

If we look at the contents at the front of the act again, we see that § 2102 is called "Notice required before plant closings and mass layoffs." From reading this section we learn that typically an employer is supposed to give at least 60 days notice to its employees before a plant closing (see § 2102 [a]). Nevertheless, we also see that under § 2102 (b), a company can order a plant closing without 60 days notice if it is caused by business circumstances that the company really could not have known about ahead of time. Could it be that the loss of a single contract is a circumstance that Norma Rae's employer could not have known about? We're going to have to have some interpretation of this issue. We're going to have to see some cases, a legislative history, and maybe more.

Finding cases that interpret your sections of the statute

Normally, because the U.S.C.S. is an annotated code, there should be citations and case notes under a heading call "Interpretive Notes and Decisions" following the text of this section; there aren't any here, but don't panic yet. We'll have to check the pocket part.

We find this section in the pocket part in the same way that we found the act in the hardbound portion of the volume. All of the sections are in numerical order, from lowest number to highest. We'll flip through the pages until we find the page where § 2102 begins. Here we see that there have been a slew of decisions interpreting various aspects of this section (see Figure 19). When there are even more case notes than this, the editors will break them down further and classify the notes in each section under descriptive subheadings, such as "Constitutionality" or "Class Actions," to speed research along. Hey, anything to save time. As elsewhere, time is money.

As we scan down the case notes, we can see two notes from the same case, *Jones v. Kayser-Roth Hosiery, Inc.*, which appears to be on point (see Figure 19). Norma Rae will want to write these citations down in full so that she can check this case later. Upon looking at this citation, one thing that may have already caused you to raise your eyebrows is that there appears to be some later proceedings of this case—one in which a prior opinion was amended, or changed (that's what the "amd" in the abbreviations means). She'll want to check these later cases as well to make sure that what the case notes say is still valid law.

Norma Rae should keep looking through the notes until she gets to the end of this section. She'll want to write down the citations of any more that she sees that appear to be on point like these two. These cases will then give her access to more cases, if there are any, through the digests and *Shepard's Citations* (see Chapter 6).

Helpful Hint

When you have later proceedings listed in a case note, they are there to make you aware that some other action was taken, but ideally, if the editors have not removed the case note, these later proceedings should not have affected the validity of the rule or conclusion in the note. It is, however, best to double check these on your own. Sometimes mistakes are made or interpretations differ.

Searching the legislative history of your statute

Any time you are going before a court to argue the interpretation of a statute, you may want more than just case law to back up

29 USCS § 2102 **LABOR**

§ 2102. Notice required before plant closings and mass layoffs

INTERPRETIVE NOTES AND DECISIONS

In order to rely on unforseen business circumstances exception (29 USCS § 2102(b)(2)(A)), employer need not show that it had insufficient assets to remain open for 60 days. Jurcev v Central Community Hosp. (1993, CA7 Ill) 7 F3d 618, 8 BNA IER Cas 1505, 126 CCH LC ¶ 10908.

Although union is entitled to bring action under WARN Act pursuant to 29 USCS § 2104(a)(5), such does not necessarily mean that union has standing, which union has burden of demonstrating; thus, action brought by union was properly dismissed, even though union alleged personal injury (employer's failure to provide notice to union pursuant to 29 USCS § 2102(a)), because relief requested by union (backpay and fringe benefits for aggrieved employees, and its own attorney's fees and expenses) would not redress union's asserted injury. United Food & Commercial Workers Int'l Union, Local 751 v Brown Group (1995, CA8 Mo) 50 F3d 1426, 10 BNA IER Cas 705, 129 CCH LC ¶ 11303, reh, en banc, den (1995, CA8) 1995 US App LEXIS 12715.

Worker Adjustment and Retraining Act of 1988 does not impose any duty or obligation on unions to warn its members about Act violations, to investigate employers' compliance with Act, or to monitor employer compliance with Act. Cruz v Robert Abbey, Inc. (1990, ED NY) 6 BNA IER Cas 1446, 138 BNA LRRM 2648, class certif gr, motion gr (ED NY) 6 BNA IER Cas 1441.

Employer which notified large number of employees that their employment was being terminated immediately and gave no prior notice of their termination as part of plant closing may not rely upon defense of "business circumstances that were not reasonably foreseeable as of time that notice would have been required" pursuant to 29 USCS § 2102(b)(2)(A), where employer knew roughly 30 days prior to notifying employees of closure that major account was lost and that without this account it could not keep plant open. Jones v Kayser-Roth Hosiery, Inc. (1990, ED Tenn) 748 F Supp 1276, later proceeding (ED Tenn) 748 F Supp 1292.

Employer's loss of its major client whom it had been serving for 30 years amounted to unforeseeable business circumstances, but once client notified employer of loss of business, employer's subjective belief that client's decision was not final was not commercially reasonable. Jones v Kayser-Roth Hosiery, Inc. (1990, ED Tenn) 748 F Supp 1276, 6 BNA IER Cas 732, 118 CCH LC ¶ 10559, later proceeding (ED Tenn) 748 F Supp 1292, 6 BNA IER Cas 744, 118 CCH LC ¶ 10560, amd (ED Tenn) 753 F Supp 218, 6 BNA IER Cas 1038, 118 CCH LC ¶ 10660.

Since Worker Adjustment and Retraining Act of 1988 does not apply to individual persons, cause of action cannot be stated against individual for violating notification requirements of Act in connection with plant closing or mass layoff. Cruz v Robert Abbey, Inc. (1991, ED NY) 6 BNA IER Cas 1441.

Employer did not have standing to claim that exceptions set forth in § 2102(b) are unconstitutionally vague, since such exceptions were not applicable to employer's conduct. Carpenters Dist. Council v Dillard Dept. Stores, Inc. (1991, ED La) 6 BNA IER Cas 1601.

Layoffs which occurred prior to effective date of WARN Act are not subject to Act's provisions, despite plaintiff's contention that such layoffs were part of single continuum of layoffs which extended beyond effective date of Act. United Auto. Aerospace & Agricultural Implement Workers, Local 1077 v Shadyside Stamping Corp. (1991, SD Ohio) 6 BNA IER Cas 1640, affd (CA6 Ohio) 6 BNA IER Cas 1648.

Plaintiffs were granted preliminary injunction which prohibited employer from dissipating its United States assets pending resolution of action brought against employer for its failure to give plaintiff employees 60 days advance notice required under WARN Act, since employer would not likely succeed on merits of business circumstances exception to notice requirement, and there was substantial likelihood that employer, who had begun winding up its affairs and negotiating settlement with its major creditor, would dissipate its assets. Parsley v Kunja Knitting Mills, Inc. (1991, DC SC) 7 BNA IER Cas 225, later proceeding (DC SC) 7 BNA IER Cas 231.

Plaintiff's motion to compel production of witness, official of parent company, for deposition was granted, since plaintiff is entitled to explore theory that parent may have directed some of subsidiary's employment decisions and that its reasons for doing so contravene WARN Act. Oil, Chemical & Atomic Workers Int'l Union, Local 7-515, etc. v American Home Products Corp. (1991, ND Ind) 7 BNA IER Cas 323.

Union and aggrieved employees have no recourse against casino that laid them off on short notice under Worker Adjustment and Retraining Notification Act (29 USCS §§ 2101 et seq.), where state casino control commission ordered casino closed with only 6 days notice, because employer's liability cannot attach unless employer rendered final decision to close plant under plain meaning of 29 USCS § 2102(a). Hotel Employees Restaurant Employers Int'l Union Local 54 v Elsinore Shore Assoc. (1991, DC NJ) 768 F Supp 1117, 6 BNA IER Cas 1217, 120 CCH LC ¶ 10956.

Former airbag-production plant employees have not established violation of 29 USCS § 2102(a), where 6 employees previously included as lay-offs must not be since they were recalled to work within less than 6-month period and therefore suffered no § 2101(a)(6)(B) "employment loss," because deduction of 6 brings key figures of full time employees suffering employment loss just under minimum numbers—50 employees or 33 percent of employees— necessary for violation of statute requiring 60-days' notice to employees to be affected by "mass layoff." Kildea v Electro Wire Products, Inc. (1991, ED Mich) 775 F Supp 1014.

Employer's challenge to constitutionality of Worker Adjustment and Retraining Notification Act (WARN) (29 USCS §§ 2101 et seq.) must fail, where employer asserts that exemptions from notice requirements of Act for "faltering business . . . actively seeking capital or business" and for "business circumstances . . . not reasonably foreseeable" are too vague, because employer lacks standing to challenge those exemptions that have already been determined inapplicable to its situation, and challenge to 29 USCS § 2102(a) 60-day written notice provision is not stated and would likely be ill-fated in any event. Carpenters Dist. Council v Dillard Dept. Stores, Inc. (1991, ED La) 778 F Supp 318, 6 BNA IER Cas 1601, 121 CCH LC ¶ 10035.

166

Figure 19

your argument, even if the argument seems pretty sound, or you may need some different interpretations of the statute because the case law seems to indicate that you wouldn't win. On the other hand, there may be a distinct possibility that there are few if any decisions that even address your issue. Hey, someone has to be the one to bring a case of first impression. If any of these situations occur, you may want to find the legislative history of your act.

To do this with Norma Rae we'll have to turn back to § 2101 of W.A.R.N. in the main volume of U.S.C.S. that we were looking at before. At the end of this section, immediately following the text, we find the date that the law was passed (August 4, 1988), the public law number, (100–379), the section number in the official text of the law. (§ 3), and the session law number (102 Stat. 890). This information provides everything that we need to begin a legislative history search.

Remember, as we discussed above, there are two commercial publications that publish the session laws: the *U.S.C.S. Advance Sheets* and U.S.C.C.A.N. One of the differences between U.S.C.C.A.N. and the *Advance Sheets* is that U.S.C.C.A.N. has selected legislative history materials, and the *Advance Sheets* do not. Furthermore, the *Advance Sheets* are paperback volumes that are frequently replaced, while U.S.C.C.A.N. is a series of permanent volumes. The advantage of this is that U.S.C.C.A.N. will have the text of the session laws and legislative history for older acts as well as the newer ones. The *Advance Sheets*, on the other hand, are replaced as new laws are passed. Therefore because W.A.R.N. is an older statute, let's go and find it in U.S.C.C.A.N.

U.S.C.C.A.N. looks similar to the West reporters. It is a set of books with tan covers, red and black bands on the spine, and gold lettering. Once we've located the set in the library we can use the year the Act was passed, 1988, to hone in on the volumes that we want to check. Once we find these, we can use either the public law number or the session law number to find out which volume will have the text of our act. The spine of each volume lists what is included in the volume. Here, we see that P.L. 100–379 would be in the volume that contains Pub. L. 100–243 to 100–418. U.S.C.C.A.N. is set up just like the codes with the numbers of the acts running in numerical order from the lowest to the highest number, with the numbers of the acts on the upper corners of the page. When you've found Pub. L. 100–379, flip to the end of the text of the act.

Following the text of the act we find some notes and citations to legislative history (see Figures 20 & 21). It is interesting that the notes tell us that former President Reagan refused to sign this act, so that it became law without his signature. He apparently objected to it in some regard. Under the legislative history, there is a notation of a presidential statement that concerns W.A.R.N., which might shed some light on his objections. This is not that important though. Courts rarely look to what the president thought of a law when interpreting a portion of it. What is important is that we learn that this act was originally Senate Bill 2527 (S. 2527). This bill number can be important for tracking the progress of the bill and finding other materials. There is also listed the volume of the *Congressional Record*, the record of floor debates, where the bill was considered and passed and the date on which these actions took place.

If Norma Rae wants to find the selected portions of floor debates, committee reports, and presidential statements, if there are any, for this act in U.S.C.C.A.N., she may notice that this information is not in the volume in which the text of the law appears. That information frequently will appear in another volume that contains that same session of Congress. In our example, if we go back to the set and look on the spines of the books, we will see that the history materials that we want would be in volume 4; the spine of which says "Legislative History Pub.L. 100–293 to 100–418." Unfortunately, as we flip through this volume we see that U.S.C.C.A.N. does not include any actual excerpts from the records and reports we'd like to see. We could dig through the *Congressional Record* at this point using the Senate Bill 2527 number that we have. In that case, we'd find the index for the *Congressional Record*, which covers the date the Act was passed, and then flip through the listings of Senate bills until we find the one for 2527. There we would find a listing of the page numbers in that volume of the *Congressional Record* where the debates can be found, but if you want more than just the debates for your legislative history, there are books that can tell you where to find this information.

One of the most comprehensive publications you can find for tracking legislative histories of federal laws is put out by Congressional Information Service; it is called *CIS/Annual Legislative Histories of Public Laws*. Each volume of *CIS/Annual* contains legislative histories for one year. It collects the legislative histories

102 STAT. 890 PUBLIC LAW 100-379—AUG. 4, 1988

Public Law 100-379
100th Congress

An Act

Aug. 4, 1988
[S. 2527]

To require advance notification of plant closings and mass layoffs, and for other purposes.

Be it enacted by the Senate and House of Representatives of the United States of America in Congress assembled,

Worker Adjustment and Retraining Notification Act. Business and industry. Employment and unemployment. 29 USC 2101 note.

SECTION 1. SHORT TITLE; TABLE OF CONTENTS.

(a) SHORT TITLE.—This Act may be cited as the "Worker Adjustment and Retraining Notification Act".

(b) TABLE OF CONTENTS.—The table of contents is as follows:

29 USC 2101.

SEC. 2. DEFINITIONS; EXCLUSIONS FROM DEFINITION OF LOSS OF EMPLOYMENT.

(a) DEFINITIONS.—As used in this Act—

(1) the term "employer" means any business enterprise that employs—

(A) 100 or more employees, excluding part-time employees; or

(B) 100 or more employees who in the aggregate work at least 4,000 hours per week (exclusive of hours of overtime);

(2) the term "plant closing" means the permanent or temporary shutdown of a single site of employment, or one or more facilities or operating units within a single site of employment, if the shutdown results in an employment loss at the single site of employment during any 30-day period for 50 or more employees excluding any part-time employees;

(3) the term "mass layoff" means a reduction in force which—

(A) is not the result of a plant closing; and

(B) results in an employment loss at the single site of employment during any 30-day period for—

(i)(I) at least 33 percent of the employees (excluding any part-time employees); and

(II) at least 50 employees (excluding any part-time employees); or

(ii) at least 500 employees (excluding any part-time employees);

(4) the term "representative" means an exclusive representative of employees within the meaning of section 9(a) or 8(f) of the National Labor Relations Act (29 U.S.C. 159(a), 158(f)) or section 2 of the Railway Labor Act (45 U.S.C. 152);.

Figure 20

Aug. 4 **WORKER NOTIFICATION ACT** P.L. 100–379

SEC. 11. EFFECTIVE DATE.

29 USC 2101 note.

This Act shall take effect on the date which is 6 months after the date of enactment of this Act, except that the authority of the Secretary of Labor under section 8 is effective upon enactment.

[Note by the Office of the Federal Register.—The foregoing Act, having been presented to the President of the United States on Friday, July 22, 1988, and not having been returned by him to the House of Congress in which it originated within the time prescribed by the Constitution of the United States, has become law without his signature on August 4, 1988.]

LEGISLATIVE HISTORY—S. 2527:

CONGRESSIONAL RECORD, Vol. 134 (1988):
June 22–24, 27–29, July 6, considered and passed Senate.
July 13, considered and passed House.
WEEKLY COMPILATION OF PRESIDENTIAL DOCUMENTS, Vol. 24 (1988):
Aug. 2, Presidential statement.

102 STAT. 895

Figure 21

of every significant act passed by Congress in that year, generally excluding only those that are ceremonial, that have to do with procedure, or that affect an insignificant number of people.

Each legislative history in *CIS/Annual* includes the following information, if it is available:

- an abstract of the public law
- citations to and abstracts of reports related to the law that was enacted
- a list of other bills which were precursors of the law that was enacted
- a history of the floor debates in both chambers of Congress pertaining to those bills
- citations to and abstracts of the hearings that were conducted that relate to those bills
- prints that came out of committees that considered matters related to the law
- other documents generated that were related to the evolution of the law
- citations to miscellaneous documents related to the law, such as presidential statements.

CIS/Annual is organized just like the other statutory materials that we have been using up to now, in numerical order, from lowest number to the highest. To find the public law that we are tracking, find the volume which contains the laws passed in 1988, and flip to the pages which cover Pub. L. 100–379—the information will be noted in the upper outside corner of each page. As you can see from the pages upon pages of citations and abstracts, this act, in one form or another, was on the minds of members of Congress for some time. Using these citations, you can access all of the information covered above: reports, other related bills, hearings, and the like. The Congressional Information Service provides microfiche copies of all of these documents, except for the floor debates (see Figure 22).

Let's try to find copies of the floor debates. Debates that take place on the floor of the House and Senate when a bill is being considered can be found in a government publication, mentioned previously, called the *Congressional Record.* To access the *Congressional Record,* it is best if we have a date on which the debates took place and even a page number. In Figure 23, we have reproduced a portion of the *CIS/Annual* from the portion headed "Pub. L. 100–379 Debate." Although we certainly could

Public Law 100-379 — 102 Stat. 890

Worker Adjustment and Retraining Notification Act

August 4, 1988

Public Law

1.1 Public Law 100-379, approved Aug. 4, 1988. (S. 2527)

(CIS88:PL100-379 6 p.)

"To require advance notification of plant closings and mass layoffs, and for other purposes."

Requires employers of 100 or more employees to notify workers and State and local governments of plant closings and mass layoffs at least 60 days in advance to facilitate planning for dislocation services.

Exempts closings that are temporary or constitute a strike or lockout, and provides for reduced notification periods under certain circumstances.

Establishes civil penalties for act violations.

Requires DOL to prescribe regulations to implement the act and a GAO report to assess the effect of the act.

P.L. 100-379 Reports

99th Congress

2.1 H. Rpt. 99-336 on H.R. 1616, "Labor-Management Notification and Consultation Act of 1985," Oct. 29, 1985.

(CIS85:H343-18 32 p.)
(Y1.1/8:99-336.)

Recommends passage, with an amendment in the nature of a substitute, of H.R. 1616, the Labor-Management Notification and Consultation Act of 1985, to:

a. Require advance notice to the Federal Mediation and Conciliation Service (FMCS), employees, and labor organizations of industrial plant closings and permanent layoffs.
b. Require FMCS to contact affected local governments and State and local agencies responsible for providing assistance to displaced workers.
c. Establish the National Commission on Plant Closings and Worker Dislocation to investigate plant closings and permanent layoffs and make recommendations.

Includes dissenting and individual views (p. 26-32).

H.R. 1616 is related to 98th congress H.R. 2847 and eight other bills.

100th Congress

2.2 S. Rpt. 100-62 on S. 538, "Economic Dislocation and Worker Adjustment Assistance Act," June 2, 1987.

(CIS87:S543-4 94 p.)
(Y1.1/5:100-62.)

Recommends passage, with an amendment in the nature of a substitute, of S. 538, the Economic Dislocation and Worker Adjustment Assistance Act, to amend the Job Training Partnership Act (JTPA) to replace JTPA dislocated worker assistance with a new DOL-State program. Includes provisions to:

a. Authorize DOL allocations to States for worker readjustment and retraining programs, including counseling, employment services, remedial education, and income maintenance.
b. Require employers to notify workers and State and local governments of plant closings and mass layoffs at least 90 days in advance to facilitate planning for dislocation services.
c. Establish a displaced worker loan demonstration project and four demonstration projects for dislocated worker retraining.

Includes minority and additional views (p. 80-94).

S. 538 is related to 99th Congress H.R. 1616.

2.3 H. Rpt. 100-285 on H.R. 1122, "Economic Dislocation and Worker Adjustment Assistance Act," Aug. 7, 1987.

(CIS87:H343-15 89 p.)
(Y1.1/8:100-285.)

Recommends passage, with an amendment in the nature of a substitute, of H.R. 1122, the Economic Dislocation and Worker Adjustment Assistance Act, to amend the Job Training Partnership Act (JTPA) to replace JTPA dislocated worker assistance with a new DOL-State worker readjustment program. Includes provisions to:

a. Authorize DOL allocations to States for worker readjustment programs, including employment and retraining services, and income maintenance.
b. Require States to establish a State Worker Readjustment Council to oversee worker readjustment program operations.
c. Require States to designate a dislocated worker unit or office for rapid governmental response to plant closings and mass layoffs within the State.
d. Establish guidelines for grants to substate areas to ensure increased local input into State dislocated worker programs.
e. Require employers to notify workers and State and local governments of plant closings and mass layoffs at least 90 days in advance to facilitate planning for dislocation services.
f. Require States to develop and maintain computerized job bank systems.

Includes dissenting, separate, and additional views (p. 48-60).

H.R. 1122 is related to H.R. 3 and S. 538 and to 10 other bills.

2.4 H. Rpt. 100-576, conference report on H.R. 3, "Omnibus Trade and Competitiveness Act of 1988," Apr. 20, 1988.

(CIS88:H783-1 i+1115 p.)
(Y1.1/8:100-576.)

Conference report on H.R. 3, the Omnibus Trade and Competitiveness Act of 1988, to amend the Trade Act of 1974 and numerous other acts to enhance U.S. international competitiveness.

Title VI, Subtitle E, the proposed Worker Adjustment and Retraining Notification Act, would require employers to notify workers and State and local governments of plant closings and mass layoffs at least 60 days in advance to facilitate planning for dislocation services.

176 CIS/INDEX Legislative Histories — JANUARY-DECEMBER 1988

Figure 22

look at the floor debates of all the related bills, we think it is a good idea, perhaps, to stick to S. 2527, which became the Worker Adjustment and Retraining Notification Act. As you can see in Figure 23, 4.28 through 4.35 cover the Senate and House consideration of this bill. These listings give you the date that the debates took place and even the page numbers in the *Congressional Record* of the debates.

The *Congressional Record* consists of a series of white, paperbound journals about the size of a magazine.* Paperback copies of the *Congressional Record* are published for each day, with the page numbers running consecutively for each volume. Each edition is split into sections concerning Senate debates, House debates, extended remarks of the members of Congress, and a daily digest of the activity of each day. With the information that we've gleaned from *CIS/Annual*, Norma Rae should have no trouble finding the debates that she wants.

Upon scanning the debates, we find a number of arguments over whether an employer can close a plant without 60 days notice if unforeseen circumstances occur. It appears that the Senators and Representatives who did not support passage of the act seemed to think that there was no such provision, and the members of Congress who supported the act pointed out that there was a business circumstances exception that would be effective in such situations so as not to impose undue hardship on the employer (see Figure 24). These arguments aren't all that enlightening as to the meaning of the business circumstances exception in specific circumstances, but perhaps they could be used creatively. As a displaced worker, Norma Rae could argue that it was apparent to many of the members of Congress (those who opposed the law) that the business circumstance that a company could rely on to give fewer than 60 days notice must be quite severe, because many members thought that such a circumstance was almost nonexistent, and in her case, the loss of a single contract simply couldn't be severe enough to qualify for the exception.

Helpful Hint

The *Congressional Record* appears to be a good publication for determining what our members of Congrèss thought about a certain pending bill, but it should be noted that the *Congressional Record* is not a verbatim transcript of what goes on on the floor of each chamber during a debate. Members of Congress can have their comments or portions of their comments deleted on request.

*Eventually, hardbound editions of these volumes are published.

Public Law 100-379 Item 4.7

4.7 June 30, Senate consideration of S. 1420, p. S8969.

4.8 July 1, Senate consideration of S. 1420, p. S9081.

4.9 July 7, Senate consideration of S. 1420, p. S9269.

4.10 July 8, Senate consideration of S. 1420, p. S9367.

4.11 July 9, Senate consideration of S. 1420, p. S9485.

4.12 July 10, Senate consideration of S. 1420, p. S9628.

4.13 July 14, Senate consideration of S. 1420, p. S9803.

4.14 July 15, Senate consideration of S. 1420, p. S9944.

4.15 July 17, Senate consideration of S. 1420, p. S10117.

4.16 July 21, Senate consideration of S. 1420, consideration and passage of H.R. 3 with amendments, and return to calendar of S. 1420, p. S10249.

4.17 Aug. 5, Senate insistence on its amendments to H.R.3, request for a conference and appointment of conferees, p. S11321.

4.18 Aug. 7, House disagreement to the Senate amendments to H.R. 3, agreement to a conference, and appointment of conferees, p. H7303.

134 Congressional Record
100th Congress, 2nd Session - 1988

4.19 Apr. 20, Submission in the House of the conference report on H.R. 3, p. H1863.

4.20 Apr. 21, House agreement to the conference report on H.R. 3, p. H2284.

4.21 Apr. 22, Senate consideration of the conference report on H.R. 3, p. S4540.

4.22 Apr. 25, Senate consideration of the conference report on H.R. 3, p. S4657.

4.23 Apr. 26, Senate consideration of the conference report on H.R. 3, p. S4718.

4.24 Apr. 27, Senate agreement to the conference report on H.R. 3, p. S4832.

4.25 May 24, House consideration of Presidential veto message and passage of H.R. 3, p. H3533.

4.26 June 7, Senate consideration of Presidential veto message on H.R. 3, p. S7231.

4.27 June 8, Senate consideration of Presidential veto message and failure to pass H.R. 3, p. S7231.

4.28 June 22, Senate consideration of S. 2527, p. S8373.

4.29 June 23, Senate consideration of S. 2527, p. S8449.

4.30 June 24, Senate consideration of S. 2527, p. S8536.

4.31 June 27, Senate consideration of S. 2527, p. S8596.

4.32 June 28, Senate consideration of S. 2527, p. S8663.

4.33 June 29, Senate consideration of S. 2527, p. S8762.

4.34 July 6, Senate consideration and passage of S. 2527, p. S8847.

4.35 July 13, House consideration and passage of S. 2527, p. H5500.

P.L. 100-379 Hearings

93rd Congress

5.1 "National Employment Priorities Act," hearings before the General Subcommittee on Labor, House Education and Labor Committee, Oct. 18, 19, 1974.

(CIS75:H341-29 iv+150 p.)
(Y4.Ed8/1:Em7/15.)

Hearings before the *General Subcom on Labor* on H.R. 13541 (text, p. 1-15), the National Employment Priorities Act of 1974, to amend the Fair Labor Standards Act, to meet the problems of unemployment and the economic hardships from plant closing by requiring prenotification of business dislocations, by providing assistance to individuals, businesses, and communities affected by dislocations, and by denying certain Federal income tax benefits to businesses involved in unnecessary or arbitrary closings or transfers of business establishments.

178 CIS/INDEX Legislative Histories JANUARY-DECEMBER 1988

Figure 23

have no doubt about the future of America. It will overcome every constraint that we put in its way. But that future will be a little less bright, opportunities will be fewer, economic growth will be less because of this bill. That to me represents an unnecessary tragedy. That is why I am opposed to this bill. I am not for plant closings. I am against plant closings. I want to debate legislation to open up plants, and to create jobs. I am not interested in spreading the miseries and rubbing everybody's nose in it. This bill is bad legislation and it assaults a fundamental premise that the American system is built on. That premise is private profit. We have no right to require an American citizen, an investor, an entrepreneur, to destroy their life's savings to force them to keep a plant open when they might salvage their business and ultimately create jobs for their employees by closing.

I hate to see a plant close or to lay people off, but there is something worse; that is, plants closing that never open, and people being laid off that are never called back.

That is what is wrong with this bill. Mr. President, I am certain that it is going to pass. I believe it is going to become law but I wanted to make it clear that I am against it. It is a law that I hope some day we are enlightened enough to repeal. I may be an old and ancient one if I am fortunate enough to be here, but if I am I will rejoice when that day comes.

I yield the floor.

The ACTING PRESIDENT pro tempore. The Senator from Illinois.

Mr. SIMON addressed the Chair.

The ACTING PRESIDENT pro tempore. The Senator form Illinois.

Mr. SIMON. I yield myself as much time as I may consume.

My friend, the distinguished Senator from Texas, says this is not a cure-all. Of course it is not a cure-all. This is just one part of what is needed in this country. We have to encourage research. We have to encourage improved productivity. We have to encourage people to get jobs here. That is why the senior Senator from Texas, Senator BENTSEN, has been pushing a trade bill, so we can get those jobs in this country.

But the argument that my friend, Senator GRAMM, uses when he says we are taking things away from business can be used against Social Security, you can use that against unemployment compensation, and you can use it against all kinds of things.

I simply point out to any Senators who may not have made up their mind yet that there are two very important—some people would call them loopholes. They are things that will permit businesses that really are under dire circumstances to avoid this. Any business where the circumstances were not reasonably foreseeable as of the time that the notice would have been required is exempt. That is a pretty massive loophole; and, also, the employer was actively seeking capital or business which if obtained would have enabled the employer to avoid or postpone the shutdown, and the employer reasonably and in good faith believed that giving the notice required would have precluded the employer from obtaining the needed capital or business. Those are pretty massive loopholes.

Then finally, Mr. President, I used to be in business. I had a small publishing business and had four small plants. I guess anyone who is in business does not like writing out those checks to the Government. But the one I always regretted writing the most was the one for unemployment compensation because very rarely was I laying people off, and very rarely was I the cause of that unemployment compensation check that I had to write out. What we are doing right now in this is to discourage needless expenditures by business. This is a business protection bill as well as a protection bill for workers. Responsible businesses give notice. But we are saying here to businesses that are not giving notice that we are going to have to do it so we will not have to pay out as much money in unemployment compensation. If workers are given enough advanced notice, they can get other jobs. We do not need to spend money for a nonproductive purpose like unemployment compensation.

I think this bill makes a great deal of sense. I hope we will pass the cloture motion and we will pass the bill, and do it quickly.

May I inquire of the Chair how much time I have left?

The PRESIDING OFFICER (Mr. DASCHLE). The Senator has 6 minutes remaining.

Mr. SIMON. I reserve the balance of my time.

Mr. BYRD. Will the Senator yield?

Mr. SIMON. I am pleased to yield to the majority leader.

Mr. BYRD. Mr. President, I thank the distinguished Senator.

ORDER OF PROCEDURE

Mr. BYRD. Mr. President, at 1:45 p.m., the Senate will vote on the motion to invoke cloture without the mandatory quorum call or without any quorum call being entered. If that cloture motion should fail, there will be an immediate vote on the second motion to invoke cloture. If that vote should fail, then there will be a third opportunity for Senators to invoke cloture. If cloture is invoked during the afternoon, then the plant-closing bill will remain the pending business before the Senate to the exclusion of all other business. And if it is not invoked this afternoon, there will be a vote on cloture on tomorrow. I hope that cloture will be invoked. The first rollcall vote this afternoon will be a 30-minute rollcall vote.

I ask unanimous consent that the call for the regular order be automatic at the conclusion of 30 minutes.

The PRESIDING OFFICER. Without objection, it is so ordered.

Mr. BYRD. Mr. President, if Senators are here, I hope they will come to the floor and vote early on the rollcall vote and not wait until the last minute; because if all Senators have voted, it will be possible then to close the vote and proceed either to the next cloture vote or further action on the bill. So if the Senators are here, they should take advantage of the opportunity to vote early and help to expedite the business of the Senate.

I thank the distinguished Senator for yielding.

Mr. SIMON. Mr. President, I reserve the remainder of my time.

As I understand our situation, if I yield back the remainder of my time, we will be in recess until 1:45. Is that correct?

The PRESIDING OFFICER. The Senator is correct.

Mr. SIMON. I yield back the remainder of my time.

RECESS UNTIL 1:45 P.M.

The PRESIDING OFFICER. The Senate stands in recess until 1:45 p.m.

Thereupon, at 1:22 p.m., the Senate recessed until 1:45 p.m.; whereupon, the Senate reassembled when called to order by the Presiding Officer (Mr. DASCHLE).

VOTE

The PRESIDING OFFICER. The question is, Is it the sense of the Senate that debate on S. 2527, a bill to require advance notification of plant closings and mass layoffs, and for other purposes, shall be brought to a close?

The yeas and nays are automatic under the rule, and the clerk will call the roll.

The legislative clerk called the roll.

Mr. CRANSTON. I announce that the Senator from Delaware [Mr. BIDEN] is absent because of illness.

Mr. SIMPSON. I announce that the Senator from Minnesota [Mr. BOSCHWITZ], the Senator from Rhode Island [Mr. CHAFEE], the Senator from Nevada [Mr. HECHT], the Senator from North Carolina [Mr. HELMS], the Senator from Arizona [Mr. MCCAIN] and the Senator from Alaska [Mr. MURKOWSKI] are necessarily absent.

The PRESIDING OFFICER. Are there any other Senators in the Chamber who desire to vote?

The result was announced—yeas 88, nays 5, as follows:

[Rollcall Vote No. 222 Leg.]

YEAS—88

Adams	Breaux	Cranston
Armstrong	Bumpers	D'Amato
Baucus	Burdick	Danforth
Bentsen	Byrd	Daschle
Bingaman	Chiles	DeConcini
Bond	Cochran	Dixon
Boren	Cohen	Dodd
Bradley	Conrad	Dole

Figure 24

SEARCHING THE *CODE OF FEDERAL REGULATIONS*

OK, Norma Rae is building up her arsenal, or finding out at this point that her arsenal is looking rather depleted and maybe it's time to wave a white flag and give up. In either case, she may not want to do this just yet, not until she's seen what the agency that is assigned to enforce the law that she is concerned with thinks about her issue. What this means is that we are going to have to find the regulations, if any exist, created by the agency in charge of this law in the *Code of Federal Regulations* (C.F.R.). So, let's turn back to the contents page of the good old U.S.C.S.

> **Helpful Hint**
>
> If you don't know what one of the abbreviations in the citations in the U.S.C.S., or U.S.C.A. mean, just look in the front of the volume. You can find a list of abbreviations used there.

As you can see, § 2107 is titled "Authority to Prescribe Regulations." This seems like a pretty likely place to see who is enforcing this law. As we turn to that section we find that is looks like the Secretary of Labor is assigned to create regulations to carry out the purposes of this act, but as before there are no listings after the text of this section, as normally there would be, of the C.F.R. sections where these regulations can be found. We'll have to look in the pocket part again.

> **Helpful Hint**
>
> It is also possible to find a C.F.R. section that may affect you through the descriptive word approach in the official index of the C.F.R., but we don't recommend it. It is very hard to access the C.F.R. in this way. Even Worker Adjustment and Retraining Notification Act was not listed in the index. It is better to use a statute or particular section of the statute in the tables portions of the C.F.R. index to find the regulations that are relevant to your problem.

As can be seen in a listing under the heading of "Code of Federal Regulations," the regulations created to interpret and administer this act are located at 20 C.F.R. Part 639. In nonabbreviated form this means Title 20 of the *Code of Federal Regulations* Part 639, and Part 639 means every section of the C.F.R. that starts with the number 639—like 693.1, 639.2, 639.3, and so on. Find the C.F.R. volume that contains this part, in this case it would be the volume marked "Part 500 to end," and flip to Part 639—everything runs in numerical order, lowest to highest like all of the other statutory-based materials.

We've found it. Welcome to the much maligned world of federal regulations. Let's see if these regulations can give us some guidance as to what sort of business circumstance might allow the employer to give fewer than 60 days notice of a plant closing, or whether the employer is barking up the wrong tree.

In looking at the contents at the beginning of this part of the C.F.R. (see Figure 25), it seems like there is a lot that might be of interest here, but § 639.9 appears to be directly relevant. Let's look at it (see Figure 26). The first subsection of § 639.9 doesn't directly address Norma Rae's problem, but § 639.9(b) does address the "unforeseeable business circumstance" exception. It appears from this that her employer may have a defense. The loss of a principal client can be the sort of circumstance that would allow for a reduction in the 60-day notice requirement. But this issue is not entirely settled. This subsection merely brings up some more specific questions that have to be answered, such as was the account that her employer lost a "principal client?" (There is no definition of what this means, so this is the sort of question that a court might have to determine on its own.) Was the loss of the client "sudden and unexpected"? Remember, the term in the law is *unforseeable business circumstance*, and according to the regulation that means a circumstance that is not "reasonably" forseeable. So, this issue is not settled yet. She's going to have to read the cases that she found in the case notes following the statute and probably gather more factual information if she decides to actually file a suit.

Updating your research

Remember that quotation from the beginning of the chapter? Now we have to follow the interpretation of that quotation that our professors suggested. We're not done yet. As with cases, statutes and the C.F.R. have to be updated to make sure that your research is as current as possible and that the language in the statutes or regulations that you are relying on is still valid.

Updating a statute

Of course, the first and easiest step in updating a statute is to check the pocket part of the commercially produced annotated code that you are using. We've already done that. When we checked for the C.F. R. citation and case notes, we would have noticed that the statute had been repealed, that is revoked so that it no longer exists, or reclassified, which simply means Congress changed the number of the statute and moved it, because the code itself would have told you, usually with an explanation like "This section has been repealed by Pub. L. 104–100." There was nothing like this, so at least up to the last time that the pocket part was issued, this would be just prior to May 1996 at the time of this writing, or more specifically through the First Session of the 104th Congress, as is noted on the front of the pocket part, the statute was still valid and the language hadn't been changed. Notwithstanding, this may not be good enough, but never fear our old friends at Shepard's have it covered.

LAW FACT

The repeal talked about here is an express repeal. There is also such a thing as an implied repeal. An implied repeal takes place when the Congress passes a later act which is so contrary to the earlier act that the earlier act must be assumed to no longer have any validity.

Just as with cases, Shepard's has citators for updating and validating statutes. There are citators for state statutes and for federal statutes. The federal statute citator is called *Shepard's Federal Statute's Citations*.

We can find Norma Rae's statute by the title and section number. In our example, that would be title 29 and section § 2102. Find the volume of *Shepard's Federal Statute's Citations* that covers this title. Before you grab all of the volumes, as you would for updating a case, stop! You don't necessarily have to. Remember, by checking the pocket part, we've already partially updated this section of the act. Instead, all we have to do is find the volumes or the supplements from the date of the coverage of the pocket part. In our case, again as of this writing, this would be two of the paperback supplements, the one issued on January 1, 1996 that contains title 29, and the one issued on September 1, 1996. Because *Shepard's Federal Statute's Citations* updates statutes, treaties, court rules, and other civil law, we will have to go to the front of the volume to the contents and find out what page the citations to the *United States Code Service* begins on. Turn to the page where the *United States Code Service* citations begin and then flip through them until you come across the citation for title 29 at the upper outside corners of the pages, and then continue looking until you find § 2102. As with all other statutory materials, everything is arranged in numerical order from lowest to highest. So, title 28 precedes title 29, and within title 29 § 2101 precedes § 2102.

In Shepard's, they even give you subsections and subdivisions that you can check. So, in our case, we'd want to check specifically if subsection (b) of § 2102 and its subdivisions have been affected countants. Such surveys, audits, or examinations normally shall be conducted annually but not less than once every two years.

§ 638.810 Reporting requirements.

The Job Corps Director shall establish procedures to ensure timely and complete reporting of such program information as is necessary to maintain accountability for the Job Corps program and funding.

§ 638.811 Review and evaluation.

The Job Corps Director shall establish adequate program management to provide continuous examination of the performance of the components of the program.

§ 638.812 State and local taxation of Job Corps deliverers.

The Act provides that transactions conducted by a private for-profit deliverer or a nonprofit deliverer in connection with the deliverer's operation of a center or other Job Corps program or activity shall not be considered as generating gross receipts. Such deliverer shall not be liable, directly or indirectly, to any State or subdivision thereof (nor to any person acting on behalf thereof) for any gross receipts taxes, business privilege taxes measured by gross receipts, or any similar taxes imposed on, or measured by, gross receipts in connection with any payments made to or by such deliverer for operating a center or other Job Corps program, or activity. Such deliverer shall not be liable to any State or subdivision thereof to collect or pay any sales, excise, use, or similar tax imposed upon the sale to or use by such deliverer of any property, service, or other item in connection with the operation of a center or other Job Corps program or activity. (Section 437(c))

§ 638.813 Nondiscrimination; nonsectarian activities.

(a) *Nondiscrimination.* Center operators and other deliverers, and subcontractors and/or subrecipients of center operators and other deliverers shall comply with the nondiscrimination provisions of section 167 of the Act and its implementing regulations, and with, as applicable, 29 CFR parts 31 and 32, part 33, and 41 CFR chapter 60. For the purposes of section 167 of the Act, students shall be considered as the ultimate beneficiaries of Federal financial assistance. (Section 167)

(b) *Nonsectarian activities.* Students shall not be employed or trained on the construction, operation, or maintenance of so much of any facility as is used or to be used for sectarian instruction or as a place for religious worship. (Section 167(a)(3))

§ 638.814 Lobbying; political activities; unionization.

No funds provided under the Act may be used in any way:

(a) To attempt to influence in any manner a member of Congress to favor or oppose any legislation or appropriation by Congress;

(b) To attempt to influence in any manner a member of a State or local legislature to favor or oppose any legislation or appropriation by such legislature;

(c) For any activity which involves political activities; or

(d) For any activity which will assist, promote, or deter union organizing. (Sections 141(1) and 143(c)(1))

§ 638.815 Charging fees.

No person or organization shall charge an individual a fee for the placement or referral of such individual in or to a training program under the Act. (Section 141(j))

PART 639—WORKER ADJUSTMENT AND RETRAINING NOTIFICATION

Sec.

AUTHORITY: 29 U.S.C. 2107(a).

SOURCE: 54 FR 16064, Apr. 20, 1989, unless otherwise noted.

Figure 25

tion may be satisfied if the employer can show that the financing or business source would not choose to do business with a troubled company or with a company whose workforce would be looking for other jobs. The actions of an employer relying on the "faltering company" exception will be viewed in a company-wide context. Thus, a company with access to capital markets or with cash reserves may not avail itself of this exception by looking solely at the financial condition of the facility, operating unit, or site to be closed.

§639.9(b) → (b) The "unforeseeable business circumstances" exception under section 3(b)(2)(A) of WARN applies to plant closings and mass layoffs caused by business circumstances that were not reasonably foreseeable at the time that 60-day notice would have been required.

(1) An important indicator of a business circumstance that is not reasonably foreseeable is that the circumstance is caused by some sudden, dramatic, and unexpected action or condition outside the employer's control. A principal client's sudden and unexpected termination of a major contract with the employer, a strike at a major supplier of the employer, and an unanticipated and dramatic major economic downturn might each be considered a business circumstance that is not reasonably foreseeable. A government ordered closing of an employment site that occurs without prior notice also may be an unforeseeable business circumstance.

(2) The test for determining when business circumstances are not reasonably foreseeable focuses on an employer's business judgment. The employer must exercise such commercially reasonable business judgment as would a similarly situated employer in predicting the demands of its particular market. The employer is not required, however, to accurately predict general economic conditions that also may affect demand for its products or services.

(c) The "natural disaster" exception in section 3(b)(2)(B) of WARN applies to plant closings and mass layoffs due to any form of a natural disaster.

(1) Floods, earthquakes, droughts, storms, tidal waves or tsunamis and similar effects of nature are natural disasters under this provision.

(2) To qualify for this exception, an employer must be able to demonstrate that its plant closing or mass layoff is a direct result of a natural disaster.

(3) While a disaster may preclude full or any advance notice, such notice as is practicable, containing as much of the information required in §639.7 as is available in the circumstances of the disaster still must be given, whether in advance or after the fact of an employment loss caused by a natural disaster.

(4) Where a plant closing or mass layoff occurs as an indirect result of a natural disaster, the exception does not apply but the "unforeseeable business circumstance" exception described in paragraph (b) of this section may be applicable.

§639.10 When may notice be extended?

Additional notice is required when the date or schedule of dates of a planned plant closing or mass layoff is extended beyond the date or the ending date of any 14-day period announced in the original notice as follows:

(a) If the postponement is for less than 60 days, the additional notice should be given as soon as possible to the parties identified in §639.6 and should include reference to the earlier notice, the date (or 14-day period) to which the planned action is postponed, and the reasons for the postponement. The notice should be given in a manner which will provide the information to all affected employees.

(b) If the postponement is for 60 days or more, the additional notice should be treated as new notice subject to the provisions of §§639.5, 639.6 and 639.7 of this part. Rolling notice, in the sense of routine periodic notice, given whether or not a plant closing or mass layoff is impending, and with the intent to evade the purpose of the Act rather than give specific notice as required by WARN, is not acceptable.

PART 640—STANDARD FOR BENEFIT PAYMENT PROMPTNESS—UNEMPLOYMENT COMPENSATION

Sec.

Figure 26

recently in any way because that is where the language of the business circumstances exception is located. As we can see (see Figure 27) there has been no action on our subsection, although there have been some cases that have dealt with this subsection —Norma Rae may want to add these to her case list. We can determine this, just as with the case citators, by the little letters that appear before citations. If you want to know what these letters stand for or any of the abbreviations used by the Shepard's volumes that you are using, turn to the front of the Shepard's volume and there you'll find a list of abbreviations. (We've included a handy list explaining these abbreviations in Appendix 5).

Because there are only cases here, all we have to concern ourselves with is the Judicial abbreviations, and the only time we would have to worry is if the case said that the subsection was unconstitutional, unconstitutional in part, void or invalid, or void or invalid in part. Any of these would mean that the subsection or part of it was no longer good law, but even that is not conclusive unless it is the Supreme Court of the United States that is saying it, or the court of appeals for the federal circuit in your jurisdiction. Remember the hierarchy of courts discussed in Chapter 1. The U.S. Supreme Court has the final say on the constitutionality of any federal law.

As to the Operation of Statute abbreviations, if you see any of these in front of a citation when checking a subsection, you'd better go find this new version of the law and see what it says. In our example, if there was a citation to a new law which affected 29 U.S.C.S. § 2102(b), it would be either in the *Advance Sheets* or the white paperback that is usually found with the *Advance Sheets* called *United States Code Service Cumulative Later Case and Statutory Service.* A similar later statute service also supplements the U.S.C.A.; it is called *United States Code Annotated Statutory Supplement.*

Helpful Hint

Shepard's Federal Statute's Citations only contains court citations to federal courts. If you want to see interpretations of this subsection by a particular state court, you would have to find the state version of *Shepard's Citations* for the state that you want.

Helpful Hint

As with the case citators, *Shepard's Federal Statute's Citations* is usually accurate, but it may be best to double-check citations that you run across to be 100 percent sure of their accuracy. Even Shepard's puts a disclaimer in the front of its citator volumes.

TITLE 29 § 2101 UNITED STATES CODE 1988 and 1994 Eds.

Cir. 4
830FS433

Cir. 5
31F3d238
790FS672
825FS126

Cir. 8
78F3d1282
138BRW925

§ 2101 (a) (6) (B)

Cir. 2
999F2d52

Cir. 3
32F3d55
833FS468

Cir. 4
830FS433

Cir. 5
825FS125

Cir. 6
748FS1284
775FS1019
792FS1050

Cir. 7
790FS1447

§ 2101 (a) (8)

Cir. 2
877FS114

Cir. 3
992F2d30
855FS1476
162BRW123

Cir. 5
778FS313

Cir. 6
775FS1018

Cir. 7
906FS1250

Cir. 8
740FS683

§ 2101 (b)

Cir. 6
945F2d122

Cir. 9
50F3d1467

§ 2101 (b) (1)

Cir. 3
763FS83
768FS1123
878FS709
162BRW123

Cir. 5
15F3d1282
778FS303
790FS666
898FS455

Cir. 6
945F2d122

Cir. 7
906FS1247

Cir. 9
50F3d1469

Cir. 10
24F3d1280

§ 2101 (b) (2)

Cir. 3
992F2d30
855FS1473

§ 2101 (b) (2) (A)

Cir. 5
790FS668

Cir. 9
50F3d777

§ 2101 (b) (3)

Cir. 1
901FS440

§ 2102

Cir. 1
723FS1580

Cir. 2
726FS462
778FS608
805FS96
805FS110
814FS256
829FS673
164BRW29

Cir. 3
725FS830
768FS1118

Cir. 4
780FS376

Cir. 5
23F3d934
31F3d227
778FS307
825FS124

Cir. 6
748FS1297

Cir. 8
50F3d1428
820FS1193
861FS66

Cir. 9
50F3d773
50F3d1467
66F3d243

Cir. 10
61F3d764
916FS1115

93ARF343n

§ 2102 (a)
115SC1929

Cir. 1
901FS434
903FS185

Cir. 2
976F2d807
778FS608
805FS110
809FS188
877FS112

Cir. 3
5F3d40
78F3d120
725FS830
763FS82
768FS1122
781FS1061
809FS7
817FS523
855FS1473

Cir. 4
830FS433
831FS1299
860FS317

Cir. 5
15F3d1286
31F3d227
778FS313
778FS321
898FS455
899FS297

Cir. 6
38F3d852
748FS1283
775FS1017
792FS1047

Cir. 7
7F3d619
790FS1443

Cir. 8
50F3d1428
75F3d1289
78F3d1280
80F3d1222
740FS683
821FS1311
821FS1313
138BRW925

Cir. 9
27F3d388
50F3d1469
66F3d243
826FS333
867FS1445

Cir. 10
847FS867

Cir. 11
6F3d723
817FS933

§ 2102 (a) (1)
115SC1929

Cir. 2
34F3d1150

Cir. 3
176BRW332

Cir. 5
778FS303

Cir. 6
792FS1047
792FS1049

Cir. 8
80F3d1223
740FS685
138BRW926

Cir. 10
847FS867

§ 2102 (a) (2)

Cir. 2
34F3d1150

Cir. 3
32F3d58
763FS82
855FS1474

Cir. 5
778FS303

§ 2102 (a) (5)

Cir. 2
726FS466

§ 2102 (a) (6)

Cir. 2
726FS466

§ 2102 (b)

Cir. 1
903FS192

Cir. 4
831FS1295

Cir. 5
778FS304

Cir. 10
847FS869

§ 2102 (b) (1)

Cir. 1
901FS440

Cir. 2
726FS464

Cir. 3
763FS82
768FS1123
162BRW123

Cir. 4
831FS1299

Cir. 5
15F3d1281
778FS305
778FS320

Cir. 6
818FS197

Cir. 9
27F3d388

§ 2102 (b) (2)

Cir. 3
162BRW123

Cir. 5
15F3d1281

Cir. 11
817FS934

§ 2102 (b) (2) (A)

Cir. 1
901FS440
901FS442

Cir. 2
976F2d811

Cir. 3
768FS1123
781FS1065

Cir. 5
778FS306
778FS320
898FS455

Cir. 6
748FS1279

Cir. 7
7F3d620

Cir. 8
75F3d1291
821FS1307

Cir. 9
27F3d388
50F3d776
826FS332

Cir. 10
847FS869

Cir. 11
817FS933

§ 2102 (b) (2) (B)

Cir. 3
768FS1123

§ 2102 (b) (3)

Cir. 3
781FS1063
162BRW123

Cir. 6
748FS1279
748FS1297
818FS197

Cir. 8
821FS1311

Cir. 9
27F3d389
826FS333

Cir. 10
847FS869

Cir. 11
817FS934

§ 2102 (c)

Cir. 3
78F3d121

Cir. 6
748FS1298
775FS1016

§ 2102 (c) (1)

Cir. 6
775FS1016

§ 2102 (d)

Cir. 1
844FS897
901FS435

Cir. 2
164BRW28

Cir. 6
748FS1283
775FS1017
792FS1048

Cir. 8
740FS683

§ 2103

Cir. 2
726FS462

Cir. 3
855FS1473

Cir. 4
831FS1296
831FS1297

Cir. 8
861FS66

Cir. 9
867FS1442

§ 2103 (1)

Cir. 3
855FS1469

Cir. 4
831FS1296

Cir. 6
792FS1048

Cir. 8
75F3d1292

1586

Figure 27

Updating a regulation

Norma Rae has rounded the last turn and now she's in the stretch heading for the finish line. We're almost done. Now all we have to do is update the C.F.R. section that interprets our subsection of the statute. In our example, that would be 20 C.F.R. § 639.9(b).

Updating the C.F.R. is tedious but not terribly difficult once you get the hang of it. What you must do first is look at the cover of the C.F.R. volume that contains the regulation that you want to update. On the front cover it will tell you when this portion of the C.F.R. was revised—that is, when it was last brought up-to-date. In our example, we're pretty lucky because it was revised as of April 1, 1996. Now we have to find a series of volumes called *Code of Federal Regulations LSA*—which stands for List of Sections Affected. It is usually shelved along with the C.F.R. We will want all the volumes that are available starting after the date that the C.F.R. section that we are using was last revised—in our example, April 1, 1996. So, at this time what we've found are two volumes: one that says May 1996 on the cover and another that says June 1996. The title pages tell us the specific dates of coverage for each volume (see Figure 28). In our example, the May volume covers changes for our title from July 3, 1995 through May 31, 1996, and the June volume covers changes for our title from July 3, 1995 through June 28, 1996. So, as it appears, we only have to check the June volume because it already covers what is in the May volume.

To find out whether 20 C.F.R. § 639.9(b) has been affected recently, all we have to do is look through the *Code of Federal Regulations LSA* as we would any other civil law volume; the citations are listed in numerical order from smallest to largest. What we find is that there has been no action concerning 20 C.F.R. § 639.9(b), but we are not quite done yet. We still have to check the *Federal Register*.

The *Federal Register* is to the C.F.R. what the slip laws are to the *United States Code*. The *Federal Register* is published daily, like a daily magazine. It not only contains rules and regulations created by federal agencies, but it also contains proposed rules—for the purpose of allowing the public to comment on them—legal notices such as notices of agency meetings that the public may attend, and presidential documents such as executive orders and proclamations. The *Federal Register* includes tables of the parts affected in the C.F.R. by any new rules or regulations or changes

LSA

List of CFR Sections Affected

June 1996

Title 1–16
Changes January 2, 1996
through June 28, 1996

Title 17–27
Changes April 1, 1996
through June 28, 1996

Title 28–41
Changes July 3, 1995
through June 28, 1996

Title 42–50
Changes October 2, 1995
through June 28, 1996

Figure 28

to the rules and regulations that are published in that edition, and at the back of each edition is a cumulative table for that month.

To complete our updating of the C.F.R. section that we are working with, we are going to have to check the index to the *Federal Register*, starting with the month that covers the last days of the *Code of Federal Regulations LSA*, which we already checked. If, say, we are doing our research on September 7, 1996, we would have to check the *Federal Register* index for June, July, and August 1996 (because the LSA that we checked covered up to nearly the end of June), and the index in the *Federal Register* for the latest date in September (ideally, you would check the issue for the day you were doing the research, in our example, September 7, 1996, but there is a short lag time between the date that the *Federal Register* is published and the date that it is received by libraries). As you can see (see Figure 29), after checking, there has been no action involving 20 C.F.R. Part 639, so Norma Rae can be safe in assuming that at least for now, this regulation is still valid, so far as the agency is concerned.

The final step in our update makes use of *Shepard's* again. In this instance, we are going to want to check *Shepard's Code of Federal Regulations Citations* to see if any courts have held that the regulation is invalid. This Shepard's is set up in a manner similar to the statutory Shepard's citator, with regulations listed by title, section, and even subsection listed in numerical order from lowest number to highest (see Figure 30). We can tell from these citations that no case has adversely affected 20 C.F.R. § 639.9(b) because there are none of those little letters preceding the case citations that say that the court found the regulation unconstitutional or invalid. (For your convenience, we've reprinted a copy of the "Abbreviations—Analysis," which is found at the front of the *Shepard's Code of Federal Regulations Citations*, in Appendix 5). So, again it appears that Norma Rae can rely on the language of this regulation.

PERFORMING CONSTITUTIONAL RESEARCH

The U.S. Constitution is also included as part of the commercially produced annotated codes and can be accessed in the same way as any statute that is contained in them. Updating a portion that you wish to rely on is generally easier and less surprising because ii **Federal Register** / Vol. 61, No. 167 / Tuesday, August 27, 1996 / Reader Aids

92 43417
94 .... 40292, 43305
304 .... 43149, 43150
308 .... 43149, 43150
310 .... 43149, 43150
317 42143
320 .... 43149, 43150
327 .... 43149, 43150
381 .... 43149, 43150
416 .... 43149, 43150
417 .... 43149, 43150
Proposed Rules:
92 43188
101 43483
102 43316
104 43316
130 43188

10 CFR
2 43406
50 41303
51 43406
Proposed Rules:
2 43409
25 40555
30 43193
40 43193
51 43409
70 43193
95 40555
430 .... 41748, 44001
434 40882
435 40882
490 41032

11 CFR
104 42371
110 40961
Proposed Rules:
109 41036
110 41036

12 CFR
26 40293
30 43948
208 43948
212 40293
310 43418
348 40293
364 43948
563f 40293
570 43948
701 41312
931 40311
932 43151
933 42531
941 43151
Proposed Rules:
3 42565
208 42565
219 43195
225 42565
325 42565
357 40756
362 43486
567 42565
613 42091
614 42091
615 42901
618 42901
619 42901
620 42901
626 42901
703 41750
704 41750
932 42570
934 41535
935 40364
941 42570
1270 42824

13 CFR
107 41496
121 .... 42376, 43119

14 CFR
17 .... 42396, 42397
25 41949,42144
27 43952
29 .... 43647, 43648, 43952
39 .... 40313, 40511, 41733, 41951, 41953, 41955, 41957, 42549, 42773, 42776, 42777, 42779, 42781, 42782, 42994, 42996, 43155, 43307, 43650, 43652
71 .... 40147, 40315, 40316, 40717, 40718, 40719, 40961, 41684, 41735, 41736, 42146, 42784, 42785, 43310,
73 42550
95 40148
97 .... 40150, 40151, 42551, 42552, 42554
121 43916
Proposed Rules:
23 41688
25 .... 40710, 41688, 41924, 42577
33 41688
39 .... 40159, 40758, 40760, 40762, 41037, 41039, 41537, 41539, 41751, 41753, 41755, 41757, 42195, 42825, 43317, 43319, 43687, 43689, 43691, 43692, 44002, 44004, 44006
71 .... 40365, 43320, 43694, 44008, 44119
91 .... 41040, 43196
93 .... 41040, 43196
121 .... 41040, 43196
135 .... 41040, 43196
255 .... 42197, 42208, 43500
Ch. 1 41750

15 CFR
679 40481
774 41326
799A 41326
902 .... 43420, 43952

16 CFR
1700 40317
Proposed Rules:
23 43500
1507 41043

17 CFR
1 .... 41496, 42999
4 42146
211 40721
230 42786
239 42786
270 42786
274 42786
Proposed Rules:
4 44009
230 43400
240 43400
250 43400
270 43400
275 43400

18 CFR
3c 43411
284 40962
381 40722
Proposed Rules:
35 41759
284 41406

19 CFR
10 41737
12 .... 41737, 43960
101 43429
102 41737
134 .... 4 .737
210 43429

20 CFR
348 42377
404 41329

21 CFR
73 40317
101 .... 40320, 40963, 42742, 43119, 43433
105 43963
136 40513
137 40513
139 40513
175 42378
177 42379
178 .... 42381, 43156
179 42381
182 43447
184 .... 40317, 43447
520 .... 43654, 43963
522 .... 41498, 42383
556 42383
558 .... 43450, 43654
584 43451
601 40153
620 40153
630 40153
640 40153
650 40153
660 40153
680 40153
1309 40981
1310 40981
1313 40981
Proposed Rules:
201 42826
331 42826
352 42398
730 44013
880 44013

22 CFR
50 43310
51 43310
126 .... 41499, 41737
212 43002
602 40332

23 CFR
667 43964
Proposed Rules:
655 40484

24 CFR
103 41480
111 41282
115 41282
203 42786
221 42786
280 42952
291 43966
700 42949
982 42129
3500 41944
Proposed Rules:
10 42722
Ch. IX 42939

25 CFR
Proposed Rules:
214 41365
215 44019

26 CFR
1 .... 40993, 42165
26 043656
31 40993
301 42178
602 40993
Proposed Rules:
1 .... 42401, 43695, 44023, 44024
20 43197
25 43197
31 42401
35a 42401
301 42401
502 42401
503 42401
509 42401
513 42401
514 42401
516 42401
517 42401
520 42401
521 42401

27 CFR
252 41500
290 41500
Proposed Rules:
4 40568
5 40568
7 40568
19 40568
20 40568
22 40568
24 40568
25 40568
27 40568
70 40568
250 40568
251 40568
252 42462
290 42462

28 CFR
29 40723
42 .... 42556, 43119
90 40727

29 CFR
4 40714
5 40714
1691 42556
1910 43454
1915 43454
1926 .... 41738, 43454
2510 41220
4044 .... 4? 384
Proposed Rules:
1 40366
5 40366

Figure 29

it takes a lot more to amend the Constitution than it does to pass a law, and you probably would have heard about any amendment of the Constitution on the news. When it happens it is big news. The Constitution, as of now, after approximately 200 years, has only been amended 26 times, with the last amendment being approved by the states in 1971. One note of caution, however: Trying to support a case based on the idea that the action of your opposing party was unconstitutional is fairly difficult. As discussed in Chapter 1, courts don't like to base their decisions on constitutional grounds and will avoid doing so if at all possible. They are far more likely to base their decisions on the interpretation of a statute or some rule of common law. So, as with court decisions, you should rely on the U.S. or other Constitutions as a basis for your case only as a last resort.

USING YOUR CIVIL LAW RESEARCH

When doing your own research into the civil law, you will, like Norma Rae, wish to make a list of the statutes that appear to affect your issue and of the regulations and cases that interpret the statutes. With statutes and regulations, we recommend making a photocopy of the language that you are relying on because you want to know when you quote it to a court later on that you are absolutely correct. Changing a word can be misleading and embarrassing, and if the court thinks the change was deliberate you could be fined. We also recommend that you write out in your own words a short paragraph laying out what you think the statutory language that you are relying on means. As with case law research we think that it is best to try to put things in your own words so that you can be sure that you understand what you're reading. Finally, when you read the cases that interpret your statute, you will want to take notes from them by making a case brief (as discussed in Chapter 5).

CHAPTER HIGHLIGHTS

How laws are created by the legislature

- In a bicameral legislature, a bill is introduced into either of the two houses by a member of that chamber

TITLE 20 CODE OF FEDERAL REGULATIONS

§ 639.4(c)
Cir. 3
724FS335*1989
725FS831*1989

§ 639.5(a)(1)
Cir. 7
790FS1445^1992

§ 639.5(b)(1)
Cir. 5
790FS669^1992

§ 639.5(b)(2)
Cir. 5
15F3d1291*1989
790FS669^1992

§ 639.5(b)(3)
Cir. 5
790FS669^1992

§ 639.5(c)
Cir. 4
831FS1298^1993

§ 639.5(c)(3)
Cir. 4
831FS1297^1993

§ 639.5(c)(4)
Cir. 4
831FS1296^1993

§ 639.6(a)
Cir. 7
790FS1443^1992
Cir. 8
821FS1311^1993

§ 639.6(b)
Cir. 5
778FS314^1991
Cir. 6
792FS1049^1992
Cir. 7
790FS1450^1992
Cir. 8
740FS685*1989

§ 639.7
Cir. 5
15F3d1287*1988
Cir. 7
790FS1452^1992
Cir. 11
817FS938^1993

§ 639.7(a)(2)
Cir. 7
790FS1451^1992

§ 639.7(a)(4)
Cir. 5
778FS305^1991
Cir. 7
790FS1451^1992

§ 639.7(b)
Cir. 5
15F3d1287*1989
778FS312^1991
Cir. 7
790FS1450^1992

§ 639.7(c)
Cir. 7
790FS1443^1992
790FS1449^1992

§ 639.7(c)(3)
Cir. 7
790FS1450^1992

§ 639.7(c)(4)
Cir. 7
790FS1450^1992

§ 639.7(d)
Cir. 7
790FS1449^1992

§ 639.8
Cir. 7
790FS1448^1992

§ 639.9
Cir. 3
763FS82*1990
162BRW124^1993
Cir. 4
831FS1296^1993
Cir. 5
15F3d1282*1989
778FS304^1991
Cir. 8
821FS1311^1993
Cir. 9
826FS332^1993
Cir. 11
817FS935^1993

§ 639.9(a)
Cir. 5
15F3d1282*1989

§ 639.9(a)(1)
Cir. 3
763FS82*1990

§ 639.9(a)(2)
Cir. 3
763FS82*1990

§ 639.9(a)(3)
Cir. 3
763FS83*1990

§ 639.9(a)(4)
Cir. 3
763FS83*1990
Cir. 6
818FS197^1993

§ 639.9(b)
Cir. 5
778FS307^1991
Cir. 6
818FS198

§ 639.9(b)(1)
Cir. 3
781FS1063^1992
Cir. 6
818FS198^1993
Cir. 7
7F3d625*1992
Cir. 8
821FS1311^1993
Cir. 9
826FS332^1993
Cir. 10
847FS869^1994

§ 639.9(b)(2)
Cir. 5
15F3d1282*1988
Cir. 6
818FS198^1993
Cir. 7
7F3d626*1992
Cir. 10
847FS869^1994

§ 639.10
Cir. 11
817FS938^1993

§ 640.1(a)
Cir. 2
441FS104*1977

§ 640.1(a)(2)
Cir. 7
691F2d1228^1982
22F3d1378^1994
Mass
500NE1332^1986

§ 640.2(b)
Cir. 6
527FS533^1981

§ 640.3
Colo
781P2d101^1989

§ 640.3(a)
Cir. 7
691F2d1228^1982
22F3d1378^1994

§ 640.3(b)
Cir. 6
527FS533^1981

§ 640.4
Cir. 2
C441FS102^1977
Cir. 7
538F2d769^1976

§ 640.5
Cir. 2
C441FS102^1977
Cir. 6
527FS533^1981
Cir. 7
538F2d769^1976

Part 650 et seq.
N Y
456NYS2d526^1982

Part 650
Cir. 2
474FS272^1979
594FS241^1984
Cir. 8
425FS45*1976

§ 650.1 et seq.
Cir. 3
C473FS248^1979
81FRD54^1978

§§ 650.1 to 650.5
Cir. 3
627F2d654^1980

§ 650.1
Cir. 2
474FS272^1979
Colo
781P2d101^1989

§ 650.1(a)
Cir. 3
C473FS248^1979

§ 650.1(b)
Cir. 3
627F2d654^1980
Cir. 7
691F2d1228^1982
Cir. 9
447FS322*1974
Mo
606SW432^1980

§ 650.1(c)
Cir. 2
474FS272^1979
Cir. 7
530FS82^1981

§ 650.1(d)
Cir. 3
627F2d654^1980
C473FS250^1979

§ 650.2(a)
Cir. 3
C473FS248^1979
Cir. 8
425FS44*1976

§ 650.2(b)
Cir. 3
C473FS248^1979
Cir. 8
425FS44*1976

§ 650.2(c)
Cir. 3
C473FS248^1979

§ 650.2(c)(2)
Cir. 8
425FS44*1976

§ 650.3
Cir. 3
627F2d654^1980
Cir. 8
425FS44*1976
Calif
152CaR197^1979

§ 650.3(a)
Cir. 3
C627F2d653^1980
C473FS249^1979
Cir. 7
843F2d982^1988

§ 650.3(a)(1)
Cir. 2
474FS272^1979

§ 650.3(a)(2)
Cir. 2
474FS272^1979
Cir. 3
C473FS249^1979
81FRD54^1978

656

Shepard's Code of Federal Regulations: Title 1-27, 1994, Part 1, Page 656 Containing 20 CFR §639.9(b)

Figure 30

- The bill is sent to the committee that is designated to review the subject matter of such legislation
- If the bill is passed by the committee, it goes to the floor of the chamber, where it is debated and possibly voted on
- If the bill passes this chamber, it moves on to the other chamber where it is submitted to the same process of committees, changes, and possible votes
- If the bill passes both houses but in different forms because of changes, it is sent to a committee of the combined houses where the differences are reconciled
- Once the bill passes both houses of the legislature, it is sent to the president for approval or veto
- If the bill is approved by the president it becomes law; if it is vetoed, it can only become law if the veto is overridden by a two-thirds majority of both houses of the legislature

How laws are published

- Generally, as with federal legislation, when statutes are passed, they are published in three different forms
  - Statutes are published as official slip laws—single statutes in pamphlet form
  - Statutes are published in the official session laws—a collection of statutes organized by the session of Congress that passed them
  - Statutes are published in the official *United States Code*—a collection of all the statutes passed by the legislature, organized by topics, usually called titles
- Statutes are also published in their various forms by commercial publishers, usually more quickly than by the government, and with editorial enhancements to make research easier

Finding a statute that affects your case

- Look in the Popular Names Table in commercially produced codes if you know the name of a statute that affects your case but don't know the cite

- ➤ Look in *Shepard's Acts and Cases by Popular Names: Federal and State* if you know the name of a statute that affects your case but don't know the cite
- ➤ Use the topic approach or the descriptive word approach to find a statute in the commercially produced codes if you don't know if there is a statute that affects your case
  - Try to fit your legal issue into one of the topics (titles) into which the commercially published code is divided
    - Search the table of contents at the beginning of that title
    - See if you can identify a law, by name, that covers the issue being researched
- ➤ To access the descriptive word index, use relevant keywords derived from brainstorming and the legal categories in Chapter 3
- ➤ Determine whether the statute that you've found controls the issue being researched
  - Look at the contents at the beginning of the act
  - Read the definitional section of the act, if one exists, to understand how specific terms are used in the act
  - Read any section of the statute on enforcement to determine whether you can personally bring a suit under the statute or whether you must go through a government agency with your grievance
  - Look for a substantive section of the statute that covers your issue
    - Find cases related to your issue that interpret this section by pursuing the case notes following the text of the section
    - Search the legislative history of the statute to find discussions in the committee reports, the committee hearings, the *Congressional Record* (when researching federal laws), and the like, which may shed light onto the interpretation of this section of the act and its relation to your issue
    - Search the *Code of Federal Regulations* (C.F.R.)—when researching federal law—or a similar state compilation of regulations

i. Use citations to sections of the regulations noted in the editorial enhancements of the commercially published act
ii. Use the descriptive word approach in the index to the regulations
iii. Use the table of statutes in the index to the regulations to find regulations that mention the act you are researching

Update your statutory research

➤ Update your statute by using the pocket parts of the commercially published code

➤ Shepardize your statute using Shepard's citators

- Find the volumes of Shepard's that cover the statute you are updating, including all of the updates to these volumes.
- Locate the statute you are updating by its cite in the list of statutes in the relevant Shepard's volumes
- Note any changes indicated by the Operation of Statute abbreviations
- Research any cases that interpret your section of the statute, especially if the judicial abbreviations appear to indicate that they invalidate it

➤ Check for changes in the regulations interpreting your statute

- Look in the C.F.R. *List of Sections Affected* (LSA), if researching federal law
- Check the *Federal Register*, or similar state register
- Shepardize the relevant section of the regulations in Shepard's citators
  - Find the volumes of Shepard's that cover the regulation you are updating—including all of the updates to these volumes
  - Locate the regulation you are updating by its cite in the list of regulations in the relevant Shepard's volumes
  - Research any cases that interpret your section of the statute, especially if the Operation (Judicial) abbreviations appear to indicate that they invalidate it

CHAPTER 8

THE LAW IN THE MACHINE

The law is not a machine and the judges not machine-tenders.
—Jerome N. Frank, Law and the Modern Mind (1930)

THE SHAPE OF THINGS TO COME

After having read this book up to now, and followed along as we researched particular issues, you would probably agree with Mr. Frank that the law is not mechanical in nature. For all the emphasis placed by judges and legislatures on introducing stability and predictability into legal outcomes, it is apparent that the law is as much art as science. Regardless, although the law may not function like a machine, machines, particularly in the form of computers, are becoming increasingly important in doing legal research. However, they have not replaced books as the primary means of legal research, and it may be a long time yet before they do. There are four primary reasons for this:

- history
- cost
- availability, and
- newness.

Let's face it, lawyers control the law. Judges were usually once practicing lawyers, many legislators are lawyers, and of course lawyers are lawyers. These are the people who deal with the law day in and day out, and many if not most of them are set in their ways. They know how to do legal research the old-fashioned way, and they don't really have time to learn about new technologies. So, if lawyers drag their feet about how the law is to be published and found, then changes in the method of legal research are not going to occur as fast as they could. This is not an insurmountable problem though. There are incentives for lawyers to change. Computerized legal research tends to be faster than book searching—and in the legal profession, as in all others, time is money. As older lawyers retire, and new lawyers take their place, they are likelier to be more open to and comfortable with new technologies. Last but not least, practically all new lawyers coming out of law school today are already trained in the use of on-line legal research in the two most pervasive and complete legal services, LEXIS and Westlaw.

Cost, on the other hand, remains a problem. At this point in time, most computer research, at least that of real value in the law, can be so costly as to be prohibitive. On-line legal services like LEXIS and Westlaw can cost around $2 to $4 per minute to use. It can take several hours just to narrow down your problem to a workable legal issue. Multiply that by minutes and then by dollars, and you can see what we're talking about.

Then there's the availability problem. To do computer researching you have to have a computer or at least access to one, and not everybody does—or if you do have access to a computer, say at work, your employer may not want you using it for your personal projects. Even if you have access to a computer, you may have to subscribe to one of the databases or services (a matter of cost as well as availability) to access the legal materials that you need.

Finally, there is the problem of the newness of the whole thing. We're not talking here about a reluctance to use new technology. That is the history problem. The problem here is that most computer databases are in their infancy. Our common-law heritage has caused the law to grow layer upon layer. As you know by now if you've sat in a good law library, the amount of law that is available out there is vast, and you may need to access a good portion of it, some of it rather old. As it stands at the writing of this book, most of the legal databases out there simply haven't had time to go back and enter in all of that material. Most of what's available on-line is only a few years old. As you know from Chapter 6, "Locating the Case You Need," the digest books alone contain law dating from as early as 1658.

Well, all that being said, it is good to know how to do computerized legal research even now. All of the problems that we've mentioned will probably be solved. People will accept new technology, competition or government edict will bring down costs, computers will likely become as prevalent as television and cars, and time will allow the databases to get up to speed and incorporate the necessary law. The Machine is coming and the law, for good or ill, will be in it.

When we talk about the Machine—computerized legal research—what we mean essentially are three things:

- the Internet
- the LEXIS and Westlaw services, and
- law on CD-ROM.

We're going to discuss them separately, even though some of them, such as LEXIS, Westlaw, and the Internet, are somewhat combined in that you can access LEXIS and Westlaw via the Internet. We'll talk about what they are, what sort of equipment you need to use them, and we'll take you through a sample search. Now that we have everybody on board, let's merge onto the information superhighway.

THE INTERNET

What is the Internet and what do I need to get on it?

We're sorry. We didn't mean to use that term in the last section, information superhighway. We're getting sick of it ourselves, but it is appropriate in one sense: It allows you to form a concrete picture in your mind as to what the Internet is. It is like a road system. It's a means of transport, a way of getting to where information is stored so that you can retrieve it and use it. Only with the Internet, you don't use cars, asphalt and concrete to get around. Instead, you use computers, modems, and phone lines.

A computer, modem, phone line and an account with an Internet provider are the most basic things that you need to get onto the Internet. As to the specifications for the computer and modem, as a general rule, the more memory and the faster transmitting speed the better. Eight megabytes of RAM for the computer and 14.4 baud for the modem are probably sufficient and they are what are commonly being offered in computer packages for sale at most retailers. Even as we speak, however, things are changing, and soon 16 megabytes of RAM and 28.8 baud modems will become the norm.

Helpful Hint

A modem is a device that converts the signals from your computer into ones that can be transmitted over telephone lines to another modem, which then reconverts the signals so that another computer —the one you're trying to talk to—can understand them. You can't use the Internet unless your computer has or is connected to a modem.

Helpful Hint

The amount of RAM and the baud number for the modem are what controls the ability of the computer to run the programs that access the Internet and the speed in which they will do it. Essentially the more RAM and the higher the baud number the faster you will be able to get the information. As of now, transmission speeds on the Internet are not exactly instantaneous. Be prepared to spend a good deal of time just staring at your computer screen while waiting for the information that you've requested to be downloaded, or to be kicked off frequently because of the amount of traffic.

As for an Internet provider, we suggest that you sign up with one of the commercial services like America Online, CompuServe, or Prodigy (there are others). It's best if the one you sign up with has some sort of Web browser. A Web browser will allow you to have access to the World Wide Web (WWW). That's how we are going to go about getting on the Internet when we do our sample search.

Searching on the Internet

To begin our section on searching the Internet, we'd like to introduce you to our co-researcher, Chris. Chris is a super guy. He was very active all of his life, and still is, but not too long ago, Chris was in a terrible accident. He fell off of a horse that he was riding and injured his spinal chord. Now he's confined to a wheelchair. Chris has a very positive attitude, though, and has even become something of an activist for individuals with disabilities. One problem with which he has come face to face is the inaccessibility of many public places to people in wheelchairs. In the past, when buildings were constructed, architects, planners, and developers just didn't design and build them with individuals with disabilities in mind. In fact, recently Chris wanted to use the public library in his hometown so that he could look up some statistics for a speech that he is giving at a political convention, but the library didn't have an elevator or a ramp or any other way for him to get into the library in his wheelchair. He has heard of the Americans with Disabilities Act, and he's pretty sure that the public library is required by it to provide some sort of wheelchair access.

Because he can't get into the library, Chris is going to use the Internet, by accessing it through his America Online account, to see if he can find some information to help him in case he has to bring a suit to force the library to comply with the act.

THE FASTEST WAY: USING A UNIFORM RESOURCE LOCATOR

The fastest way to find any information on the Internet through the World Wide Web is to use an URL. Short for Uniform Resource Locator, an URL is simply like an address that you type in that tells your Internet service to connect you to that site. Nowadays you see URLs all over the place, in advertisements, on commercials, in the newspaper. They are those things that say something like http://www.law.cornell.edu/uscode/ (which happens to be an URL for a site with a copy of the United States Code).

Helpful Hint

It is important to remember that anytime you use an URL to access a site on the Internet, you must type it in exactly the way you see it written. Don't substitute capital letters for lowercase letters or vice versa, and don't put in spaces between words, letters, numbers, or symbols where there are none or take out spaces if they are there.

You don't have to merely stumble across a URL in a newspaper article or have a friend who constantly surfs the net give it to you. There are books of computer addresses out there, with the addresses collected and classified by topics, such as "Law." They're something like yellow pages. Come to think of it, they are probably better than the yellow pages because not only do they gather the addresses, but usually each address is accompanied by a blurb explaining some of the features and information included on each site.

In our example, however, let's say that Chris doesn't even have one of those books of Internet yellow pages—remember, he can't even get into the library. All is not lost. He can find addresses on-line. America Online has collections of legal addresses that you can use to do your legal research.

Let's take Chris through the steps to find the legal addresses on America Online so that he can find a copy of the Americans with Disabilities Act and determine if the law says that a public library has to have some sort of wheelchair access.

First, Chris will have to sign on to his service and type in his password. The service will then connect him to the main menu. At the top of his computer screen there will be a menu bar with names, identifying the menus like **File**, **Edit**, and **Go To**. Choose **Go To** from the menu bar, click on it with the pointing device. Then choose **Keyword**. At this point a keyword box will pop onto the screen. Type in the word *legal*, and then press Enter or click on **Go**. A menu called **Online Legal Areas** will appear with choices such as **Legal Information Network**, **Clubs and Interest**, **Cyberlaw**, and **Law on the Net**.

Helpful Hint

Gopher is the name of a protocol. A protocol, like gopher or http, is what computers use to communicate to each other on the Internet. So, when you type in an URL that starts with gopher, your computer is telling the computer at the site that you are trying to access that they are going to be communicating to each other in the gopher protocol.

Helpful Hint

A Listserver is like a chat line where people with common interests, say disability law, get together to discuss questions and developments in that field. To get on to one of these specialized listservers, you usually have to subscribe and to get off you usually have to unsubscribe. This can be accomplished via electronic mail (E-mail). If you don't want to participate in these list server conversations but merely want to read what has been said on them in the past, sometimes these sites offer free archives of the old discussions.

Most of these sites are just chat lines where people go to ask legal questions and hope that someone has an answer. In our sample search, Chris already knows that he want to see a copy of the Americans with Disabilities Act, so he wouldn't necessarily want to ask any questions on any of these sites. If you don't have any idea where to begin, such sites can be helpful, but be forewarned, the Internet is anonymous. So, you can never be sure if you leave a question out on the Internet whether the person answering is an attorney or even knows what he or she is talking about.

Back to Chris's search. In the **Online Legal Areas** menu click on **Law on the Net**. Another menu will appear. Here we will want to click on **Search Law on the Net**. Now a **Search** box will appear. Here we will type in our desired search terms; in Chris's case he will type in *Americans with Disabilities Act*, and then he will press Enter. Several matching entries are found. The most promising of these looks like **Americans With Disabilities Act- Gopher, Listserver.**

Click on this entry with the pointer. Now, a menu entitled **List Articles** will appear with a box that can be scrolled through. This box has two URLs where you can find copies of the Americans with Disabilities Act:

gopher://gopher.ucsc.edu

In this menu click on **Library**, and in the **Library** menu click on **Electronic Books and Other Texts**. In the **Electronic Books and Other Texts** menu select **American with Disabilities Act**.

or the alternate:

gopher://riceinfo.rice.edu:70/11/

At this menu click on **Information by Subject**, and in the **Information by Subject** menu choose **Government, Political Science and Law**. In the **Government, Political Science and Law** menu click on **Americans With Disabilities Act**. Now close out of these windows and return to the service's main menu. Along with Chris, we're going to try these addresses and see what we turn up.

Back at the main menu we will click on **Go To** again and choose **Keyword**. At this point Chris could type in **WWW**. This would bring him to the World Wide Web, which is the system through which we are going to conduct our search. This just adds another step though. America Online, like other services, recognizes an URL when it sees one, so if you type in your URL in the **Keyword** box and press Enter, you will automatically be connected to the World Wide Web and the search for the URL site will begin simultaneously.

As it appears, when the first URL is typed in, we reach the site and the menu for **Electronic Books and Other Texts** that we desired, but there is no entry for **Americans with Disabilities Act**. Apparently, the site on America Online for **Law on the Net** was not up to date when we checked it. Furthermore, when the alternate site is accessed, we also learn that the **Access Files by Subject** is listed as "Obsolete." Chris hasn't hit a dead-end quite yet though. Although the **Access Files by Subject** is listed as "Obsolete" it can still be accessed. We can then choose **Government, Political Science and Law** and then **Americans With Disabilities Act** from the menus that appear. And voila, there is a copy of the ADA, and its true direct-access URL, which at the time of this writing happens to be:

gopher://wiretap.spies.com/00/Gov/disable.act

What this little exercise has demonstrated is the volatility of the Internet. One of the great strengths of on-line information is that it can be changed and updated quickly, far more quickly than books can be. Conversely, anything that can be changed and updated so quickly can be unstable. The Internet changes daily and an address that was good one day may not be good the next. In fact, the entire site that you searched could be gone. That is why we prefer a system of searching on the Internet that does a lot of the legwork for you. They're called search engines.

The relaxed way: Using a search engine

Search engines are like automated indexes that tell you where to find stuff on the Internet. They can help you to narrow things down and find the information sites that you might want to use. The menus that appear while you are scrolling and clicking through the search engine will be peppered with links (usually on phrases that are underlined) that you can point to and click and automatically access the site or document that the link describes. That may sound a little confusing, but it really isn't too bad. The best way to show you though is to get back on-line and walk through the steps.

There are quite a few search engines out there that we could use. There is a lot of overlapping access to sites where the information you want is stored, but not all search engines are connected to all the same sites. If you find it necessary to use more than one, many of the search engines will have links to other available search engines that you may want to try, so it probably doesn't matter which one you start with. Because we are going to be searching on the World Wide Web—and it is weblike, with just about everything connecting to everything else—there probably aren't going to be many situations when "you can't get there from here" will be your answer.

Here are the URLs to just a few of the more popular search engines:

<u>On the World Wide Web</u>
http://www.yahoo.com
htpp://www.webcrawler.com/
http://www.lycos.com/
http://www.infoseek.com/*

<u>On Gopher</u>
gopher://veronica.scs.unr.edu:70/11/veronica

<u>On FTP</u>
gopher://gopher-gw.micro.umn.edu:4324/larchie

These are not search engines specifically designed to find legal materials, but they can certainly be used that way.

*You may have to pay a fee if you use this address for Infoseek.

Both we and Chris have had luck on the search engine called Yahoo in the past, so let's start there. Go back to your main menu and click on **Go To** from the menu bar. Access **Keyword** and in the box that appears type in the URL for Yahoo.

http://www.yahoo.com

The Yahoo home page will appear. It has a box where we can type terms that the search engine will look for. Remember, this is like an index, so you're going to want to be specific, so that you will not get a lot of extraneous answers, but not so specific that you get nothing. For example, in Chris's case, if he typed in the term *disability*, the search engine might tell him that he got about 100 responses. Then he would have to scroll down through these, and it might take him a long time to find what he wants. He doesn't have the time and neither do we. A better search phrase might be *Americans with Disabilities Act*. Because, again, we and Chris know that is what he thinks is the relevant law in this area. Type this phrase in and press Enter on your keyboard.

Helpful Hint

Learn to be patient when doing research on the Internet. Even when you know exactly where you think you may want to go and even if you use good search terms to find your data, the Internet can be as slow as molasses. We've found that we can get a lot of chores done around the house while the Internet is connecting to various sites and downloading information.

This search turns up a few interesting sites for Chris, not too many to look through even if he wanted to look at them all. Chris seems to think that the site called **Americans with Disabilities Act Document Center** sounds like a good bet because it says that it has a link to the Americans with Disabilities Act Accessibility Guidelines, as well as other interesting stuff. Because he wants access to his public library, this site seems like it would be right up his alley. Let's all click on this link and go empty the dishwasher while the **Americans with Disabilities Act Document Center** (we're going to call it ADADC) home page is accessed. Just kidding, but this will take a while.

Bingo! From the ADADC home page it looks like we might have hit on a one-stop shopping center for all our ADA needs. According to the description and indexes, this site has or links to sites that have copies of the ADA, regulations (the C.F.R.), Technical Assistance Manuals created by the Department of Justice, sites

Helpful Hint

News groups are collections of individuals interested in particular topics who get together on-line to discuss and keep track of the latest developments for that topic. They can be good places to get some background information and guidance about searching a topic, but usually you have to subscribe (and unsubscribe) to a newsgroup. This can ordinarily be accomplished by leaving an E-mail message at the newsgroup's address. Be forewarned, you may be charged for joining a newsgroup. Make sure you ask before committing yourself to one.

concerned with mobility impairments, Internet legal information sites, sites with case law, sites concerned with architecture and construction, other search engines, explanations of how to file ADA complaints with the Department of Justice, and links to news groups.

Chris realizes that he wants to check the ADA, but doesn't have any background information about it yet, so he decides that a good place to begin would be the site that gives a synopsis of the law at the link that says *Go to a brief overview of the ADA*. Click on this link. From the looks of it Chris may have a case. He may be covered by the ADA, but he will want some explanation of *substantial impairment of a major life activity*, and it looks like the public library might also be within the scope of the act because it says that local governments are covered under Title II. He has some question as to whether the public accommodations under Title III would cover a public library. He thinks that it may not though because the places that are listed as being public accommodations all look like places run in the private sector, such as restaurants and the like.

Chris thinks at this point that to continue his research he is going to want to read the act itself, the regulations and technical assistance manuals having to do with Title II, and some cases that interpret the act, and then if it looks like he may have a case, he'll want to file a complaint with the Department of Justice. To accomplish this, all he has to do is to return to the home page and index of the ADADC and click on the link for the site that he wants, read it, and then go back to the ADADC home page and index and find the next site, and so on until he has read everything that he wants to read.

One thing he does notice, however, as he is checking out the sites is that there doesn't appear to be much in the way of case law that he can easily link to. All that is listed is a link to recent U.S. Supreme Court cases. Chris's observation dredges up that old problem we were talking about at the beginning of the chapter, the newness problem. At this time there just isn't much in the way of case law that you can find by surfing the net.

This problem is slowly being solved, however. Lately, Law Journal EXTRA started putting recent U.S. Courts of Appeal opinions and state court opinions on-line on the World Wide Web. Law Journal EXTRA can be contacted at the following URL:

http://www.ljextra.com

Once you access its home page, all you have to do then is click on the link for the *Table of Contents* and then click on the *Courthouse*. The cases can be searched by word, phrase, or the party names.

If you want to get cases the old-fashioned, hard way, you can find more federal court opinions and some state court opinions by dialing in directly to a bulletin board system.

Bulletin board systems

Most of the federal courts are slowly making their opinions available on-line, and most of them have decided to make the opinions available through things called bulletin board systems—called BBSs by Internet aficionados. There are a few idiosyncrasies that make BBSs different from most things that you access through the Internet, however. First, you have to subscribe to BBSs, and second, in the case of most federal cases, you have to pay for the privilege.

Still if you want to get cases from the federal courts, the way to access the most recent opinions is through a system called PACER (Public Access to Court Electronic Records). With PACER you have to register first because you are going to need an ID and a password. It will take about a week, usually, for you to get your application, and then you have to return it and wait to actually receive your essentials.

Helpful Hint

It might be a good idea while searching the Internet to keep a pad and a pen handy so that you can write down the URLs of the sites that you contact. This way you may be able to access them directly and more quickly in the future by not having to return to the search engines that helped you find them. You may also, as on American Online (AOL), be able to designate these places as sites that you would like to visit frequently. On AOL you can add sites to your "Favorite Places" icon and then return to them with a couple clicks of your pointing device.

Helpful Hint

To save yourself some time, and money, when you retrieve a document from a site and it looks from a quick perusal that you may want to read it, you can then copy it to your own hard drive and read it at your leisure, taking as much time with it as you want, and returning to it as many times as you want. Be careful though, before opening any transferred documents from your hard drive it might be best to scan them with an antivirus program. You don't want to learn the hard way what a virus can do to your system.

When you have your ID and password in hand, you can access the courts that you want by dialing in directly with the list of the telephone numbers that PACER provides.

LEXIS AND WESTLAW SERVICES

Prior to the explosion of the Internet onto the public consciousness, one of the few ways that legal research could be done by computer was through the two services called LEXIS and Westlaw. LEXIS came on-line in 1973 and was soon followed by Westlaw in 1975. Their scope was limited when they were first introduced—LEXIS had only a limited amount of case law and Westlaw only offered the West headnotes up until 1979, after which full-text opinions were finally added—but after more than 20 years both systems continued to expand, so much so that now they can be used as complete sources for legal research. It would be an extravagant researcher, however, who would do all of his or her research on these systems. As mentioned above, the cost of using them can be astronomical, so great in fact that many lawyers don't even use them.

Their usefulness for the layperson is further complicated by a problem of access. Most people don't have access to these systems at work or otherwise. For both systems, as with bulletin board services, you have to subscribe and be given an ID number before you can sign on and start your research. If you do sign up with one of these services the company will send you manuals that will teach you not only how to use the system, but how to use it effectively.

For the sake of completeness and on the chance that you have access to these services, say at your local law library, we will give you a brief run-down of what one typically contains and how to formulate the queries that you will use for a search.

What can I find on LEXIS and Westlaw?

Both of these services house many thousands of state and federal legal documents, including both published and unpublished opinions, constitutions, statutes, regulations, and court rules; citators, presidential papers, law reviews, and other legal periodicals; and even bill tracking systems. For instance, Westlaw includes databases covering all of the following areas of law:

General Westlaw Databases

All Federal Cases
Supreme Court Cases
Federal Courts of Appeal
Federal District Courts
All State Cases
First Amendment Cases
Attorney General Decisions
Federal Public Laws
Federal Statutes
Annotated Federal Statutes
Congressional Record
U.S. Code Congressional and Administrative News
Code of Federal Regulations
Federal Register
U.S. Court Rules
Articles Interpreting Federal Court Rules
State Statutes
Annotated State Statutes
State Court Rules
Presidential Documents
Digest Topics
Texts and Periodicals
Legal Periodicals
Index to Legal Periodicals
Legal Resource Index

As well as organizing material in this manner, Westlaw also organizes material by commonly used legal topics such as "Admiralty," "Civil Rights," "Family Law," "Insurance," "Securities," and "Worker Compensation." And having been created and maintained by a book publisher, Westlaw tries to integrate its computer materials with its print materials, which can be a real boon to the cost-conscious researcher.

> **Helpful Hint**
>
> One of the ways in which Westlaw integrates its print and on-line materials is through the use of star paging. Star paging lets you know, while reading a case on-line, exactly what that page would correspond to in the printed reporter. It does this by placing a little * in the text along with a page number. You may need such specific information when citing to a rule of law from a case in a brief to the court.

How can I search these systems?

OK you're saying, "It's nice to know that LEXIS and Westlaw have so much stuff on them, enough that I could conceivably do all of my research on them if I wanted to, but how do I actually do a search?" That's a fair question. But before we show you how to conduct an actual search, we're going to have to tell you how these systems "see" the questions that you ask them.

Natural language searching

Computers are not people. They aren't exactly smart in the way that we think of smart—although there are computers and programs that are being developed that can actually teach themselves how to do things by learning from mistakes, much the way that people do. But for now computers don't see things the way we do, and they don't read as we read. This caused problems in the past as computers were being developed and marketed for mainstream society because to run them you had to learn, in some sense, to think and talk to the computers more on their level, in a type of "computerese." LEXIS and Westlaw formerly exclusively used a type of search language called Boolean searching which reflected this bias (more on this later). To combat this problem both systems came up with a search program that could tell the computer what to search for while allowing the researcher to use regular, everyday, as they call it, natural language.

> **LAW FACT**
>
> Boolean searching is named after an English mathematician, George Boole, who lived in the nineteenth century. He created a system of algebra in which variables are represented by series of ones and zeroes. It is this same system that is used in most computers.

Because natural language is supposed to be just that, we aren't going to waste time teaching you how to speak or record your questions in written form. If you've read this far into the book we guess that you already know how to do that. What we will tell you though is how the computer program that reads natural language goes about doing it.

When you type in your query (that's what these systems call a legal question) the natural language program immediately starts throwing things out. It knows better than you anyway, human! So it throws out unsearchable terms, words that are too common to bother with, like *the*. Then it looks over the remaining terms, the ones it thought were searchable, and ranks them according to what it thinks is important. Then, it searches through the database that you've chosen for your terms and for terms that it thinks are related to them, in order of importance and frequency of occurrence. Then it tells you how many matches it has found and lists them. Simple enough.

But there can be a slight problem. The natural language programs were created by humans, who could not possibly attempt to quantify all of the idiosyncrasies of language. Consequently, these natural language programs tend to retrieve more documents that are irrelevant to your query than do the traditional Boolean searches—if the Boolean searches are done correctly.

BOOLEAN SEARCHING

Computer programs tend to be very literal. When Boolean searching in LEXIS and Westlaw, generally, the search programs will find only exactly what you tell them to find. The problem that most first-time users of these systems run into, however, is that they tell the machine to look for too many things or too few. So, operating under the theory that learning how something works will allow us to use the thing better, let's take a look at how these systems read your queries.

—Singular terms and plurals

Both LEXIS and Westlaw will read the singular form of a word as containing its plural. Therefore, if you type in the word *wheelchair*, the systems will retrieve documents that contain the word *wheelchair* and its plural *wheelchairs*. On the other hand, they will only retrieve the plural, wheelchairs, if that term is typed in. It will not retrieve the singular, wheelchair.

—Possessives

Possessives are retrieved in a manner similar to that of singulars and plurals. If the nonpossessive form of a word is typed in, such as *individual*, the systems will retrieve documents with both the possessive, *individual's*, and the nonpossessive, *individual*. On the contrary, if you type in *individual's*, the systems will not retrieve the nonpossessive, individual.

—Acronyms

The two systems will retrieve both an acronym with periods between the letters or without periods between the letters if you type the acronym in with the periods between each letter. For example, if you type in A.D.A. (the acronym for the Americans with Disabilities Act) the systems will retrieve documents with *A.D.A.* and *ADA*.

—Equivalents

Certain terms, such as numbers and abbreviations for states and months, on both systems will retrieve terms that the program recognizes as the equivalent form of that term. For example, typing in the word *twenty* will also retrieve documents that have the number *20* in them, *Maryland* will also find *MD*, and *February* will retrieve *Feb*.

—Root expanders

People don't usually get all that excited when formulating queries for LEXIS and Westlaw, so both systems decided that it would be a pretty safe bet to use an exclamation point (!) for something other than showing surprise. A ! at the end of a term will retrieve documents with that word or that word with various endings. Therefore, if you type in *disab!* it would find *disabled* and *disability*, which may both be useful terms for an issue concerning the Americans with Disabilities Act. Be careful with the use of this expander, however, because the use of ! on disab! would also retrieve documents containing the terms *disable* and *disabuse*, terms which probably would not be helpful with the issue of disability.

—Universal characters

An asterisk (*) used in a term tells the program to find variations of a word where only one letter might be different. For example, m*n would retrieve documents with men or man in them.

—Connectors

Both LEXIS and Westlaw's Boolean searching also use a bunch of different connectors to define the search. These connectors are like codes that tell the program "search for this word but only when it appears with this word," or "search for this word but retrieve the document only if this term does not appear with this other word." The following is a chart listing and comparing the different types of connectors on LEXIS and Westlaw:

LEXIS CONNECTORS	WESTLAW CONNECTORS	PURPOSE
or	or	Finds documents with either or both of the specified terms (e.g., *lawyer or counsel* will find documents that contain either of those terms or both)
w/n	/n	Finds documents in which the terms are located within a specified number of word of each other (e.g., *americans w/3 disabilities* or *americans 3/n disability* finds documents with those terms within three words of each other)
and	and, &	Finds documents that contain both of the specified terms (e.g., *americans and disability* only finds documents with both americans and disability in them)
w/seg	/p or /s	In the case of LEXIS, finds documents that are located within the same segment. In the case of Westlaw, finds documents when they are within the same paragraph or sentence (e.g., *americans /p disability* only finds documents with both americans and disability in the same paragraph; *americans /s disability* finds documents with both americans and disability in the same sentence)

LEXIS CONNECTORS	WESTLAW CONNECTORS	PURPOSE
pre/n	+n	Finds documents in which the term on the left of the connector comes before the term on the right of the connector by the specified number of terms or less (e.g., *americans pre/3* or *+3 disability* finds documents in which americans precedes disability by 2 or 3 terms)
and not	%	Will not retrieve documents that contain the term following the connector (e.g., *disability and not* or *% physical* will find documents that contain the term *disability* but will not retrieve documents that contain both disability and physical)

—Putting it all together

Now let's try to stop your head from swimming by calling Chris back over here and putting what we've learned together to form a simple query.

> **Helpful Hint**
>
> Always do all of your preliminary research so that you have narrowed down your issue and formulated its terms and alternative terms and put them into a possible query or queries before getting on-line with LEXIS or Westlaw. These systems are too expensive to use to waste time doing all of this when you are already on-line.

Remember that Chris was looking for the meaning of the phrase *substantial impairment of a major life activity.* To start his search for the interpretation of this phrase on Westlaw, he would first sign on and then when he reached the main menu, he would choose whether he wanted to search by a specific topic or a state or federal database. In this example, he might, logically, want to search in the federal database because the Americans with Disabilities Act is a federal law. He would choose this database and then another menu would appear. Here he might decide to search the federal cases database, and may wish to narrow down his search even more by choosing the database for the circuit that he lives in. After choosing these, he would be ready to type in his query.

Here, he decides to try this:

substantial** /s impair! /s major /s life /s activity

This would tell the program to search the selected database and retrieve cases that include the terms *substantial* or *substantially*; *impair*, *impaired*, *impairment*, or *impairing*; *major*; *life*; and *activity* as long as these terms all appear in the same sentence. Chris chose to search in this way because he felt that a court might change the order of the wording of the phrase or might say something like "the disability substantially impaired the major life activity of the plaintiff," but because the phrase is directly from the ADA it would be unlikely that a court would discuss the terms separately throughout the opinion without ever linking them together in some semblance of their form in the act.

If Chris is lucky he'll turn up just enough cases and not too many, but his research on-line isn't done quite yet. We bet you know what's coming up.

Helpful Hint

If it turns out that a query is not very good and retrieves too many or too few documents, you can change it, in Westlaw by typing in the letter *q* or in LEXIS by typing in the letter *m* and then pressing the Enter key. You can then use connectors that are less limiting or use more terms or more root expanders.

UPDATING YOUR RESEARCH

Whether we've found our cases by a natural language search or a Boolean search we are not done until we've updated them to make sure that the law that they embody has not been overruled or changed in some other way. Luckily for all of us on both LEXIS and Westlaw you can take care of this with a touch of a button. Both LEXIS and Westlaw offer Shepard's on-line. If you are reading a case all you have to do is type in the command shep on LEXIS and sh on Westlaw and the Shepard's listing for that case automatically appears on your screen. If you want to read

Helpful Hint

You don't always have to search the full text of cases. For instance, if you know the name of the case that you want to find, you can tell the program to search only the titles of cases. In fact, you can restrict your search by any of the data that is usually found in the heading of a case: titles, judges, counsel, docket numbers, dates, and on Westlaw, by headnotes.

what one of the other cases said about your case to better understand its impact all we have to do is choose that case from the list of numbers (the cases in the Shepard's on-line list are given identifying numbers) and press Enter. The case then instantly appears. Now that's easy updating.

Finally, we'd just like to mention that there are a few services which are even more current than Shepard's. These are Auto-Cite, Shepard's PreView, and Insta-Cite. Auto-Cite looks a little different from Shepard's. It lists case history in a long-string cite rather than in columns, and it also gives history for the cases that affected the original case that we were looking for. For instance, an Auto-Cite citation might tell you that your original case was overturned by a later case but then that later case was invalidated by a statute, which could mean that your original case may be a valid statement of the law again. Shepard's PreView is simply that. It is a database that contains listings of cases that affect the cited case, but which have not been editorially enhanced with History and Treatment analysis (that is, it doesn't tell you how the case was affected). Insta-Cite prides itself on its currentness, but it limits its enhancements to listing cases that directly overrule, question, or limit the case you were updating. It does not contain citations to all of the cases that cited to your case.

LAW ON CD-ROM

The last leg of our tour through the Machine takes us into the world of law on CD-ROM. CD-ROMs should appear familiar to you. They look rather like audio CDs, but instead of storing music, the CDs that we are talking about store cases, digests, statutes, regulations, forms, and treatises. Not only can a lot of information be stored on each disc, but many of the discs out there, at least ones from the same publisher, can be linked together so, you can run an entire stack of discs all at one time in interconnected CD-ROM drives, jumping from cases to statutes to regulations, and so on can be accomplished all with a few keystrokes. In this way, these disc products have the capability to have almost as great a scope as the traditional databases of LEXIS or Westlaw.

One advantage that the CD-ROMs have over the on-line services, however, is cost. True, the initial expense of buying the CD-ROMs and subscribing for updates is too great for the average person to afford, especially a nonlawyer who won't use them that often, but it seems to us that law libraries would be far more likely to let patrons onto a computer with a CD-ROM system set-up because there is no charge for the amount of time that one spends at the computer screen. Once you buy the CD-ROMs they are the buyer's to use as often and for as long as required without the $2 to $4 per minute charge for time on the traditional databases.

CD-ROMs also have the advantage of search speed that the other computerized legal services have, but they do have one drawback similar to that of books. They are only updated monthly or quarterly like the printed books are, so you don't have the immediacy of on-line services which can conceivably have the latest opinion on-line and ready for customers to access within hours of it being handed down. What it appears to be then is that CD-ROMs are something of a hybrid between the old world of printed matter and the new world of computers. Because of this, they may be one of the most comfortable ways for the layperson to learn to search with a computer.

How to search on CD-ROM

One of the more prevalent of the search systems used by legal publishers for their law on CD-ROM is a system called Folio. According to the literature, you don't have to use Boolean logic to search on a system that uses Folio. This is because Folio eliminates the need to tell the computer how close together the terms that you want to search have to be, but it appears you can still use a combination of connectors, universal characters, and root expanders to help make your searches more efficient. For our illustration, we are going to identify and show you the connectors and universal characters that are used on the Law Desk CD-ROM systems that use Folio.

Connectors

The following is a list of the characters that a legal researcher can use to define his or her search when using Law Desk.

LAW DESK CD-ROM CONNECTORS	PURPOSE
blank space	Represents "and' in a search. Finds all documents that contain all of the search terms specified, in no particular order (e.g., *wheelchair access* would find all documents in the specified databases that contain both of these terms)
/	Represents "or" in a search. Finds all documents that contain either of the search terms specified (e.g., *wheelchair/access* would find documents that contained the word wheelchair, the word access, or both)
^	Represents "not" in a search. Finds all documents that contain the terms to the left of the symbol, but do not contain the term to the right of the symbol (e.g., *wheelchair access^ramp* would find all of the documents that contain both wheelchair and access but would exclude documents that talk about wheelchair access with ramps)
~	Represents an "exclusive or." Finds all documents that contain one specified term or the other term, but not documents that have both (e.g., *wheelchair~access* would find documents that contain the term wheelchair, documents that contain the term access, but would exclude documents that contain both wheelchair and access.)

The system also processes the connectors in a particular order of importance, so that terms preceded by the "not" character are searched for first, terms connected by the "or" character are searched for second, terms connected by the "exclusive or" character are searched for third, and terms connected by the "and" blank space are searched for last. You're not stuck with this automatic priority, however. By placing terms inside of parentheses, you can cause those terms to be searched for first.

Universal characters and root expanders

Just as with LEXIS and Westlaw, Law Desk on CD-ROM uses universal characters to represent specific characters in a word and root expanders to tell the program to search for all words starting with a particular root term but with any number of undefined characters following that term. On Law Desk, though, the universal character is represented by a question mark (?) and the root expander is an asterisk (*). So that this term m?n would find both man and men, and the term disab* would find disabled, disability, disable, and disabuse.

Putting it all together

We're back to the model search again, and again we'll want to get Chris over here to help us out. Remember that when we last left him he was looking for cases that interpreted the phrase from the Americans with Disabilities Act (ADA) *substantial impairment of a major life activity.* At this point he thinks that his disability, confinement to a wheelchair for life, is probably considered a substantial impairment of a major life activity, namely walking, but he still isn't quite sure whether a public library is covered by Title II of the ADA. He has a number of CD-ROM titles to choose from in the Law Desk series, and decides to use the one called *Americans with Disabilities on Law Desk.*

> **Helpful Hint**
>
> One of the advantages of the Folio search system on Law Desk is that is shows you the number of positive responses—called hits—that the terms that you are typing in come up with. This is helpful because if you find that a particular search is coming up with nothing, you can see which particular term is throwing everything off.

After slipping the CD-ROM into the CD-ROM reader and starting up the program, Chris finds himself at the main menu (Figure 31). Here he sees that he has the option of choosing to search a treatise on Americans with disabilities topics, cases that deal with this subject, statutes, regulations, and legal forms. He isn't quite sure what to pick but decides to go with cases, because case law interpretation of the ADA will carry the most weight in an argument. So, he chooses **Cases** and presses Enter.

At the search menu, he decides to search the **Headnotes** because this might be faster than searching the whole text of the

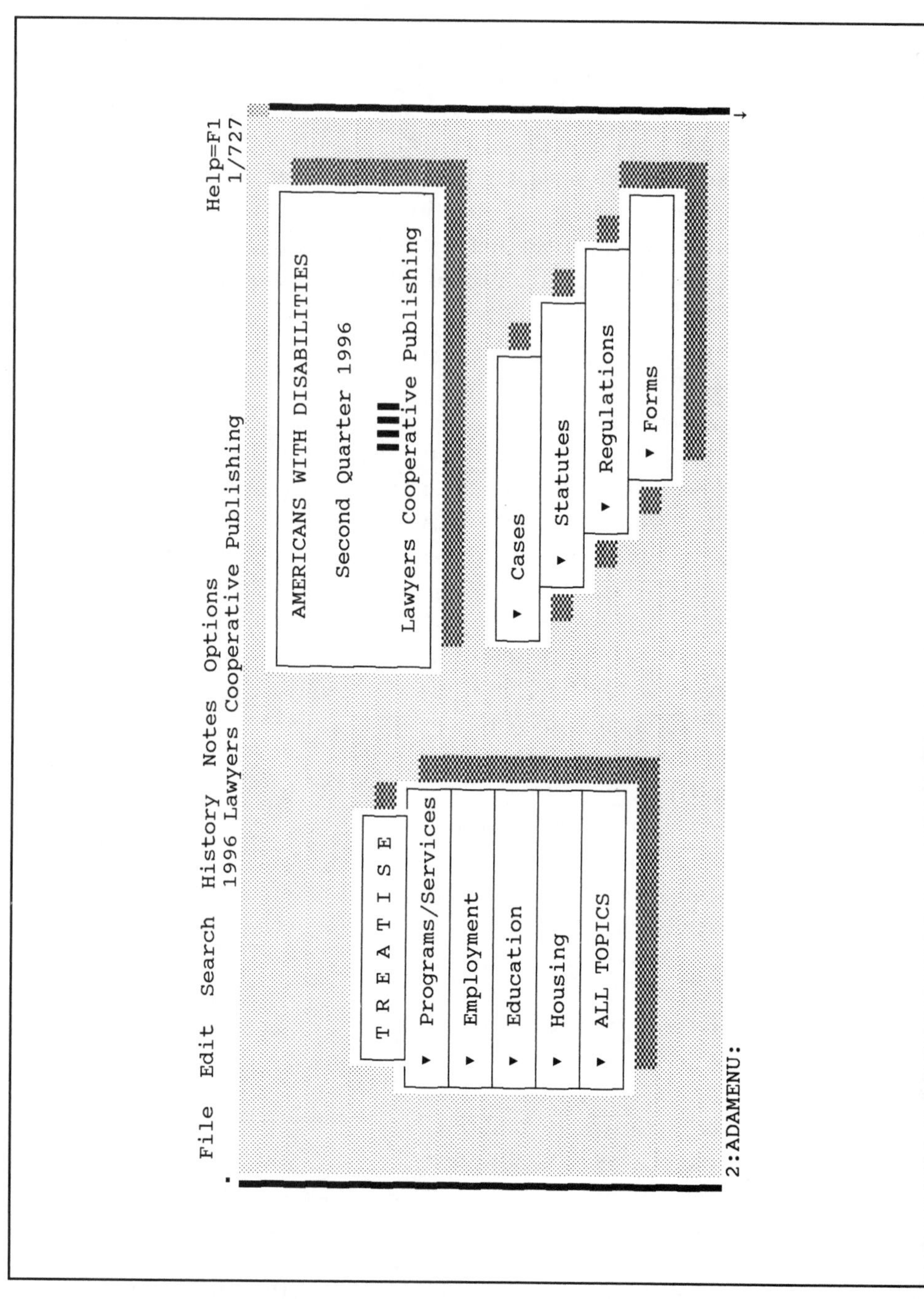

Permission to reprint has been granted by the copyright holder, Lawyers Cooperative Publishing, a division of Thomson Information Services, Inc.

Figure 31

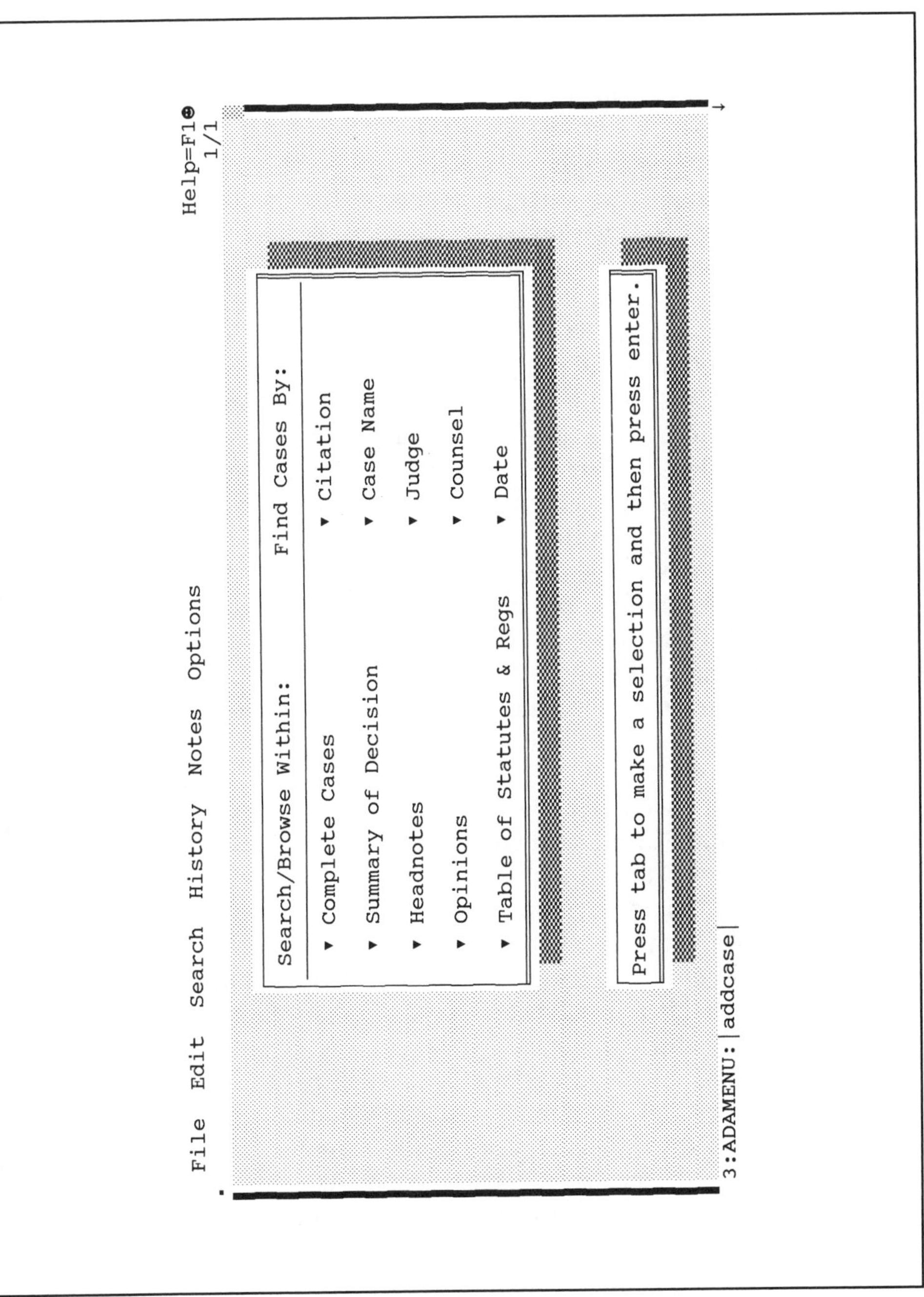
File Edit Search History Notes Options
Help=F1
1/1
Search/Browse Within:
Find Cases By:
▸ Complete Cases
▸ Citation
▸ Summary of Decision
▸ Case Name
▸ Headnotes
▸ Judge
▸ Opinions
▸ Counsel
▸ Table of Statutes & Regs
▸ Date
Press tab to make a selection and then press enter.
3:ADAMENU: addcase

Figure 32

opinions, and chooses this option (Figure 32). He then types in a simple search just to see what comes up:

title ii public library

In Chris's search he comes up with two hits, and by pressing Enter he is able to see a list of the positive response. From the titles of the cases they both look like they may be about universities. He selects the first case and then the other, perusing both quickly. They are both about universities that receive federal money, so this is not quite what he wants. So, he presses the Escape (Esc) button until he is back at the main menu.

Chris realizes that he might need some more background information or direction as to where to search, so he decides to try searching the **Treatise** section. The **Programs/Services** division looks the most promising, because a library does provide a service. He chooses this option and presses Enter.

On the next screen he is given the choice of searching the entire topic, going to a particular text section, or looking at an outline (Figure 33). Because he doesn't know which section he would like to look at and since he is looking for some sort of general discussion, he chooses Outline and presses Enter. On the next screen he sees that there are six chapters in this section (Figure 34). The one that jumps out at him as being right on target is Chapter 2, which includes a discussion of the applicability of the ADA to **State and Local Governments**. He chooses this Chapter and presses Enter.

At the Chapter 2 outline Chris finds exactly what he is looking for in **Overview**. He chooses this option and presses Enter. Under this subsection he notices a division entitled **Public Entities**, and under this a subdivision called **What entities are covered**. He chooses this subdivision.

In a box entitled **Practice Pointer** he sees that there are several factors for determining whether something is a public entity, and it specifically lists libraries as an example of something that is difficult to discern whether it is a public entity or not a public entity covered by Title II of the ADA (Figure 35). This Practice Pointer is followed by a footnote, and when he chooses the footnote link and presses Enter, he sees that this text was extracted from the *ADA Title II Technical Assistance Manual* § II-1.2000.

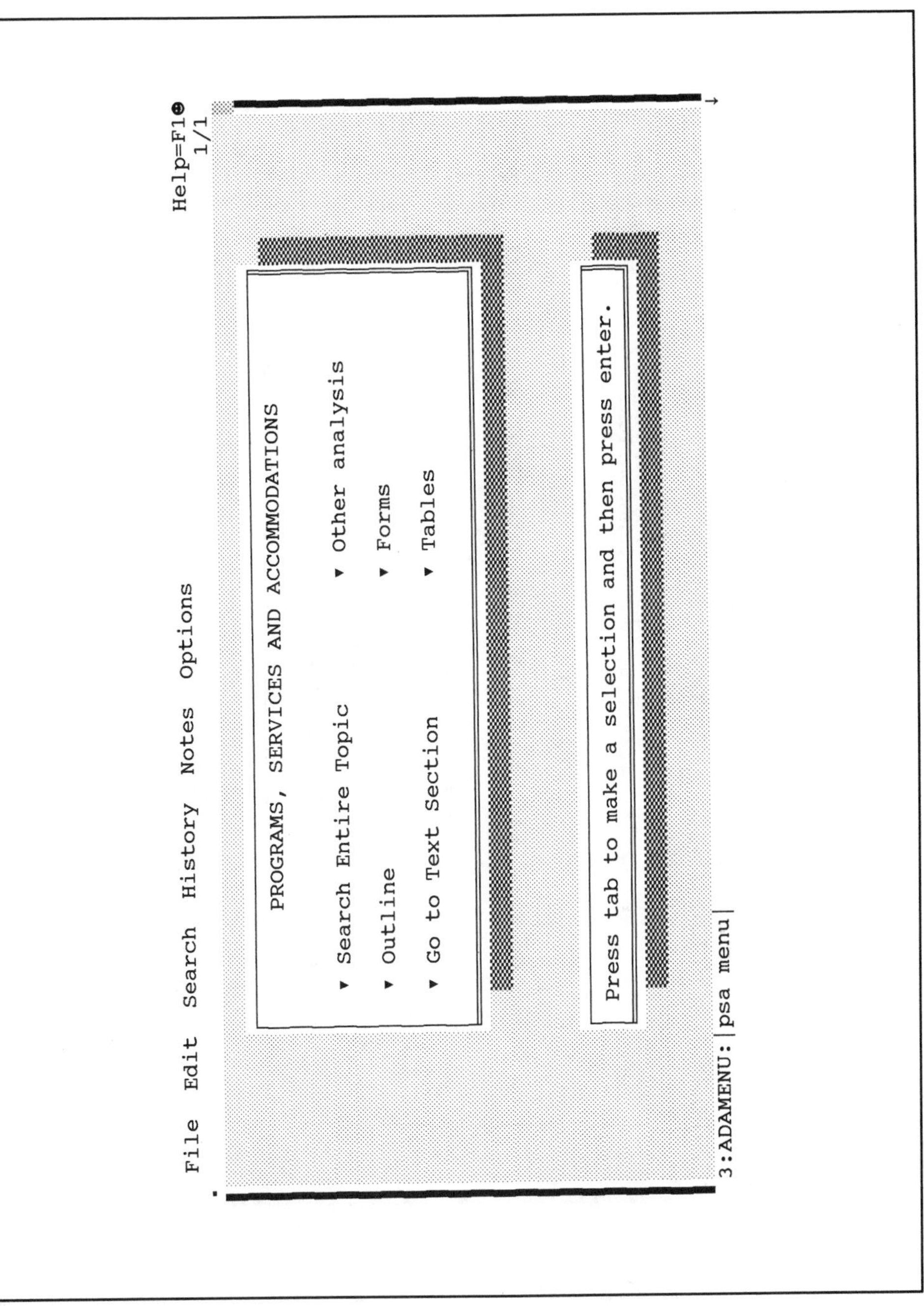
File Edit Search History Notes Options
Help=F1
1/1
PROGRAMS, SERVICES AND ACCOMMODATIONS
▸ Search Entire Topic
▸ Other analysis
▸ Outline
▸ Forms
▸ Go to Text Section
▸ Tables
Press tab to make a selection and then press enter.
3:ADAMENU: psa menu

Figure 33

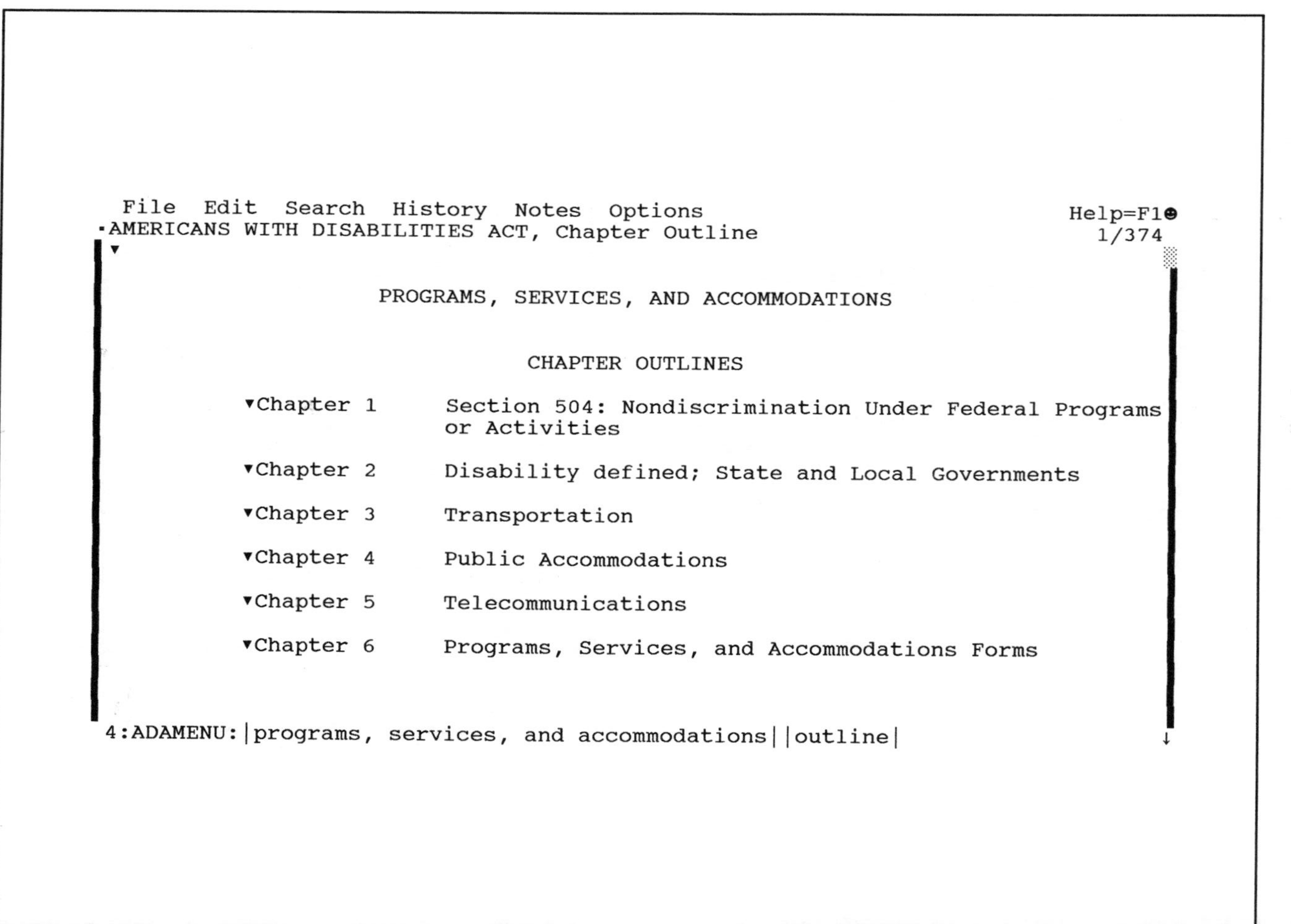

Permission to reprint has been granted by the copyright holder, Lawyers Cooperative Publishing, a division of Thomson Information Services, Inc.

Figure 34

Finally, Chris presses the Escape button to get back to the outline and chooses—**Illustrations**. As he scrolls down this screen, he sees that there are no mentions of a public library. At this point, it is looking like he may not find that one perfect case. He may have to do some analogizing from other cases that may be similar to his. What is clear, however, from the *Technical Assistance Manual* is that he has some more research to do about how his local library is run before he will feel comfortable filing a complaint with the Department of Justice.

TAKING NOTES ON INFORMATION FOUND IN COMPUTERIZED SOURCES

Of course, as with the rest of your research, if you are going to save yourself some backtracking, it is best to take notes from the documents that you find. One of the advantages of using computers is that you can take notes—in a sense—much more quickly than you can by hand. In the case of the Internet, you can save documents to your hard drive, for perusal later. With LEXIS and Westlaw, it may be a good idea to print the screen by pressing the print screen command, so that you can get a blurb of information from the case and a citation and get off-line as quickly as possible; then you can go look the stuff up in the books to save on-line costs. With CD-ROMs you can take the time to read the information while it is on the screen and even read whole cases if you want—it's not costing too much money—but it may be a good idea to print the screen when you find a passage that is particularly helpful or telling, so that you can refer to it later when you are organizing your research. (For more on this, see Chapter 9).

Helpful Hint

If you are working with primary materials like cases, regulations, or statutes it is best to write down your interpretations of these so that you can clarify in your mind what they mean. It is too easy to think that you understand something, only to find out later that you are still confused when you go to organize your thoughts later.

Supplement
Go to Outline
Cases Statutes Regulations Analysis

§ 2:30. What entities are covered

For purposes of Title II of the ADA<fn 5> and implementing regulations<fn 6> relating to nondiscrimination on the basis of disability in state and local government services, the term "public entity" means

(1) any state or local government;
(2) any department, agency, special purpose district, or other instrumentality of one or more state or local governments; and
(3) the National Railroad Passenger Corporation (AMTRAK)<fn 7> and any commuter authority, as defined in the Rail Passenger Service Act (45 USCS § 502(8)).<fn 8>

Under the ADA<fn 9> and the regulations implementing Title II, the term "state" means each of the several states, the District of Columbia, the Commonwealth of Puerto Rico, Guam, American Samoa, the Virgin Islands, the Trust Territory of the Pacific Islands, and the Commonwealth of the Northern Mariana Islands.<fn 10>

ADA Title II does not require that a public entity be a legislative or governing body,<fn 11> or an employer of a protected individual with a disability.<fn 12> However, the ADA does not apply to the Federal Bureau of Prisons, since Title II excludes the federal government from its definitions of a public entity.<fn 13>

▌▌▌▌ **Note:** An adjudication that an entity is a state actor for purposes of an equal protection analysis does not automatically make it a public entity for purposes of ADA Title II.<fn 14>

▌▌▌▌ **Observation:** The above definition of a public entity for purposes of ADA Title II and the regulations implementing Title II is the same definition contained in the regulations<fn 15> implementing Title III of the ADA<fn 16> relating to public accommodations,<fn 17> and in the regulations<fn 18> implementing the transportation provisions of Titles II and III of the ADA.<fn 19>

▌▌▌▌ **Practice pointer:** In some cases it is difficult to determine whether a particular entity that is providing a public service, such as a library, museum, or volunteer fire department, is in fact a public entity. Where an entity appears to have both public and private features, it is necessary to examine the relationship between the entity and the governmental unit to determine whether the entity is public or private. Factors to be considered in this determination include whether (1) the entity is operated with public funds; (2) the entity's employees are considered government employees; (3) the entity receives significant assistance from the government by provision of property or equipment; and (4) the entity is governed by an independent board selected by members of a private organization or a board elected by the voters or appointed by elected officials.<fn 20>

Figure 35

CHAPTER HIGHLIGHTS

To perform legal research on the Internet, we suggest using a computer with at least 8 megabytes of RAM, a 14.4 baud modem, and a commercial Internet service with a Web browser (all examples in this section use America Online)

- To start searching, access your Internet service
- Choose **Go To** from the menu bar; then choose **Keyword**
- In the keyword box that appears, type in the Internet address, known as the URL (Uniform Resource Locator), to the site you wish to contact, and then press Enter or click on **Go**
  - URLs of law sites can be found in Internet "Yellow Pages" books
  - URLs for law sites can also be found on-line in sites provided by your Internet Service; on American Online simply type the word legal into the keyword box and press Enter or click on **Go**; then choose the site: Law on the Net
- If you do not have an URL for a particular law site and the "Yellow Pages" or law forum provided by your Internet server was not helpful, use a search engine—a type of automated index
  - At the keyword box type in the URL of the search engine (ex., http://www.yahoo.com)
  - At the home page of the search engine, type your terms into the search box and then press Enter on your keyboard
  - Scroll through the list of sites that is retrieved and choose whichever seems appropriate
  - As you find documents (that appear to be relevant to your issue, save them to your hard drive choosing **Save As** from the menu bar (CAUTION: If you are going to download documents from the Internet be sure to scan them with software designed to detect and clean computer viruses)
  - If you are specifically looking for case law on-line, especially federal cases, you can access it through the Law

Journal EXTRA site at http://www.1jextra.com, or by signing up for the bulletin board service (BBS) called PACER.

Searching the LEXIS and Westlaw databases

- Determine whether you are going to conduct your search using "natural language" for your query—a string of search terms which represent your legal issue—or whether you will conduct a Boolean search using root expanders, connectors, universal characters, and the like
- Formulate your query while off-line, as a cost-saving strategy
- Access either LEXIS or Westlaw
- Choose the database you wish to search
- Enter your query
- Modify your query as necessary either to expand or to reduce the number of documents that it retrieves
- Print the citations of the documents that you wish to read
- As a cost-saving measure, get off-line and conduct your research with the citations that you have collected in your computer search
- Access LEXIS or Westlaw again to update the cases, statutes, and so on that you think are relevant and that you may wish to rely on

Performing research using CD-ROM products

- Determine which CD-ROMs you wish to search
- Place the CD-ROMs in the appropriate drives and start the program
- Formulate your search query—it is unnecessary to use a Boolean search on CD-ROMs that uses the Folio system, but it is helpful
    - If you decide to use a Boolean search, determine which connectors, root expanders, universal characters, and the like that you will use

- At the main menu, choose which database you wish to search
- Choose which portion of the database you wish to search (e.g., if searching for cases perhaps choose to search only headnotes)
- Enter your query, modifying if necessary in response to the number of hits—positive responses to your query—that you get
- Peruse the positive responses
- Read in depth any cases, statutes, regulations, and so on that appear relevant
- Take notes by using the **Print Screen** option to make a hard copy of any text and citations that you think are relevant

CHAPTER 9

ORGANIZING YOUR RESEARCH

I took a good deal o' pains with his eddication, sir; let him run in the streets when he was very young, and shift for hisself. It's the only way to make a boy sharp, sir.

—Charles Dickens, Pickwick Papers (1836-1837)

PRELIMINARY THOUGHTS

Although you've no doubt made plenty of mistakes while researching your issues, these errors are an inevitable part of legal research; because of them, you've learned to correct your errors midstream, a talent that will come in handy should you find yourself doing further legal research. You've also discovered how to find background information regarding your issues and how to read cases, learned about the terminology that's used in the cases, and determined how to spot the courts' holdings. As with any other subject, however, the final leap in understanding the materials must be made by the researcher. In other words, notwithstanding that the actual method of doing legal research can be taught, understanding the cases and drawing conclusions from them are largely dependent on your own good judgment and astuteness.

Still, there are certain guidelines that will help you focus your thoughts and determine the importance of each case. By the very act of compiling the information you've gathered and analyzing the data, you can take giant strides toward making valid conclusions. This compilation and analysis step is crucial, because without a summary of your research and an assessment of the relevant cases, your research is just a jumble of facts without an organizing principle. Leaving your research without organizing it would be like going to several doctors for an opinion on whether you need surgery for a medical condition without comparing their advice and without making a qualitative judgment as to the basis of their opinions.

Even though you're not a lawyer, you'll have to make some judgment calls concerning what your research leads you to decide. To do this, you'll write yourself a memorandum that describes the situation that prompted you to do legal research in the first place, the issues involved in that situation, and an analysis of the cases and statutes that apply to your legal questions.

MATERIALS YOU NEED TO WRITE A LEGAL MEMORANDUM

In order to write a memorandum, you'll need to have the notes you took when reading the cases, a copy of any statutes that apply to your facts, and possibly, copies of some of the relevant, on-point cases (for quick reference in case you need them). Aside from these things, you'll need certain intangible qualities to write a good memorandum. An emotional distance from your material is the most important of these qualities. Granted, you may know that you were right about the situation that caused you to do research or you know that you shouldn't be held responsible for the results of something you did, but you'll want to be completely honest with yourself when assessing your liability or responsibility for whatever happened. Remember that if a judge were to assess your case, he or she would have no biases in your favor, and therefore, you shouldn't either. For your own sake, maintain a distance from your material because you're not doing yourself any favors by giving yourself the benefit of any doubts. If necessary, pretend that you're writing this memo for someone else, not for yourself. This strategy will pay off richly when you have to decide what your next move will be—whatever decision you make, you'll know that it's sound, because it will be based on an informed, dispassionate analysis. As always, you'll also need perseverance to get to the finishing line. Now is not the time to take shortcuts in your work. Understand that this step, like so many of the other steps you've taken, is completely new to you, so it will take time and patience. Considering how hard you've worked on the other steps and considering that you're almost finished with your research, you can hopefully endure a little more vigilance and attentiveness now in order to bring all your earlier efforts to fruition.

JUST THE FACTS, MA'AM

The first part of your memo will incorporate your phrasing of the facts, which you first worked on in Chapter 3. There, you ummarizing your legal problem into one fact-filled that you could focus on what the real issue was. Dig mary from your notes and look it over. In light of learned from the cases and background materials, it pathetically inadequate to describe what prompted your legal research in the first place.

Therefore, write a one-paragraph summary of your facts, including all the facts that turned out to be important to your research. Don't incorporate any extraneous or unnecessary facts that didn't affect the course of your research.

Conclude with the one-sentence summary that you were asked to write in Chapter 3, paring the summary down so that it concisely asks the question that your research answered. For instance, your one-sentence conclusion might be "I want to know whether I can be held liable on a contract that my business partner signed and that obligates the partnership to pay $50,000 for new equipment."

As we mentioned in Summarizing Your Problem, pages 25–26, you should be straightforward and factual when writing out your facts. Include not only those facts that are favorable to your side of the story, but also include those facts that impair your case. Write your facts in a way that anyone reading them would not know whether you or your adversary had written them. Only then will you have a good statement of the facts.

As an example, let's turn to Donald. Donald's snowplowing business failed last year after his area experienced its mildest winter in 35 years. The man with whom he ran the snowplowing business, Tony, bought $50,000 worth of snowplowing equipment just before the winter started, assuming that the coming winter would be just as snowy as the previous winter, which dropped 82 inches of snow on the area. Tony used a check drawn on a joint checking account with Donald to buy the equipment, although Donald hadn't authorized Tony to go out and buy all that equipment. Now that the business has failed, Donald is being sued by the equipment supplier for $45,000 in damages. Donald wonders whether he can be held liable for this amount.

Here's the fact summary that Donald wrote:

FACTS: Donald and Tony orally agreed to be business partners in a snowplowing business but never got around to signing a partnership agreement. When they agreed to work together, they decided that neither one of them could bind the other to any contracts without first discussing the contract with the other. Nevertheless, after making a lot of money plowing snow the previous winter, Tony bought $50,000 worth of plowing equipment in August. To do so, he signed a credit agreement from the supplier. Under his signature, he wrote: "Partner in the 'Donald and Tony Snowplowing Services'." Tony also made a down payment using a check that was imprinted with both Donald's and Tony's names and was drawn on a joint checking account. The following January, the snowplowing business shut down because of a lack of business. In February, Tony declared personal bankruptcy. There is still $45,000 outstanding on the snowplowing equipment which the supplier is now demanding from Donald. Donald wants to know whether he can be held liable for paying any of the amount and, if so, whether he can be held liable for paying the entire sum.

This summary discusses all the facts necessary to answer Donald's question, but doesn't include extraneous information, which would merely complicate the issue.

STATING THE ISSUES

Next, you'll write down the issue or issues that were raised by your research. The statement of the issue shouldn't simply restate what kind of outcome you would like to achieve (I want my $500 back, I want to keep my tenant's security deposit, or I want to force my spouse to pay alimony). Instead, the statement of the issue should ask one of two questions:

- Do you or any other person involved satisfy all the elements of the law to make a good case for filing a complaint against another?
- Do you or any other person involved satisfy all of the elements of the law to be held liable for your (or their) actions?

For instance, Donald's issue might appear this way:

ISSUE: Whether, under New York law, Donald satisfies the requirements of partnership law to be held liable for his partner Tony's unauthorized contract where (1) the partnership agreement required both parties to agree before entering into any contracts, (2) Tony entered into the contract without Donald's knowledge, and (3) Donald failed to repudiate the contract, where a New York statute provides that a partner (in this case, Donald) will be held liable for the other partner's contracts (Tony's) if the contracting partner (Tony) holds himself out to the other party to the contract as being authorized to bind the partnership.

To understand how Donald was able to phrase his issue in this way, let's retrace the steps he took to reach his issue statement.

Donald discovered early in his research that state law applies to partnerships, so he made sure the issue statement explicitly points out the law that governs the issue. Donald also found, in his research of the statutory law, that partners are liable for all acts of the partnership under certain circumstances defined in the statutes and in the cases. Therefore, he listed the requirement that must be met to make one partner liable for the acts of the other partner (that is that the contracting partner hold himself or herself out to the other party as being authorized to bind the partnership). However, depending on what the law requires, it might have been easier for him to list those elements that must be met for one partner *not* to be liable for the other partner's acts.

By learning something of business law, Donald has transformed his legal question into a more concrete inquiry as to whether his case satisfies the particular requirements of the law requiring him to be responsible for his partner's debt.

It's important to separate all your issues and to deal with them one at a time to avoid confusion. For instance, suppose the case law (or a statute) had said that Donald must both (1) be a partner and (2) have ratified (explicitly approved) the contract, in order to be held liable under it. Donald should separate his case out into two issues and deal with them separately in the discussion section of his memo. His issues might then be stated this way:

ISSUE: Whether, under New York law, Donald satisfies the requirement of the law that one must be a partner in order to be held liable as a business partner for the contracts of another partner, where Donald and Tony never signed a partnership agreement and Donald is not sure whether they ran the business as a partnership.

> **Helpful Hint**
>
> When stating the issue, refer to any applicable statutes or case law. If the courts have set forth a test or list of requirements that a party must fulfill in order to make a good claim, or to adequately defend a claim, include this test or these requirements in your statement of the issue. Also, restate those facts that bear directly on the issue; for example, in the case of Donald, he restated the fact that the partnership agreement didn't allow them to enter into contracts without the other partner's agreement, that Tony signed a contract without Donald's knowledge, and that Donald never repudiated the contract.

ISSUE: Whether, under New York law, Donald satisfies the legal requirement that one must ratify a contract in order to be held liable as a business partner for the contracts of a partner, where Donald's and Tony's oral agreement required both parties to concur before entering into a contract, Tony entered into a contract with someone who knew that Tony did not have the authority to bind the partnership, the contract was made without Donald's knowledge, but Donald never repudiated the contract.

DISCUSSING THE LAW AS APPLIED TO YOUR FACTS

Find your notes on the cases you read that were applicable to your facts as well as your copies of any relevant statutes. Set the statutes aside for the time being and gather together your notes of those cases that support conclusions favorable to you. In a separate pile, put all those cases that support conclusions that would make you lose the case if they were to be argued in court. If you have any other issues to deal with, do the same thing with each of your issues, making two piles for favorable and unfavorable cases. Then pick one of the issues to analyze first.

The first sentence of your discussion should be a general statement of the law, either discerned from the statutes or from case law. For instance, if Donald is discussing the first issue concerning ratification, the first sentence of his discussion of that issue would go something like the following (Remember that he'll have to write a statement for the second issue as well!):

Under New York law, for Donald to be held liable for a contract made by Tony, where Tony wasn't authorized by Donald to enter into contracts without Donald's concurrence, the other party to the contract knew that Tony did not have the authority to bind the partnership, and Donald was not told of the contract, Donald must subsequently have ratified the contract to be held liable under it.[1]

If a statute applies to your issue

If a statute applies to your issue, you'll take a slightly different approach to writing your memo than if none applies. First, read the statute that applies to the issue. Is it favorable or unfavorable to

[1]This is not a statement of New York law—it's just an example of how such a statement should be written.

Helpful Hint

After your general statement of law, insert a case cite or a statutory cite to support the statement. Although lawyers include these cites in case briefs so that a judge can check on the authority for the propositions found in the brief, in your case, this cite isn't for a judge but for you. It serves to remind you where you learned this information and allows you to return to the reference cited, should you later have a question about your general statement. Case cites and statutory cites should be used in the rest of your discussion as well, and for the same reasons as are mentioned above. As you start to refer to other cases and compare these cases to your own (as you'll be doing soon), you'll want to keep track of which case you're discussing and allow yourself the opportunity to double-check your arguments later on by referring back to the cited cases. Case cites should be inserted after a complete discussion of the case cited. They can also be inserted after you set forth a judicial viewpoint, and you need some authority to back up the statement, in which case you'll probably mention more than one case cite to support the statement.

your case? If the answer to this question were clear from the statute itself, chances are that there would be no cases that discuss facts parallel to your own, and therefore, you would have found no case law on the subject. But because you have, then the courts must have interpreted the statute as applied to facts like yours, and the answer to your particular issue is, or has been, interpreted by the courts.

Decide exactly what the controversy concerning the statute is. Is the controversy over to whom the statute applies? Or is there disagreement about under which circumstances the statute's provisions apply? State the nature of the controversy after your statement of the statute's relevant provisions. Now you've set the stage for the controversy to be answered. Amazingly enough, your own research will ultimately answer your questions.

If there is no relevant statute regarding the issue

If there is no statute that applies to your facts, write that there is no applicable statute. Then, using the cases, describe the points on which the courts disagree regarding your issue. Assuming you've gotten this far into the research, the courts must disagree on some point for you to still hold out hope of having a winning case.

Now briefly explain the different interpretations the courts have given to the issue. Don't evaluate their reasoning or omit discussion of any judicial points of view that you found in your research simply because you dislike the reasoning. As long as any court holds a view on the particular issue, include it. The time for evaluation will come later.

Example of a statement of the controversy

Donald's brief statement of the courts' differing interpretations of a statute or, if there is no statute, the issue in general, might go like this: "Courts have interpreted the ratification requirement loosely in New York and in other jurisdictions that also employ the ratification requirement [provide case cites], though some jurisdictions require explicit ratification of a contract in order for a partner to be held liable for the contract [provide case cites]."

> **Helpful Hint**
>
> When we refer to a statute applying to your issue, we mean a statute that substantively regulates your issue. For instance, statutes regulate corporations, certain professions, tax issues, and real estate law. Statutes of limitations also apply to these issues, but they also apply to any legal issue, and shed no light on your issue. We're not concerned with such procedural statutes here (unless your issue is itself a procedural issue). This section applies to you only if there is a statute on the books that regulates the substance of your issue.

Evaluating the conflicting sides

If there is a statute that affects your issue, this is the most compelling authority that you'll have regarding the issue. Even if you've found such a statute, however, case authority is still important, because the courts are the ones that interpret the statutes and give them life. Whether or not a statute controls your issue, your next step is to analyze the courts' reasoning and decide which reasoning is most compelling. Several factors affect how you rank the persuasiveness of the case authority you've found:

- jurisdiction of the court (see Chapter 1)
- rank of the court (see Chapter 1)
- age of the case (see Chapter 1)
- similarity of the case authority's facts to your facts (see Chapter 1)
- whether the court's decision is dicta or holding (see Chapter 5)

We'll discuss each of these factors in turn.

Jurisdiction of the Court

Remember in Chapter 1 where we discussed the fact that the most persuasive case authorities come from courts in your own jurisdiction? You'll want to weigh the persuasiveness of the cases when writing your discussion to reflect this. If you're dealing with a federal claim, the authorities you're dealing with will be from the federal court system. If you're dealing with a state claim, the authorities will come from the state court system. This means that if you live in California, a decision made in California is more persuasive than one made by a state court in Arkansas or New York, and your discussion will focus more on the California cases than on cases from other states (unless there are no California cases on the issue, then you'll have to rely on cases from other jurisdictions).

Similarly, if you live in New York and are dealing with a copyright issue, cases decided by a federal court in the second circuit (where New York is located) would be more persuasive in your discussion than decisions made in the eleventh circuit (where Florida, Georgia, and Alabama are located).

One important point to remember is that, no matter what your jurisdiction, the U.S. Supreme Court can take appeals from the highest state courts for certain issues and from any of the highest federal courts (called the court of appeals of that circuit).

What if you're dealing with a state claim, and have found several state court decisions on the issue, but suddenly you find a federal decision on the same (state) issue? You're probably wondering how a federal court nosed its way into the state's jurisdiction. Briefly, this sometimes happens when a plaintiff brings several different claims in one complaint, some of which are federal claims and some of which are state claims, or when the complaint involves parties from two different states. If the complaint involves mixed issues of state and federal law, the federal court, as a matter of convenience, may choose to (or may be forced to) decide the state issue along with the federal issues. Where a federal court applies state law to a state claim, its decision is authoritative but not binding on the state courts, as the highest state court's decision on the same issue would be. Your discussion should not rely on a federal court decision that conflicts with state court decisions on a state issue.

RANK OF THE COURT

The most persuasive authorities are the highest courts in your jurisdiction.

—Federal system

In the federal system, the U.S. Supreme Court decisions are binding in all the federal jurisdictions, though decisions made in any one of the federal circuits are not binding on other federal circuits. U.S. Supreme Court case cites can be recognized by any of the following abbreviations in the cite: U.S., U.S.L.W., S. Ct., L. Ed., and L. Ed. 2d. (Other abbreviations may occur in the case cite as well, but at least one of these abbreviations should appear.)

The next most persuasive court in the federal court system after the U.S. Supreme Court is the circuit courts of appeals, of which there are thirteen (see the map in Chapter 1). You can recognize a court of appeals case because the cite for the case will include F., F.2d, or F.3d. Next in line is federal district court, which is the trial court level in the federal circuit. Federal district courts are bound by their own circuit's court of appeals on matters of federal law, and also by the U.S. Supreme Court. District court cases have cites that contain the following abbreviations: F. Supp., F.R.D., B.R., Fed. R. Serv., or Fed. R. Serv. 2d.

There are many other courts in the federal court system, including the U.S. Court of Appeals for the Federal Circuit, which hears customs and patent appeals and appeals from the court of claims. Its cites will appear as follows: F.2d and F.3d; cases older than 1982 will have cites that appear as Ct. C1. and C.C.P.A. Not as persuasive as these cases are U.S. Claims Court cases, whose cites appear either as F. Supp. or C1. Ct. The federal court system also includes bankruptcy courts, whose cites will often appear as Bankr. or B.R. Finally, the tax court cases can be identified by their abbreviations, T.C. and T.C.M. Cases and memorandum decisions decided by the tax court which are older than 1942 are identified by the cite B.T.A. and B.T.A.M. (Note that there are other courts in the federal system, but we won't bother with them because you probably won't encounter them in your research.)

Remember, too, that federal statutes are binding on all federal courts in deciding a federal issue.

—**State system**

State courts are similarly ranked according to persuasiveness. The U.S. Supreme Court hears appeals from the highest state courts on certain issues, and when it does, its decisions are binding on all the courts of that state.

Similarly, the decisions made by the highest court of a state is binding on all other state courts in that state. But how can you tell from a case cite whether a court is the highest court in a state? In most states, this court is called the state supreme court, however, in New York and Maryland, it's called the Court of Appeals; and in Maine and Massachusetts, it's called the Supreme Judicial

> **Helpful Hint**
>
> If you're balking at the thought of having to do even more research in order to figure out whether your state's intermediate court decisions are binding on all your state's lower courts, consider this: The intermediate appellate court for your district always has the last word on any issue, so long as a higher court doesn't disagree with your intermediate court's decision. A decision made by another intermediate appellate court that conflicts with your intermediate appellate court will never bind you because you're not in that other intermediate appellate court's jurisdiction. And, no matter what rule your state follows as to the reach of an intermediate appellate court's decisions, if your own intermediate appellate court has not ever decided an issue like yours, other intermediate appellate courts' interpretations will either be binding or extremely persuasive.

Court; in West Virginia, it's called the Supreme Court of Appeals.

The next court in line in your state is also probably an appeals court, but it can go by many different names depending on your state. In most states, it's called the court of appeals, but in Alabama for instance, it's known as the court of civil appeals; in Connecticut, it's called the appellate court, and in Florida, it's called the district court of appeal. So much for uniformity! The decisions made by these intermediate appellate courts are binding on all lower court decisions that that particular intermediate court reviews. Additionally, depending on which state you live in, intermediate appellate court decisions may also be binding on all lower courts in the state, as long as the intermediate court's decisions don't conflict with the decisions of the intermediate court that hears the lower court's appeals. Whether this is the case depends on the particular state concerned.

Beneath this level, states have an even wider variety of courts, ranging from county courts, courts of claim, courts for the correction of errors, family court, courts of chancery, tax courts, and so on.

Needless to say the highest court in your jurisdiction will be binding on all other courts, and thus its decisions should be emphasized in your discussion. As the courts descend down the ranks, the binding nature, or persuasiveness, of the courts' decisions lessen.

Remember, too, that state statutes bind all state courts for that state, although courts can interpret those statutes.

Age of the Case

There is no hard-and-fast rule concerning how the age of the cases affects their persuasiveness. In Chapter 1, we discussed precedents, which are previously decided cases, recognized by the courts as being authoritative on an issue. Precedents are binding on all lower courts as well as the courts themselves that originally decided the case. Although long-standing precedent can be powerful authority for a proposition, you should remember that precedent can always be overturned by the courts if the reasons to do so are strong enough. Especially if you have an ancient precedent that the courts haven't discussed in many years and if there have been many changes in that area of law (or many relevant societal changes) in the intervening years, the power of the precedent may be in doubt.

Helpful Hint

Another area where the similarity of a case to yours may be irrelevant is where a court from a different jurisdiction deals with the same issue as yours, but a completely different kind of statute than yours controls the issue. For instance, a case can be a virtual carbon copy of your own, but if your statute demands something different than the other case's statute, the other case is not a compelling authority.

The best position to be in is to have a 100-year-old case that adopts your argument as well as recent cases from the past few years that similarly accept the precedent and support your position.

If you're dealing with an issue in an area that has arisen only in the past few years, like computer law or AIDS law, you may find that most of your cases are newer cases. Even though the cases are relatively new, there can still be a binding precedent that has already been set down by the courts.

SIMILARITY OF THE CASE AUTHORITY'S FACTS TO YOUR FACTS

Obviously, cases whose facts are more similar to yours tend to be more persuasive cases than those with facts that are slightly different. For instance, if your issue involves AIDS law, a case that discusses tuberculosis isn't as compelling as an AIDS case, even though both cases deal with liability for intentionally exposing another to the illness.

In Donald's situation, a compelling case would involve a partner, who wasn't authorized to enter into contracts, entering into one and the other partner not immediately repudiating the contract. A less persuasive case would involve a member of a joint venture entering into an unauthorized contract, where the other member of the joint venture does not immediately repudiate the contract.

Whether the court's decision is dicta or holding

In Chapter 5, we discussed the difference between dicta and holding. A holding is the ruling of the court, while dicta is any remarks or observations that are not necessary for the holding. In your discussion, remember that courts' dicta is not binding on subsequent cases, and therefore doesn't have precedential value. So, your discussion should emphasize the cases with holdings that affect your issue. You may also include those cases that discuss your issue in dicta, but be sure to distinguish these cases in your discussion, and make sure that these cases do not form the linchpin of support for your position. You need some holdings on your side as well.

All of the five factors affect the strength of a particular case authority. Often you'll find a case that is persuasive according to one of the five categories but unpersuasive according to the other categories. Perhaps the most important of the categories is a combination of the first two categories—jurisdiction of the court and its rank. If you have a decision from the highest court in your state that discusses your issue, even if the facts aren't quite parallel to your own, this case is much more compelling than another case with facts exactly like your own but from another jurisdiction.

Keeping in mind that jurisdiction combined with rank is the most important factor, weigh your cases carefully to decide their importance. As always, try to be impartial so that you can get as honest a picture of your situation as possible.

Putting your discussion together

Now that you've weighed the importance of the case authorities, it's time to compile your results using your notes. Remember that you should concentrate on one issue at a time, even though some of your cases may discuss more than one of your issues. Focusing on one issue will keep you from confusing your issues.

Your goal is both to meld the comparisons and contrasts between your facts and the cases and to point out the persuasiveness of any one of the cases you're discussing. To do this, spend up to three paragraphs per case, depending on the persuasiveness of the authority. Don't spend less time on a case simply because it is contrary to your position; you want to understand and analyze all perspectives. The three paragraphs (or, if a case is less persuasive, three sections of a paragraph) should contain the following information:

- The first paragraph (or section of a paragraph) should describe the case's facts and what the court held (your notes should come in handy for this step). Discuss the reasons why the court decided the case as it did, describing the factors that the court seemed to find most compelling in arriving at its decision.
- The second paragraph (or section) should describe the factual similarities of the case to your situation.
- The third paragraph (or section) should describe the factual differences of the case with your situation.

Repeat this process with each relevant case you've found that pertain to the issue you're focusing on.

DRAWING CONCLUSIONS FROM THE DATA

By the time you finish your discussion, you've probably developed enough of an understanding of your area of the law that you can take an educated guess (but, remember—it's only a guess!) concerning how a court in your jurisdiction would hold on your issue.

If you're still not sure what sort of conclusion to draw, you might have a close issue. Leave your research for a day or two and try not to think about it. When you come back to it, read your discussion section critically. What would an unbiased third person probably conclude from reading your discussion?

Remember that your answer may not be an unconditional statement. You'll probably conclude that a court would probably decide X, or might possibly hold Y. Don't worry that your answer sounds somewhat wishy-washy. Even a trained lawyer can't possibly know what a judge will hold in a given set of circumstances (after all, someone has to lose in a case).

Then again, the answer might be that the case could go either way. This is a perfectly respectable conclusion, and not an unusual one. If this is what you believe, briefly state the reasons why a court might hold one way and why it might hold another.

Whatever your conclusions, devote about one paragraph of the conclusion to each issue. The length of the conclusion is not a hard-and-fast rule, however, and you should feel free to make it longer or shorter, depending on the complexity of your issue.

Donald's conclusion turned out this way:

CONCLUSION FOR ISSUE 1: Donald probably satisfies the requirement of partnership liability that one partner must ratify the other partner's unauthorized contract to be held liable on it. Although Donald did not initially concur in the contract, he never repudiated it, and in fact, he used the snowplowing equipment that his partner contracted for. Most New York courts have ruled that acceptance of the fruits of a contract is equivalent to ratifying the contract. Those courts that have ruled that acceptance of the fruits of the contract did not amount to ratification of the contract have pointed out that, in those cases, the partner who was sought to be held liable was not aware that an unauthorized contract had been made and therefore did not knowingly accept the consideration under the contract.

CONCLUSION FOR ISSUE 2: Donald would probably be found by a court to be a partner in the snowplowing business. Although he didn't sign a partnership agreement and he deposited all payments from his customers into a personal checking account, he held himself out to the public as being a member of a partnership. New York cases have found that where someone drives a truck that is painted with a business name, holds himself out to customers as being a member of a partnership, and jointly holds property with another, there is an implied agreement by the two to be partners.

Although we gave you both of Donald's conclusions above, remember that before reaching your second conclusion (assuming you have two issues), you will have to go back to Stating the Issues, above, and repeat the memo-writing process for each of your issues.

A SAMPLE MEMORANDUM

LEGAL MEMORANDUM

To: Myself
Date: 11/1/96
Re: Recovery of damages for negligent infliction of emotional distress when a woman is present at the scene of a fire in which her fiancé's daughter is killed

Facts

Ms. Queue wants to know whether, under Florida law, she can recover damages for negligent infliction of emotional distress against her landlord, Chatworth Complex. Chatworth Complex failed to maintain electrical wiring, and as a result, a fire broke out in Ms. Queue's building. Ms. Queue was present at the scene of the fire in which Stephanie Johns, her fiancé's daughter, was killed. Ms.Queue did not actually see Stephanie killed, but heard screams from the burning building. Only the next morning did she learn of Stephanie's death. Although Stephanie wanted to live with Ms. Queue and Ms. Queue's fiancé, Stephanie was not related to Ms. Queue. During the fire, Ms.Queue portrayed her relationship with Stephanie to others as if she were Stephanie's stepmother. After the fire, Ms. Queue began suffering from insomnia, migraine headaches, nightmares, and weight loss. Her psychiatrist stated that these ailments are symptomatic of the guilt she feels about Stephanie's death. Ms. Queue want to know whether she can recover damages for negligent infliction of emotional distress for Stephanie Johns' death.

Issues

1. Whether, under Florida common law, plaintiff satisfies the requirement of direct involvement for negligent infliction of emotional distress when plaintiff was present at a fire where the victim was killed, heard screams from the burning building in which the victim died, and learned the next day that the victim of the fire was a loved one.
2. Whether, under Florida common law, plaintiff satisfies the relationship requirement for negligent infliction of emotional distress, when plaintiff was not related to the victim, although she was engaged to marry the victim's father, held herself out to be the victim's stepmother on at least one occasion and the victim wanted to live with the plaintiff.

Discussion

To state a claim for negligent infliction of emotional distress under Florida common law, Ms.Queue must meet three criteria of foreseeability. Champion v. Gray, 478 So. 2d 17 (Fla. 1985). These criteria are a close emotional attachment between plaintiff and victim, plaintiff's direct involvement in the accident that caused the victim's injury, and physical injury caused by the emotional trauma of witnessing the event. *Id.* at 20. This memo will evaluate two of these three elements: Ms. Queue's relationship with the victim and Ms. Queue's involvement in the accident. The third element of physical injury is satisfied because Ms. Queue suffered physical ailments after witnessing the fire.

1. *Direct Involvement*

Ms. Queue wants to know whether, under Florida law, she was sufficiently involved in the accident in which Stephanie died so that she can recover damages for negligent infliction of emotional distress. To do this, she must show she sensorily perceived the accident or arrived at the scene while the victim was still there. *Id.* at 17. Courts have interpreted the direct involvement requirement narrowly in Florida and in other jurisdictions that also employ the same type of foreseeability rule. *See, e.g.*, Dillon v. Legg, 68 Cal. 2d 728, 441 P.2d 912, 69 Cal. Rptr. 72 (1968); Ledford v. Delta Airlines, Inc., 658 F. Supp. 540 (S.D. Fla. 1987). However, Florida cases have not yet addressed the problem of whether involvement is established when plaintiff, who is at the scene, is uncertain that the loved one has been injured.

In *Champion*, the Florida Supreme Court set forth the rule that established the criteria for foreseeability of negligent infliction of mental distress. *Champion*, 478 So. 2d at 20. In *Champion* the plaintiff's daughter was struck and killed by a car driven by a drunk driver. *Id.* at 18. The plaintiff heard but did not see the impact. *Id.* She immediately came to the accident scene and, upon seeing her dead daughter, died from shock and grief at the scene. *Id.* at 18. On appeal from dismissal, the Supreme Court of Florida established the foreseeability test that expanded the impact rule to include negligent infliction of emotional distress, and the case was remanded for a finding consistent with the test. *Id.* at 20. The court held three elements must be satisfied to state a cause of action. *Id.* at 20. Plaintiff must show (1) significant discernible physical injury resulting from (2) involvement in an accident in which (3) a person who is emotionally attached to the plaintiff is injured. *Id.* at 20. The court ruled that the issue of involvement can be satisfied if the plaintiff sees the accident, hears it, or arrives at the scene while the victim is there. *Id.* at 20. Because the plaintiff heard the accident and arrived upon the scene immediately thereafter, the court held she met the involvement requirement of the test. *Id.* at 20.

Several similarities between *Champion* and the instant case exist. Both the *Champion* plaintiff and Ms. Queue were present at the scene of the accident. The *Champion* plaintiff arrived immediately after the victim was killed, and Ms. Queue arrived while the fire was still burning. Both heard the sounds of the accident occurring and were initially unaware that the victims were loved ones. The *Champion* plaintiff heard the sound of the impact as the victim was struck by a car, and Ms. Queue heard screams from the building. The *Champion* court determined that the mother was directly involved. Because Ms. Queue heard the victim in the fire and arrived at the scene, it is reasonably foreseeable that she would suffer emotional distress.

However, a major difference between the two cases is also present. While both women were aware of the accidents occurring, the *Champion* plaintiff learned immediately after hearing the sounds of the accident that her daughter had been killed. Ms. Queue, on the other hand, did not learn until the next morning that Stephanie was the person killed in the fire. Ms. Queue, by her actions, appeared to be reasonably certain that the screams emanating from the burning building were Stephanie's; however, whether the screams were in fact Stephanie's was not established at the scene and Ms. Queue could only assume they were. Therefore, if involvement was satisfied by merely hearing the accident occurring, Ms. Queue has satisfied the involvement requirement. But if involvement requires knowledge, at the scene, that the victim was indeed a loved one, as the *Champion* plaintiff realized before she died, then Ms. Queue has not satisfied the requirement. Because the *Champion* court did not deal with the issue of lack of knowledge that plaintiff was involved in the accident, other cases may further clarify the requirement. Therefore it is difficult to predict whether a court would find that Ms. Queue was directly involved in the accident based on *Champion v. Gray*.

In *Ledford*, 658 F. Supp. at 540, the plaintiff was informed by telephone that his wife's plane had crashed in Texas. *Id.* at 541. The plaintiff, in Florida, then viewed the news reports of the crash on television. *Id.* at 541. The court granted summary judgment to the defendant, partly because the plaintiff had failed to show involvement in the accident. *Id.* at 542, 543. The court followed the *Champion* foreseeability rule and reasoned that, because plaintiff only viewed the accident on television after it had occurred and did not see his wife on television nor the accident as it was happening, he did not, as a matter of law, state a viable claim of negligent infliction of emotional distress. *Id.* at 543.

The most significant similarity between the two cases involves plaintiffs' uncertainty of the victims' involvement in the accidents. Both the *Ledford* plaintiff and Ms. Queue could not be sure that their loved ones were injured in the accidents. It may therefore be difficult to establish Ms. Queue's involvement in the event, because she did not see Stephanie at the scene.

The most important distinction between the two cases is that the *Ledford* plaintiff saw the accident only after it occurred and was not at the scene, while Ms. Queue witnessed the accident, was at the scene and heard screams. The *Ledford* court noted that one of its reasons for dismissing the action was that the plaintiff did not "see his wife on television," and presumably, could not know whether or not she was injured. *Id.* Ms. Queue, because of her proximity to and contemporaneous observance of the fire, was more involved in the accident than the *Ledford* plaintiff. Although Ms. Queue may be able to establish a stronger case for involvement, she did not see Stephanie in the fire and could not know whether she was injured. According to the *Ledford* rationale, which suggested that plaintiff might have satisfied the requirement for direct involvement if he had seen the victim on television and the accident as it was happening, Ms. Queue might not be able to sustain her claim in court, because, although she was present at the scene, she did not see the victim.

While the Florida courts have not ruled explicitly on whether plaintiffs' uncertainty that a loved one is involved in an accident satisfies the involvement requirement, a California court dealt with this problem of uncertainty in Scherr v. Las Vegas Hilton, 168 Cal. App. 3d 909, 214 Cal. Rptr. 393 (Ct. App. 1985). In *Scherr*, the plaintiff, whose husband was staying at a hotel in Las Vegas, watched a live television broadcast of the hotel burning from California. *Scherr*, 215 Cal. Rptr. at 394. Plaintiff was aware that her husband was staying at the hotel, but did not see him being injured in the broadcast. *Id.* at 394. The court applied a common law rule of foreseeability similar to the *Champion* rule. *Id.* at 394. This rule, derived from Dillon v. Legg, 68 Cal. 2d 728, 441 P.2d 912, 69 Cal. Rptr. 72 (1968), requires the plaintiff to experience a sensory and contemporaneous observance of the accident. *Scherr*, 214 Cal. Rptr. at 394 (citing *Dillon v. Legg*, 69 Cal. Rptr. 72). The *Scherr* court affirmed dismissal of the case, because plaintiff not only failed to contemporaneously witness the fire but also failed to see her husband being injured and could not be certain he was even in the fire. *Id.* at 395. The court further stated that whether the television was an intervening element that would bar foreseeability was not at issue. *Id.* at 394. To recover damages, the court held that plaintiff must not only witness the accident but also the infliction of injuries upon the victim. *Id.* at 395. The court clarified the term witnessing, as requiring "full perception of the injurious impact." *Id.* Furthermore, the court contended that simply realizing that there exists a high probability that the victim is being injured is insufficient to show involvement. *Id.*

Both the *Scherr* plaintiff and Ms. Queue were uncertain that their loved ones were in the fires. Neither of the plaintiffs witnessed the victims being injured as the court interpreted *witness* in *Scherr*. Ms. Queue, like the *Scherr* plaintiff, did not see the actual infliction of injuries on the victim, and both had to wait to have their suspicions confirmed from a third party source—Ms. Queue until the next day and the *Scherr* plaintiff until an undisclosed time. Therefore, because Ms. Queue did not know that Stephanie was injured in the fire, a Florida court using the same reasoning employed in *Scherr* might decide that Ms. Queue does not satisfy the involvement requirement of negligent infliction of emotional distress.

Two main differences between *Scherr* and the instant case exist. First, Ms. Queue heard screams from the building, while the *Scherr* plaintiff heard no screams. However, because the *Scherr* court placed greater emphasis on plaintiff's certainty of the victim's involvement in the accident than on plaintiff's perceptions of the accident, Ms. Queue's case would probably not be stronger than *Scherr* on this point.

Secondly, the *Scherr* plaintiff viewed the accident on television, while Ms. Queue was present at the scene. However, the *Scherr* court did not view the intervention of television as limiting foreseeability. Rather, because the *Scherr* plaintiff did not observe the infliction of victim's injuries, she could not recover damages.

Although Ms. Queue's presence at the scene probably strengthens her claim of involvement, the *Scherr* court downplayed the significance of viewing an accident "live" on television, as opposed to actually being at the scene. Therefore, the screams that Ms. Queue heard coming from the burning building would probably not constitute sufficient involvement. Because Ms. Queue did not actually see Stephanie killed in the fire, and discovered the next morning that she had died, Ms. Queue could most likely not satisfy the direct involvement element under the *Scherr* rule.

Ms. Queue's involvement in the accident in which Stephanie was killed probably does not satisfy the direct involvement requirement for negligent infliction of emotional distress. While the *Ledford* court implied that a plaintiff would have to be certain that a loved one was being injured, the *Scherr* court stated explicitly that where the plaintiff does not witness the infliction of injuries and is uncertain that the victim has been injured a claim does not exist. Both cases indicate a similar trend toward lessening the number of claims for negligent infliction of mental distress by narrowing the possibilities for establishing involvement. *See also* Crenshaw v. Sarasota County Public Hospital Board, 466 So. 2d 427 (Fla. Dist. Ct. App. 1985). *Scherr* is more analogous to the instant case, because the *Scherr* plaintiff, like Ms. Queue, was uncertain that her husband was in the hotel and viewed the accident as it was happening. Recourse to either *Scherr* or *Ledford*, though, indicates that Ms. Queue could probably not establish sufficient involvement in the fire. Also, because Ms. Queue did not discover until the following day that Stephanie had been killed, the *Champion* court would probably hold that third-party confirmation of the victim's death the day following the accident would not satisfy the foreseeability requirements. See *Champion*, 478 So. 2d at 20. By applying the reasoning used in *Ledford* and *Scherr*, and the legal rule established in *Champion*, a Florida court would probably decide that Ms. Queue's involvement is not sufficient, because she was neither certain of Stephanie's presence in the fire, nor did she learn of Stephanie's death until the following day.

2. *Plaintiff's relationship to victim*

Besides establishing direct involvement in the accident, Ms. Queue must also show a sufficient relationship to the victim to recover for negligent infliction of emotional distress. *Champion*,

478 So. 2d at 20. Again, the common law rule set forth in *Champion* would apply to the instant case. *Id.* One element of the *Champion* foreseeability rule requires that "an especially close emotional attachment" exist between plaintiff and the victim, a requirement that must be met by the relationship between Ms Queue and Stephanie. *Id.* However, courts in other states have demonstrated a reluctance to interpret this element too broadly. *See, e.g.*, Drew v. Drake, 110 Cal. App. 3d 555, 168 Cal. Rptr. 65 (Ct. App. 1980).

In *Champion*, the victim, the plaintiffs daughter, was negligently struck by a car, and the plaintiff died upon seeing the victim's dead body. *Champion*, 478 So. 2d at 18. The *Champion* plaintiff's estate sued for negligent infliction of emotional distress. *Id.* In holding for the plaintiff, the court formulated the *Champion* rule, which included a requirement that the plaintiff and the victim be sufficiently emotionally attached to state a valid claim for negligent infliction of emotional distress. *Id.* at 20. The requirements set forth by the *Champion* court seem to indicate the court's interest in limiting the claims that could be brought under this cause of action. *Id.* In *Champion*, because the victim was the plaintiff's daughter, the court reasoned that plaintiff satisfied the "emotional attachment" rule. *Id.* However, the ambiguity of the *Champion* rule leaves room for diverse interpretation in deciding what constitutes a sufficient relationship for the purposes of this rule. The court stated that people outside the immediate family may or may not qualify under the rule, depending upon "their relationship and the circumstances thereof." *Id.*

The major similarity between the two cases deals with the nature of the relationships between bystander and victim. Both Ms. Queue and the *Champion* plaintiff enjoyed a close relationship with the victims. While the *Champion* plaintiff was the mother of the victim, Ms. Queue was close to Stephanie and was planning to let Stephanie live with her and her fiancé. On this point alone, then, the instant case might satisfy the rule, because Ms. Queue probably was emotionally attached to Stephanie.

However, Ms. Queue was not related to Stephanie by blood or marriage, as the plaintiff in *Champion* was related to the victim. Also, Stephanie did not live with Ms. Queue, as the plaintiff and victim presumably did in *Champion*. Because Ms. Queue and Stephanie were not related to one another and did not live together, it probably was less foreseeable that Ms. Queue would suffer emotional distress upon witnessing Stephanie's death.

Although the *Champion* court expanded the claims that could be brought for negligent infliction of emotional distress by abandoning the impact rule and adopting a foreseeability rule, the court also seemed anxious to limit the instances in which a claim could satisfy the rule. *Id.* While Ms. Queue did have a close emotional attachment with Stephanie and the two seemed to have a family-like relationship, as measured by Stephanie's intention to live with Ms. Queue, Ms. Queue may still be unable to establish a sufficient relationship under the *Champion* foreseeability rule, because the *Champion* court was ambiguous about whether a nonfamilial relationship would satisfy the relationship requirement.

In Ferretti v. Weber, 513 So. 2d 1333 (Fla. 3d Dist. Ct. App. 1987), a Florida court further defined what constitutes a sufficient relationship. In *Ferretti*, the plaintiff witnessed a car accident in which his "live-in lady friend" was killed, and he sought to recover damages. *Id.* at 1333. The court held that the trial court's dismissal of the case was appropriate and ruled where no legal relationship exists between the plaintiff and victim, no claim exists for negligent infliction of emotional distress. *Id.* In this case, because no marriage existed between the plaintiff and the victim, the plaintiff, as a matter of law, could not recover. *Id.*

The most important similarity between the *Ferretti* plaintiff and Ms. Queue is that both were unrelated to the victims. Despite this absence of legal relationship, in both *Ferretti* and the instant case, evidence of close relationships between the bystanders and victims existed. The *Ferretti* plaintiff actually lived with the victim, and Ms. Queue was planning on living with Stephanie. But, because Ms. Queue was not legally related to Stephanie, Ms. Queue's close attachment to her probably does not increase foreseeability. There appears to be no relevant distinctions between these cases, while the similarities between *Ferretti* and the instant case on the relationship issue are compelling. The necessity of a legal relationship between the plaintiff and victim narrows the scope of the *Champion* rule and could further limit the possibility of Ms. Queue's ability to maintain a claim if the *Ferretti* reasoning were adopted by the Florida Supreme Court.

Elden v. Shelden, 46 Cal. 3d 267, 250 Cal. Rptr. 254, 758 P.2d 582 (Calif. 1988) gave a lengthier interpretation of the California requirement of sufficient relationship than *Ferretti* gave of the Florida requirement. California requires that the plaintiff and the victim be "closely related." *Dillon v. Legg*, 69 Cal. Rptr. at 80. In

Elden, the plaintiff was involved in an accident in which his "live-in lady friend" was killed. *Elden*, 758 P.2d at 582. The Supreme Court upheld dismissal of the case for failure to state a claim, ruling that plaintiff and victim must be legally related for plaintiff to recover under the *Dillon* rule. *Id.* at 586. In deciding *Elden*, the court stated three major policy considerations: the state's interest in marital relationships, the unwillingness of the courts to intrude in the private lives of plaintiffs to determine whether relationships are of a familial nature or not, and the desire to limit the number of people to whom a negligent defendant owes a duty of care. *Id.* at 586–88. Because the *Elden* plaintiff and the victim were unmarried, the plaintiff could not recover damages for negligent infliction of emotional distress. *Id.*

The major similarity between *Elden* and the instant case is that the *Elden* plaintiff was unrelated to the victim, as Ms. Queue was unrelated to Stephanie. According to the *Elden* court's ruling, even when foreseeability may be reasonably supposed, policy considerations override foreseeability when the plaintiff and victim are not legally related. Therefore, if a Florida court were to adopt the *Elden* court rationale (which explicitly expressed the state's interest in marital relationships, the state's concern with the problem of discovering whether relationships are familial, and the state's interest in limiting claims), the foreseeability of Ms. Queue being distressed by Stephanie's death would probably not override the fact that a legal relationship did not exist between Ms. Queue and Stephanie.

In one California case, Trapp v. Schuyler, 149 Cal. App. 2d 1140, 197 Cal. Rptr. 411 (Ct. App. 1983), even a blood relationship was held not to satisfy the relationship element of the foreseeability test. *See Dillon v. Legg*, 69 Cal. Rptr. 72. In *Trapp*, a brother and sister, plaintiffs, witnessed the drowning death of their cousin, with whom they had a relationship analogous to that of siblings. The court affirmed dismissal of the case, ruling that family members who are beyond the nuclear family unit cannot establish a claim for negligent infliction of emotional distress. *Trapp*, 197 Cal. Rptr. at 412. In *Trapp*, the court noted that foreseeability does not exist simply because the plaintiffs were cousins of the victim and had a meaningful relationship with him. *Id.* The ordinary person could not have foreseen the relationship between the victim and his cousins. *Id.* Furthermore, the court noted that the relationship element does not encompass friends, housemates, or those who have meaningful relationships with the victim. *Id.*

Like the *Trapp* plaintiffs, Ms. Queue enjoyed a close attachment with the victim, somewhat akin to an actual nuclear family relationship. The *Trapp* plaintiffs alleged that their relationship with their cousin was as close as a relationship usually found between siblings, while Ms. Queue's and Stephanie's relationship was similar to that usually found between a mother and daughter. Under the *Trapp* ruling, the quality of relationship alone cannot satisfy the relationship requirement. Therefore, under this ruling, the lack of a legal relationship between Ms. Queue and Stephanie would lessen foreseeability that Ms. Queue would suffer emotional distress at Stephanie's death.

However, the *Trapp* plaintiffs were actually related to the victim, while Ms. Queue was not related to Stephanie. This distinction between the two cases further weakens foreseeability in the instant case. A court, using the *Trapp* criterion for relationships, would probably decide that the instant case, which does not involve even a distant familial relationship between Ms. Queue and Stephanie, could not satisfy the relationship requirement. Consequently, the instant case would fail on the merits of relationship if a Florida court were to adopt the *Trapp* court's rule and reasoning.

A jurisdiction that holds more liberal views of what constitutes a sufficient relationship in cases of negligent infliction of emotional distress is Hawaii. In Leong v. Takasaki, 520 P.2d 758 (Haw. 1974), the plaintiff was the step-grandson of the victim. The plaintiff saw his step-grandmother, who had lived with him and his family for several months, being run over by a car. *Leong*, 520 P.2d at 760. Her relationship to the plaintiff was similar to a grandmother-grandson relationship, and plaintiff had been adopted by the victim's son. *Id.* at 758, 760. The court reversed summary judgment for defendant, ruling that a blood relationship need not exist between victim and plaintiff to establish a sufficient relationship. *Id.* at 766. The court reasoned that close emotional ties may exist without blood ties, and therefore, foreseeability can exist. *Id.* In *Leong*, although a blood relationship between plaintiff and victim was absent, the court noted that the strong Hawaiian tradition of close extended families substituted for the close ties of the nuclear family. *Id.* The relationship element, then, was satisfied in part by the quality of relationship between victim and plaintiff, which was demonstrated by the traditional role in Hawaii for adopted children.

The major similarity between the *Leong* plaintiff and Ms. Queue is that neither had blood relationships with the victims. The *Leong* plaintiff had been adopted by the victim's son, and so was legally related to the victim, but had no consanguinal relationship to her. Ms. Queue, although not legally related to Stephanie like the *Leong* plaintiff, enjoyed a close attachment to the victim and so might be able to establish the sufficiency of her relationship with Stephanie under the *Leong* ruling.

The main distinction between the two cases is that, whereas the *Leong* plaintiff lived with the victim, Stephanie was only visiting Ms. Queue for the week. Because the *Leong* ruling on the relationship element is concerned with the quality of relationship between plaintiff and victim, Ms. Queue may be able to establish a sufficient relationship with Stephanie, although because Ms. Queue did not live with Stephanie, it was less foreseeable that Ms. Queue would experience emotional distress upon witnessing Stephanie's death.

Most likely, Ms. Queue, even under this liberalized ruling, would still be unable to recover damages, because she did not live with Stephanie. Additionally, no tradition of close relationships between a woman and her fiancé's children, like the Hawaiian tradition of adoption, is operating that could substitute for blood ties and therefore enhance foreseeability. Even under the *Leong* ruling, Ms. Queue could probably not establish a sufficiently close relationship with Stephanie.

At first blush, it appears that, because Stephanie planned on living with Ms. Queue, and Ms. Queue held herself out as Stephanie's stepmother, Ms. Queue's relationship with Stephanie satisfies the "close attachment" criterion set forth in the *Champion* foreseeability rule. However, under the *Ferretti* ruling, which required plaintiff and victim to be bound by family ties to satisfy the relationship requirement of *Champion*, Ms. Queue's relationship with Stephanie would fail, because they were not legally related. Although *Ferretti* was decided at the district court level in Florida and, additionally, is not binding on Ms. Queue's jurisdiction (the fifth district), the *Ferretti* decision is compelling. California, which is a leading jurisdiction for negligent infliction of emotional distress cases, also decided an analogous case similarly at the supreme court level in *Elden v. Shelden*. While none of the cases addressed the problem that arises when the plaintiff holds him or herself out as being related to the victim, policy considerations, such as those noted in *Elden*, could also work against Ms. Queue's case. These policy considerations, such as the state's interest in marital relationships, its unwillingness to intrude in plaintiffs' personal lives to assess the sufficiency of their relationships, and its interest in limiting claims, all suggest that, if these considerations are applicable in Florida, Ms. Queue could probably not expect to establish that, because she held herself out to be Stephanie's stepmother, she meets the requirement of sufficient relationship. Even where neither blood relationship nor close consanguinal bonds are necessary to establish relationship sufficiency, as in *Leong*, Ms. Queue could probably still not demonstrate a sufficient relationship to Stephanie, because she cannot rely on strong cultural traditions to establish a close enough relationship to enhance foreseeability. Therefore, Ms. Queue probably could not show a sufficient relationship between herself and Stephanie to meet the Florida relationship requirement for cases of negligent infliction of mental distress.

Conclusion

1. The plaintiff probably doesn't satisfy the requirement of direct involvement for negligent infliction of emotional distress. Presence at the scene fairly contemporaneously with the accident as well as sensory perception of the accident are necessary elements in determining plaintiff's involvement. Additionally, some courts have ruled that plaintiff must also establish complete awareness of victim's involvement in the accident. In the instant case, Ms. Queue was not certain that Stephanie was involved in the fire until the next morning, when Stephanie's body was discovered. Therefore, Ms. Queue's presence at the accident scene would probably be insufficient to establish direct involvement.

2. The plaintiff does not satisfy the relationship requirement for negligent infliction of emotional distress under Florida common law. While Florida law requires a close emotional attachment between victim and plaintiff, Florida and other courts have interpreted the requirement to encompass only legal familial relationships. Some courts have required that plaintiff and victim must not only be related but also living together. Although Ms. Queue had a close relationship with Stephanie, their relationship was not familial, and they were not living together. Therefore, the emotional attachment between Ms. Queue and Stephanie would probably not be sufficient to satisfy the relationship requirement.

THE END?

Writing the memo may mean the end of your legal work, in which case, congratulations! You can pat yourself on the back for a job well done, and use your newfound knowledge as you wish. You may be considering hiring a lawyer or mediator to pursue your interests, or perhaps you've decided not to pursue the case. Either way, you learned firsthand about the law, and perhaps demystified it somewhat. Additionally, it must be comforting to realize that you can always pursue other areas of legal research should the need arise.

You may even have decided to do further research on the practical side of filing, pleading, and arguing a lawsuit. Indeed, in small claims court, you may have a significant edge on your opponent after having researched the law so intensively.

The practical steps involved in bringing a lawsuit are beyond the scope of this book. But if you're interested in doing so, the next chapter can provide a little insight on how to find some of the forms, books, trial guides, and civil and criminal procedural rules that would govern your case.

Additionally, the next chapter will help you if you want to find standard will forms, lease forms, incorporation forms, partnership agreements, and other such practical forms.

CHAPTER HIGHLIGHTS

Materials needed to write a legal memo

- Notes from your readings of the case
- A copy of any statutes which apply to your facts
- Possibly, copies of some of the very relevant and on-point cases
- Objectivity

Writing the legal memo: Recite the facts of your case in one paragraph

Writing the legal memo: State the issues

Writing the legal memo: Discuss the law as applied to your facts

- Address each issue, one at a time from start to finish before turning to another
- Evaluate the conflicting cases, keeping in mind the following factors

  - Jurisdiction of the court
  - Rank of the court
  - Age of the case
  - Similarity of its facts to your facts
  - Whether the court's discussion is dicta or holding

- Write a summary of the relevant cases you found, comparing and contrasting the cases to your own facts

Writing the legal memo: Draw conclusions from the data

- Sum up what all of the cases, taken together and weighed according to their impact on cases in your jurisdiction, tell you about the fate of your own case
- Before writing the conclusion, take a day away from your work if necessary, in order to view your case from a fresher perspective.

CHAPTER 10

PRACTICE FORMS, TRANSACTION FORMS, AND PRACTICE REFERENCES

Every citizen is entitled to resort to all the courts of the country, and to invoke the protection which all the laws or all those courts may afford him.

—*Ward Hunt (1874)*

WHAT NEXT?

Finding out the legal ramifications of a dispute you're involved in would be worthless without the possibility of action to redress the problem. For any legal wrong you suffer, the law tries to provide a legal remedy by which to set the problem straight. Many plaintiffs pursue that remedy in the courts, though if you wish to do so yourself, without the help of a lawyer, you'll have to look beyond the bounds of this book and consult some sort of practice manual.

Beyond actions in court, parties to legal disputes are increasingly turning to mediation or arbitration to settle their differences with others. The advantages of alternative dispute resolution (alternative to pressing a claim in the courts, that is) is that it is not necessarily as procedurally demanding as court practice, and the process is supposed to be more informal.

Helpful Hint

If you've decided to hire a lawyer, a good reference to help you find one is the *Martindale–Hubbell Law Directory*. It lists law firms and practitioners by geographical area and describes what kind of practice the firms engage in. Your law library should have copies of the multivolume set, or you can check with your local public library.

Back in Chapter 4, we first mentioned form books and practice references, but suggested that you set them aside until you knew more about how the courts went about analyzing legal issues. Now that you've gained a certain familiarity with your legal topic, these references will make more sense to you, which means that searching through them won't be nearly as hard as your search of the encyclopedias.

Whether you want to find practice forms (which we define here to include standard forms for papers and motions filed in court), transactional forms (by which we mean forms that one might use to draw up a legally binding [and correct!] documents like incorporation forms, wills, or leases), or practice references (which include books that show you how to bring a case in court and when and how to file the appropriate papers), the search method is the same. To find form books and practice references, you'll use three methods:

- Use the form book cites and practice reference cites that you might have jotted down from your encyclopedia searches, and look up the references;
- use the encyclopedia search method of searching the indexes with your keywords. (If you need to refresh your memory regarding how to carry out a search, see Chapter 4, which explains how to carry out an encyclopedia search); and/or
- use the indexes at the back of the individual volumes if the particular resource has no separate index volume. In this case, if the resource is a multivolume work, try to scan the titles of the articles, usually listed in the front of each volume, to find the likeliest bet, then find the appropriate volume, and check the index for that title.

In the next section, we'll give you a partial list of various volumes that you might find useful for your research. Locate your state under each of the three headings—practice forms, transactional forms, and practice references—to see some of the titles that are out there. Practice forms books will be most helpful to those who want to bring a claim in court; they contain forms for complaints, defenses, motions, answers, and amendments to complaints or answers. Transactional forms books will be most helpful to those who want to write a will, a lease, a partnership agreement, an incorporation form, a standard sales contract, a real estate sales contract, or a trust agreement. Finally, practice reference books explain to the reader how various claims are filed, how claims are answered, when motions are made, and how much time is available to do any of the preceding. Other practice references are actually manuals designed to show legal practitioners the ins and outs of practicing in certain areas of the law (but why can't you learn those ins and outs too?). Although similar to the legal encyclopedias in providing some background in a legal area, practice references are a more practical application of the law to actual practice in a specific area.

PRACTICE FORMS, TRANSACTION FORMS, AND PRACTICE REFERENCES—LISTS

Practice forms

Federal and generic state
American Jurisprudence, Pleading and Practice 2d (Lawyers Coop)
Federal Procedural Forms, L. Ed. (Lawyers Coop)
West's Federal Forms (West)
West's Legal Forms (West)

California
California Practice with Forms (Bancroft-Whitney/Lawyers Coop)
California's Forms of Pleading and Practice (Matthew Bender)

Florida
Bender's Florida Forms-Pleadings (Matthew Bender)
Florida Civil Procedure Forms (West)
Florida Creditors' Remedies and Debtors' Rights (West)
Florida Criminal Procedure (Lawyers Coop)
Florida Jurisprudence Pleading and Practice Forms (Lawyers Coop)
West's Florida Legal Forms (West)

Illinois
Callaghan's Illinois Civil Practice Forms (Lawyers Coop)
Horner Probate Practices and Estates (Lawyers Coop)
Nichols Illinois Civil Practice with Forms (Lawyers Coop)

Indiana
Indiana Forms of Pleading and Practice (Matthew Bender)

Iowa
Iowa Practice (West)

Kentucky
Kentucky Practice (Banks-Baldwin)
Kentucky Practice (West)

Massachusetts
Massachusetts Pleading and Practice, Forms and Commentary (Matthew-Bender)
Massachusetts Practice (West)

Michigan
Michigan Court Rules Practices (West)
Michigan Pleading and Practice (Lawyers Coop)
Michigan Practice (West)
Michigan State Court Administrative Office Approved Forms (West)
Michigan's Criminal Law and Procedure with Forms (Lawyers Coop)

Minnesota
Minnesota Practice (West)

Missouri
Missouri Practice (West)
Missouri Probate Forms Manual (West)
Missouri Probate Law and Practice (West)
Missouri Procedural Forms (West)

New Jersey
New Jersey Criminal Procedure (Bancroft-Whitney/Lawyers Coop)
New Jersey Practice (West)

New York
Bender's Forms for the Civil Practice (NY) (Matthew Bender)
Bender's Forms for the Consolidated Laws of New York (Matthew Bender)
Bender's Forms of Pleading (NY) (Matthew Bender)
Carmody–Wait 2d (Lawyers Coop)
McKinney's Forms (West)
New York Civil Practice (Matthew Bender)

Ohio
Couse's Ohio Form Book (Anderson Publishing Co.)
Ohio Civil Practice (Banks-Baldwin/West)
Ohio Civil Rules Practice with Forms (Anderson Publishing Co.)
Ohio Criminal Law (Banks-Baldwin/West)
Ohio Forms of Pleading and Practice (Matthew Bender)
Ohio Probate Law (Banks-Baldwin/West)
West's Ohio Practice (West)

Oklahoma
Oklahoma Probate Law and Practice with Forms (West)
Vernon's Oklahoma Forms (West)

Pennsylvania
Anderson Pennsylvania Civil Practice (West)
Pennsylvania Forms (Matthew Bender)
Standard Pennsylvania Practice (Lawyers Coop)

Tennessee
Tennessee Practice (West)

Texas
Texas Criminal Practice Guide (Matthew Bender)
Texas Family Law with Forms (Bancroft-Whitney/Lawyers Coop)
Texas Jurisprudence Pleading & Practice Forms 2d (Bancroft-Whitney/Lawyers Coop)
Texas Litigation Guide (Matthew Bender)
Texas Practice (West)

Washington
Washington Practice (West)

Wisconsin
Callaghan's Wisconsin Pleading and Practice (Lawyers Coop)
Wisconsin Civil Practice Forms (Lawyers Coop)
Wisconsin Practice (West)

Transactional forms

Federal and general state forms
American Jurisprudence Legal Forms (Lawyers Coop)
Current Legal Forms with Tax Analysis (Matthew Bender)
Nichols Cyclopedia of Legal Forms Annotated and Tax Notes (Clark Boardman Callaghan)
West's Legal Forms (West)

California
California Forms—Legal and Business (Bancroft-Whitney)

Colorado
Colorado Corporate Forms, Legal and Business Series (Lawyers Coop)

Florida
Florida Business Organizations (West)
Florida Creditors' Remedies and Debtors' Rights (West)
Florida Jurisprudence Forms—Legal and Business (Lawyers Coop)
Florida Real Estate (Lawyers Coop)

Illinois
Horner Probate Practice and Estates (Lawyers Coop)
Illinois Forms, Legal and Business (Lawyers Coop)

Indiana
Indiana Practice—Legal and Business Forms (Lawyers Coop)
Indiana Practice—Uniform Commercial Code Forms (West)

Iowa
Iowa Practice (West)

Massachusetts
Massachusetts Practice (West)

Michigan
Michigan Practice (West)

Missouri
Missouri Legal Forms (West)
Missouri Practice (West)

Nebraska
Nebraska Practice, Uniform Commercial Code Forms (West)

New Jersey
New Jersey Forms—Legal and Business (Lawyers Coop)
New Jersey Law with Forms (Matthew Bender)
New Jersey Practice (West)

New York
Criminal Law of New York (Bancroft-Whitney/Lawyers Coop)
McKinney's Forms (West)
New York Forms—Legal and Business (Lawyers Coop)
Stocker on Drawing Wills (Practicing Law Institute)

Ohio
Couse's Ohio Form Book (Anderson Publishing Co.)
Ohio Forms—Legal and Business (Lawyers Coop)
Ohio Probate Law (Banks-Baldwin/West)

Oklahoma
Oklahoma Probate Law and Practice with Forms (West)
Vernon's Oklahoma Forms (West)

Pennsylvania
Pennsylvania Forms (Matthew Bender)
Standard Pennsylvania Practice 2d (Lawyers Coop)

Tennessee
Tennessee Practice (West)

Texas
Texas Forms—Legal and Business (Bancroft-Whitney/Lawyers Coop)
Texas Practice (West)

Practice references

The American Bar Association (ABA) and most state bar associations offer continuing legal education (CLE) publications that can be ordered by their members and the public. These publications include in-depth technical information regarding the legal fields that they cover, though they are usually somewhat expensive. However, CLE information published by local bars contain helpful information regarding state or local laws. Additionally, they may include special practice rules applicable in your particular jurisdiction.

Federal and generic state references
American Jurisprudence, Pleading and Practice (Lawyers Coop)
American Jurisprudence, Proof of Facts (Lawyers Coop)
American Jurisprudence, Trials (Lawyers Coop)
Defense of Drunk Driving Cases (Matthew Bender)
Federal Procedure, L. Ed. (Lawyers Coop)
Handling Accident Cases (Matthew Bender)
Immigration and Procedure Law (Matthew Bender)
Prosecution and Defense of Criminal Conspiracy Cases (Matthew Bender)
Trademark Registration Practice (Clark Boardman Callaghan)
Wright and Miller on Federal Procedure (West)

Arizona
Arizona Probate (Bancroft-Whitney/Lawyers Coop)

California
California Deposition and Discovery Practice (Matthew Bender)

Colorado
Colorado Methods of Practice (West)

Connecticut
Connecticut Estates Practice (Lawyers Coop)
Connecticut Practice (West)

Florida
Florida Creditors' Remedies and Debtors' Rights (West)
Florida Criminal Practice and Procedure (West)
Florida Corporations (Lawyers Coop)
Florida Estates Practice Guide (Matthew Bender)
Florida Lawyer's Guide (Lawyers Coop)
Trial Handbook for Florida Lawyers 3d ed. (Lawyers Coop)
Wills and Administration in Florida (The Harrison Co.)

Georgia
Georgia Divorce (Lawyers Coop)
Georgia Probate (Lawyers Coop)

Illinois
Callaghan's Illinois Civil Practice Forms (Lawyers Coop)
Illinois Law and Practice Encyclopedia (West)
Illinois Tort Law and Practice (Lawyers Coop)

Indiana
Indiana Practice (West)
Indiana Practice—Uniform Commercial Code Forms (West)

Iowa
Iowa Practice (West)

Kentucky
Kentucky Practice (Banks-Baldwin)
Kentucky Practice (West)
Kentucky Probate (Lawyers Coop)

Massachusetts
Massachusetts Corporations
(Bancroft-Whitney/Lawyers Coop)
Massachusetts Practice (West)
Settlement of Estates and Fiduciary Law in Massachusetts
(Bancroft-Whitney/Lawyers Coop)

Michigan
Hackett's Evidence, Michigan and Federal (Lawyers Coop)
Michigan Court Rules Practice (West)
Michigan Divorce (Bancroft-Whitney/Lawyers Coop)
Michigan Lawyer's Manual (Lawyers Coop)
Michigan Pleading and Practice (Lawyers Coop)
Michigan Practice (West)
Michigan Probate (Lawyers Coop)
Michigan's Criminal Law and Procedure with Forms (Lawyers Coop)
Trial Handbook for Michigan Lawyers (Lawyers Coop)

Minnesota
Minnesota Dissolution (Bancroft-Whitney/Lawyers Coop)
Minnesota Practice (West)
Minnesota Probate (Bancroft-Whitney/Lawyers Coop)

Missouri
Missouri Criminal Practice and Procedure (West)
Missouri Practice (West)
Missouri Probate Law and Practice (West)

New Jersey
New Jersey Practice (West)

New York
Law and the Family—New York (Bancroft-Whitney/Lawyers Coop)
New York Civil Practice (Matthew Bender)
New York Elder Law Handbook (Practicing Law Institute)
New York Estates Practice Guide (Bancroft-Whitney/Lawyers Coop)
New York Law and Practice of Real Property (Bancroft-Whitney/Lawyers Coop)
New York Zoning Law and Practice (Lawyers Coop)
Stocker on Drawing Wills (Practicing Law Institute)
Warren's Weed New York Real Property (Matthew Bender)

Ohio
Ohio Civil Practice (Banks-Baldwin/West)
Ohio Civil Rules Practice with Forms (Anderson Publishing Co.)

Ohio Corporations (Bancroft-Whitney/Lawyers Coop)
Ohio Criminal Law (Banks-Baldwin/West)
Ohio Probate (Bancroft-Whitney/Lawyers Coop)
Ohio Probate Law (Banks-Baldwin/West)
Ohio Real Estate (Bancroft-Whitney/Lawyers Coop)
West's Ohio Practice (West)

Oklahoma
Vernon's Oklahoma Forms (West)

Pennsylvania
Anderson Pennsylvania Civil Practice (West)
Law of Vehicle Negligence in Pennsylvania (George T. Bisel Co.)
Pennsylvania Civil Practice (The Michie Co.)
Pennsylvania Civil Practice Handbook (George T. Bisel Co.)
Pennsylvania Estates Practice (Bancroft-Whitney/Lawyers Coop)
Pennsylvania Zoning Law and Practice (George T. Bisel Co.)
Standard Pennsylvania Practice (Lawyers Coop)

Tennessee
Tennessee Corporations (Bancroft-Whitney/Lawyers Coop)
Tennessee Practice (West)
Tennessee Probate (Bancroft-Whitney/Lawyers Coop)

Texas
McDonald Texas Civil Practice (Bancroft-Whitney)
Texas Criminal Practice Guide (Matthew Bender)
Texas Family Law with Forms (Bancroft-Whitney/Lawyers Coop)
Texas Lawyer's Guide (Lawyers Coop)
Texas Practice (West)
Texas Trial Handbook (Lawyers Coop)

Virginia
The Virginia Lawyer (The Michie Co.)

Washington
Washington Practice (West)

Wisconsin
Callaghan's Wisconsin Pleading and Practice (Lawyers Coop)
Wisconsin Corporations (Bancroft-Whitney/Lawyers Coop)
Wisconsin Divorce (Bancroft-Whitney/Lawyers Coop)
Wisconsin Practice (West)
Wisconsin Probate Law (Lawyers Coop)
Wisconsin Probate Law and Practice (Lawyers Coop)
Trial Handbook for Wisconsin Lawyers (Lawyers Coop)

Treatises

In addition to practice forms, transactional forms, and practice references, there are state and national treatises covering just about every area of substantive and procedural law. A treatise is a scholarly work, usually by a respected law professor or an expert in the field, that covers a specific area of the law, either in one volume or in several. Most treatises deal with a legal topic starting from a very basic level and then gradually moving to a more sophisticated and detailed treatment.

These can be excellent resources for someone who is not overly familiar with an area of law, because treatises usually attempt to explain every facet of a particular legal area without taking the reader's knowledge of the subject for granted.

Examples of legal treatises include *Corbin on Contracts*, *Collier on Bankruptcy*, *Powell on Real Property*, *Page on Wills*, and *Couch on Insurance* (note the emphasis on the author). Although the treatises just mentioned are intended for a national audience, other treatises are state specific. Chances are, you'll run across some references to treatises in your research, even if you aren't specifically looking for them. If you feel there's a gap in your research (or a gap in your understanding of your legal area), looking at a treatise can be helpful.

Guides for laypeople

Most state bar associations and even some local bar associations publish legal guides for the public, with topics ranging from how to select a lawyer to the basics on family law. These guides (or pamphlets) are either free or available for nominal fees. To receive a list of these guides from your local or state bar association, check your telephone book under your state, county, or city bar association (or ask a librarian at your local public library where you can find the number) and give the association a call.

Finally, don't forget that there are plenty of legal guides published for laypeople, including how to buy real estate without a lawyer, get divorced without legal representation, represent yourself in small claims court, form corporations, or write a will. Below is a small sample of some of the guides available. We haven't evaluated the following list for usefulness or thoroughness, so be sure to check any publication before you buy it. Because the quality among these volumes may vary, take the time to read their tables of contents and look over their chapters. Does the book include the features you want—for example, forms, legal overviews, practical suggestions, and procedural information—all in an easy-to-read straightforward manner?

ABA Family Legal Guide (Times Books)
ABA Guide to Family Law (Times Books)
ABA Guide to Wills and Estates (Times Books)
Complete Estate Planning Guide, The (Mentor)
Complete Idiot's Protecting Yourself from Everyday Legal Hassles, The (Alpha Books)
Complete Probate Kit, The (John Wiley & Sons, Inc.)
Complete Will Kit, The (John Wiley & Sons, Inc.)
Consumer's Guide to Today's Health Care, The (Houghton Mifflin Co.)
Court TV Cradle-to-Grave Legal Survival Guide, The (American Lawyer/Little, Brown, and Co.)
Divorce Handbook, The (Random House)
Divorce Sourcebook, The (Lowell House)
Elder Law Handbook, The (Facts on File)
Employment Law (E-Z Legal Books)
Everybody's Guide to the Law (Harper & Row)
Everybody's Guide to Small Claims Court (Nolo Press)
E-Z Legal Advisor (E-Z Legal Books)
Family Legal Companion, The (Allworth Press)
Guide to Divorce Mediation, A (Workman Publishing)
Handbook of Everyday Law (Fawcett Crest)
Homeowner's Legal Guide (Consumer Reports Books)
How and When to Be Your Own Lawyer (Avery Publishing Group)
How to Avoid Probate (HarperPerennial)
How to Collect Your Child Support (Adams Publishing)
How to Mediate Your Dispute (Nolo Press)

How to Settle Your Own Personal Injury Case (Citadel Press)
Keys to Understanding Bankruptcy (Barron's Educational Series, Inc.)
Law for Dummies (IDG Books)
Legal Ease: Bankruptcy Step-by-Step (Barron's Educational Series, Inc.)
Legal Ease: Corporations Step-by-Step (Barron's Educational Series, Inc.)
Legal Ease: Estate Planning Step-by-Step (Barron's Educational Series, Inc.)
Legal Guide for Lesbian and Gay Couples, A (Nolo Press)
Legal Rights: The Guide for Deaf and Hard of Hearing People (Gallaudet University Press)
Legal-Wise: Self-Help Legal Forms for Everyone (Allworth Press)
Living Together Kit, The (Nolo Press)
Neighbor Law (Nolo Press)
Netlaw: Your Rights in the Online World (McGraw-Hill)
Patent It Yourself (Nolo Press)
Renter's Survival Kit, The (Dearborn Financial Publishing)
Represent Yourself (Plume)
Retirement Rights (Avon)
Rights of Crime Victims, The (Bantam Books)
Rights of Prisoners, The (Bantam Books)
Rights of Teachers, The (Bantam Books)
Small Claims Court (E-Z Legal Books)
Women's Legal Guide (Fulcrum Publishing)
Writer's Legal Companion, The (Addison Wesley)

For a longer list of legal resources for laypeople, see *Law for the Layman: Annotated Bibliography of Self-Help Law Books* (Fred B. Rothman & Co.), which allows you to search for books by state, title, author, publisher, and topic.

Look for any of the above books at your local public library or bookstore. Although you should also check your law library, a public library might be more apt to carry these publications, because law libraries tend to cater to lawyers while public libraries are more oriented to the general public and laypeople's interests. At any rate, if you discover that you can't find these books at any of the above three sources, try ordering directly from the publisher.

HOW TO TACKLE FORMS AND PRACTICE REFERENCES

Finding forms is similar to finding articles in an encyclopedia or jurisprudence, except that with finding forms you have the advantage of already having some leads based on the previous research you've done (see What Next?, pages 233–235) regarding how to search for and find forms).

Which form books should you try first—state or federal? Unlike your background research, where you started with a national encyclopedia and then moved on to the state jurisprudence, you'll want to try the state form books first. This is because specialized state forms will be tailored to your state laws, and even some federal forms may be included in the state form book. If you do find federal forms in a state resource, this is probably because the state has developed its own idiosyncratic approach to federal claims, and the forms book will reflect this.

Hopefully, you're lucky enough to live in a state that has state form volumes. But if you're not, stationery stores usually carry at least some state legal forms, like wills and standard leases. If necessary, call them and check.

Meanwhile, if you have some forms references already jotted down from your background research stage, just find the corresponding volume and look at the form to see if it's relevant. If the form isn't useful, check the contents for the article to see if there might be other forms that are pertinent to your needs.

> **Helpful Hint**
>
> Cites for form books are in the same style as case cites—the number that comes before the reference's abbreviation is the volume number and the number which comes after the abbreviation is the page number.

A SAMPLE CASE

Halle and Thomas, who both live in Illinois, have decided to enter into a partnership agreement for a catering business. Although they considered hiring a lawyer to draft the partnership agreement, they recently heard from their friend, Liliana (who embarked on a film production partnership last year) that writing one's own partnership agreement is not difficult. Halle and Thomas, who readily admit that they know nothing about business but everything about gift from a spouse or other relative. However, the share of partnership profits allocable to a capital interest acquired by gift is subject to special limitations.[21] Purchase of a capital interest from a member of the buyer's family is treated as a gift under the rules applicable to partnerships in which capital is a material income-producing factor. For this purpose, "family" includes spouses, ancestors, and lineal descendants and trusts for the primary benefit of such persons.[22]

Where capital is not a material income-producing factor, the Internal Revenue Code is silent on the effect of a gift of a partnership interest. Where the partners are related, the IRS will look closely at a personal service partnership, especially where a partnership interest was acquired by gift from a member of the same family. If the donee partner contributes little or no services to the enterprise, the donee's share of the profits may be taxed to the donor. However, if the donee partner is a bona fide partner in the conduct of the business, either because of services to be performed, or because of contributions of capital of which he or she is the true owner, then the donee's share of the profits will not be taxed to the donor.[23]

B. FORMS

§ 30:131 Professional or personal service partnership agreement

PARTNERSHIP AGREEMENT

The parties to this agreement, __1______, of __2______, *[address]*, __3______, of __4______, *[address]*, and __5______,

21. *26 USCS 704(e)(1).*

22. *26 USCS 704(e).*

23. *Commissioner v Culbertson 337 US 733, 93 L Ed 1659, 69 S Ct 1210, on remand Culbertson v Commissioner 9 TCM 647, revd Culbertson v Commissioner (CA5) 194 F2d 581; Stanton 14 TC 217 affd (CA7) 189 F2d 297.*

(For Tax Notes and Practice Notes, see end of form)

Figure 36

of __6______, *[address],* agree to form a partnership on the following terms and conditions.

I. NAME OF PARTNERSHIP

The name of the partnership shall be __7______. The use of the partnership name is subject to the provisions of Article XV(g).

II. PURPOSE

The purpose of the partnership shall be to __8______ [practice the profession of __9______ *or* perform the services of __10______] and to do all other acts incidental thereto pursuant to the laws of the State of Illinois __11______ *[if appropriate add:* and the rules and regulations of __12______ *(regulating authority, such as:* the Illinois State Bar Association

III. LOCATION OF OFFICES

The offices of the partnership shall be at __13______, City of __14______, State of Illinois. Such office location may be changed, and additional offices may be established by the agreement of the partners.

IV. DURATION

The partnership __15______ [commenced *or* shall commence] as of __16______, 19_17_, and shall continue until it is dissolved as provided in Articles XV, XVI, or XVII, or liquidated as provided in Article XVIII, of this partnership agreement.

V. CAPITAL

(a) Partnership Capital. The initial capital of the partnership shall consist of the sum of __18______ Dollars ($____).

(b) Initial Contributions. The initial contributions of each partner shall be as follows:

(1) __19______ *[Name]:* __20______ *[contribution—if cash,*

(For Tax Notes and Practice Notes, see end of form)

Figure 36 *(continued)*

cooking, would like to have their partnership agreement firmly in place before the holiday catering season begins. Where do they look?

Because Halle and Thomas are looking for a form that has nothing to do with bringing a claim in court, they would look under the transactional forms list to see whether their state has any relevant material. If they can't find a state-specific (Illinois, in this case) form book, they'll settle on finding a national form book.

Luckily for them, Halle and Thomas located a transactional form book, *Illinois Forms, Legal and Business*, which sounds like it may fit their needs. Thomas, unable to find a separate index volume (you've already learned how to search a general index from your encyclopedia search anyway), searches the list of titles found at the beginning of each of the form volumes, to find a title that might include forms relating to partnership issues. First, he looks for "Partnerships" and is unsuccessful. Next, he tries "Businesses" and similarly has no luck. But Halle spots the article "Business Enterprises," which seems like it might be helpful. She finds one of the volumes that contains the article "Business Enterprises" and looks up "Partnership" in the index. In short order, she is led to the partnership sections that are reproduced above.

The first section to which she's led, while not the form she's looking for, discusses some general principles of drafting partnership agreements. The partnership form itself appears a few sections further into the text, after the authors have pointed out some concerns which a drafter should keep in mind when writing the agreement.

CONCLUSION

We're glad that you were persistent enough to reach this point. Even if you're still unsure of some of the aspects of your issue (and you rarely can be certain of the conclusions you've drawn without actually trying your case out in court), realize that, if it's important to you, you can continue your research further and clarify any points of confusion as long as you're willing to persevere. Moreover, if you should ever decide to do your own legal research again (hard to think about just now, we realize), the skills you learned from this first effort will make your next somewhat faster and slightly easier. After all, demystifying one legal issue, which is quite an accomplishment, means that you're capable of demystifying others as well.

CHAPTER HIGHLIGHTS

Decide whether to pursue your case or whether to continue working without a lawyer

- Use your legal memo to evaluate your case
- Decide whether to prepare legal documents without a lawyer's advice

Decide which resources you need

- Practice forms books contain standardized forms for papers that are filed in court and other papers that may be needed for a court case
- Transactional forms books contain standardized forms for papers that are often used by nonlawyers for their everyday business and nonbusiness needs; examples include wills, incorporation forms, partnership agreements, trust agreements, and leases
- Practice references are used by lawyers as handbooks in specific areas of practice and provide important background material regarding how to practice in a legal area

Locate references

- Check the practice forms list in this chapter and/or your law library for relevant sources
- Check the transactional forms list in this chapter, your law library, and even a stationery store for relevant sources
- Check the practice references list in this chapter and/or your law library for relevant sources
- Locate any lay guides in your legal area of interest, using the list in this chapter and checking bookstores and libraries

Search method

- Start your forms search and practice references search with state form books, rather than national or federal forms books
- Move to national or federal practice references if you want to supplement your forms or if you are unable to find state-specific sources
- Use the keywords you used in Chapter 4 to search the references' indexes

APPENDIX 1

DEFINITIONS FROM *BARRON'S LAW DICTIONARY*

Administrative law: law created by administrative agencies by way of rules, regulations, orders, and decisions.

Affirm: the assertion of an appellate court that the judgment of the court below is correct and should stand.

Amend: to alter; to improve upon. Thus, one amends a bill by altering or changing an established law—the law is continued in changed form. One amends a pleading by making an addition to or subtraction from an already existing pleading.

Appeal: a resort to a higher court for the purpose of obtaining a review of a lower court decision and a reversal of the lower court decision and a reversal of the lower court's judgment or the granting of a new trial... . Although the term is now used generally to denote all forms of review, in determining its more specialized meaning "it is necessary in each instance to look to (the) particular act giving an appeal, to determine powers to be exercised by (the) appellate court." 104 A. 617, 620.

Appellant: the party who appeals a decision; the party who brings the proceeding to a reviewing court; at common law, the plaintiff in error.

Bill: a proposition or statement reduced to writing. In commercial law, an "account for goods sold, services rendered and work done," 11 Cal. Rptr., 893, 897; in the law of negotiable instruments, bills are "all forms of paper money," 127 S.W. 961, 962; a single bond without condition, 36 U.S. 257, 328; an order drawn by one person on another to pay a certain sum of money absolutely and in all events. 61 N.Y. 251, 255.

In legislation, a draft of a proposed statute submitted to the legislature for enactment. 226 F. 135, 137.

In equity pleadings, the name by which the complainant sets out his cause of action.

Case: an action, cause, suit, or controversy, at law or in equity, see 220 S.W.2d 45, 51.

Certiorari: Latin: to be informed of a means of gaining appellate review; a common-law writ, issued from a superior court to one of inferior jurisdiction, commanding the latter to certify and return to the former the record in a particular case. 6 Cyc. 737. The writ is issued in order that the court issuing the writ may inspect the proceedings and determine whether there have been any irregularities. In the U.S. Supreme Court, the writ is discretionary with the Court and will be issued to any court in the land to review a federal question if at least 4 of the 9 justices vote to hear the case. A similar writ used by some state courts is called certification.

Civil law: Roman law embodied in the Justinian Code (Codex Justianeus) and presently prevailing in most Western European States. It is also the foundation of the law of Louisiana. The term may also be used to distinguish that part of the law concerned with noncriminal matters, or may refer to the body of laws prescribed by the supreme authority of the state, as opposed to natural law.

Common law: the system of jurisprudence, which originated in England and was later applied in the United States, is based on judicial precedent rather than statutory laws, which are legislative enactments; it is to be contrasted with civil law (the descendent of Roman Law prevalent in other western countries). Originally based on the unwritten laws of England, the common law is "generally derived from principles rather than rules; it does not consist of absolute, fixed and inflexible rules, but rather of broad and comprehensive principles based on justice, reason, and common sense. It is of judicial origin and promulgation. Its principles have been determined by the social needs of the community and have changed with changes in such needs. These principles are susceptible of adaptation to new conditions, interests, relations, and usages as the progress of society may require." 37 N.W. 2d 543, 547.

Concurrent jurisdiction: equal jurisdiction; that jurisdiction exercised by different courts at the same time, over the same subject matter and within the same territory, and wherein litigants may, in the first instance, resort to either court indifferently. 242 Ill. App. 139.

Constitution: the organic law framing a governmental system; the original and fundamental principles of law by which a system of government is created and according to which a country is governed. A constitution represents a mandate to the various branches of government directly from the people acting in their sovereign capacity. It is distinguished from a law which is a rule of conduct prescribed by legislative agents of the people and subject to the limitations of the constitution. In American law, the word Constitution specifically refers to a written instrument which is the basic source from which government derives its power, but under which governmental powers are both conferred and circumscribed... . Like the federal Constitution, a state constitution is the supreme law within the state. 140 F. Supp. 925, 928.

Damages: monetary compensation that the law awards to one who has been injured by the action of another; recompense for a legal wrong such as a breach of contract or a tortious act.

Defendant: in civil proceedings, the party responding to the complaint; "one who is sued and called upon to make satisfaction for a wrong complained of by another, [the plaintiff]." 203 S.W.2d 548, 552. In criminal proceedings, also called the accused.

Dictum: (plural: dicta) a statement, remark, or observation in a judicial opinion not necessary for the decision of the case. Dictum differs from the holding in that it is not binding on the courts in subsequent cases. *See* 14 Ohio N.P., N.S. 97.

Due Process of Law: a phrase that was first expressly introduced into American jurisprudence in the Fifth Amendment to the Constitution, which provides that "nor [shall any person] be deprived of life, liberty, or property, without due process of law." This provision is applicable only to the actions of the federal government. 7 Pet. 243 (1833). The phrase was made applicable to the states with the adoption of the Fourteenth Amendment, Section 1, which states that "Nor shall any State deprive any person of life, liberty or property, without due process of law." The phrase does not have a fixed meaning but expands with jurisprudential attitudes of fundamental fairness. 302 U.S. 319. The legal substance of the phrase is divided into the areas of substantive due process and procedural due process. The constitutional safeguard of substantive due process requires that all legislation be in furtherance of a legitimate governmental objective... . The original content of the phrase was a procedural due process protection i.e., in guaranteeing procedural fairness where the government would deprive one of his property or liberty. This requires that notice and the right to a fair hearing be accorded prior to a deprivation. 237 U.S. 309. The enumeration of those procedures required by due process varies according to the factual context. The extent to which procedural due process must be afforded a person is influenced by the extent to which he may be "condemned to suffer grievous loss... and depends upon whether the [person's] interest in avoiding that loss outweighs the governmental interest in summary adjudication. ..." 397 U.S. 254, 262–263.

Et seq: Latin: the abbreviated form of et sequentes or et sequentia, which means "and the following." It is most commonly used in denominating page references and statutory section numbers.

Exhaustion of administrative remedies: the doctrine of all courts, adopted either as judicial policy or by statutory directive, that the courts will not interfere with or review an administrative decision or process until the available administrative channels of review have been attempted. 299 N.W.2d 259, 264. This requirement stems from the usual requirement that courts review only "final" administrative actions. The doctrine avoids piecemeal interruption of administrative processes, conserves scarce judicial resources, and ensures that the expertise of administrative agencies will be fully employed. In some extreme cases, where irreparable harm to public or private interests may be caused by honoring the doctrine, it will be held inapplicable.

First impression: first discussion or consideration; refers to the first time a question of law is considered for determination by a court. A case is one of "first impression" when it presents a question of law that was never before considered by any court, and thus is not influenced by the doctrine of stare decisis.

Habeas corpus: Latin: you have the body. The writ of habeas corpus, known as the great writ, has varied use in criminal and civil contexts. It is a procedure for obtaining a judicial determination of the legality of an individual's custody. Technically, it is used in the criminal law context to bring the petitioner before the court to inquire into the legality of his confinement. 488 F.2d 218, 221. ... The writ is used in the civil context to challenge the validity of child custody, deportations, and civil commitment to mental institutions.

Headnote: summary of an issue covered in a reported case; summaries of all the points discussed and issues decided in a case, which are placed at the beginning of a case report.

Holding: in procedure, any ruling of the court, including rulings upon the admissibility of evidence or other questions presented during trial, may be termed a *holding. See* 218 P.2d 888, 893.

Injunction: a judicial remedy awarded for the purpose of requiring a party to refrain from doing or continuing to do a particular act or activity. 104 A.2d 884. ... The injunction is a preventative measure that guards against future injuries rather than affording a remedy for past injuries.

Issue: in practice, an issue is a single, certain point of fact or law disputed between parties to the litigation, generally composed of an affirmative assertion by one side and a denial by the other. *See* 249 F. 285, 287.

Jurisdiction: the power to hear and determine a case. This power may be established and described with reference to particular subjects or to parties who fall into a particular category. ... Without jurisdiction, a court's judgment is void.

Key numbers: a numbering system used by West Publishing Company in their publications to break down legal research into manageable topic areas with subcategories. It is a quick and useful method of finding cases pertaining to a given subject.

Law: the legislative pronouncement of the rules that would guide one's actions in society; "the aggregate of those rules and principles of conduct promulgated by the legislative authority [court decisions], or established by local custom. Our laws are. ... derived from a combination of the divine or moral laws, the laws of nature, and human experience, as [each] . . . has been evolved by human intellect influenced by the virtues of the ages. Human laws must therefore of necessity continually change as human experience shall prove the necessity of new laws to meet new evils, or evils which have taken upon themselves new forms, or as the public conscience shall change, thus viewing matters from a different moral viewpoint."

Long arm statutes: statutes that allow local courts to obtain jurisdiction over nonresident defendants when the cause of action is generated locally and affects local plaintiffs. In *International Shoe Co. v. State of Washington*, 236 U.S. 310, 316, the Supreme Court authorized such expanded jurisdiction where "the contacts of the nonresident defendant with the forum are such that exercise of jurisdiction does not offend our traditional notions of fair play and substantial justice." Green, Basic Civil Procedure 37 (2d ed. 1979). Such statutes are commonly employed to allow a local court to exercise jurisdiction over nonresident motorists who cause automobile accidents within the state.

On all fours: an expression used to describe a case that is on point and therefore useful as precedent. It is derived from the Latin maxim *nullum simile est idem nisi quatour pedibus currit*, meaning: nothing similar is identical unless it runs on all four feet.

Ordinance: a local law that applies to persons and things subject to the local jurisdiction. See 90 F.2d 175, 177. It is used to mean an act of a city council or local governmental entity that has the same force and effect as a statute when it is duly enacted; it differs from a law in that laws are enacted by a state or federal legislature and ordinances are passed by a municipal legislative body. See 7 S.E.2d 896, 898. Ordinances are enacted to regulate zoning, highway speed, parking, refuse disposal, and other matters typically and traditionally of local concern. Some criminal violations (such as loitering) are based on ordinances rather than state penal law, though the more serious offenses are covered by state laws.

Overrule: to overturn or make void the holding of a prior case; occurs when a court in a different and subsequent case makes a decision on a point of law exactly opposite to the decision made in a prior case. A decision can only be overruled by the same court or a higher court within the same jurisdiction.

Plaintiff: the one who initially brings the suit; "he who, in a personal action, seeks a remedy in a court of justice for an injury to, or a withholding of, his rights." 147 F. 44, 46.

Precedent: a previously decided case that is recognized as authority for the disposition of future cases. At common law, precedents were regarded as the major source of law. A precedent may involve a novel question of common law or it may involve an interpretation of a statute. In either event, to the extent that future cases rely upon it or distinguish it from themselves without disapproving of it, the case will serve as a precedent for future cases under the doctrine of stare decisis.

Preemption: a judicial doctrine asserting the supremacy of federal legislation over state legislation of the same subject matter; it "rests upon the supremacy clause of the federal constitution, and deprives a state of jurisdiction over matters embraced by a congressional act regardless of whether the state law coincides with, is complimentary to, or opposes the federal congressional expression." When Congress legislates in an area of federal concern, it may specifically preempt all state legislation (thus, occupying the field), or may bar only inconsistent legislation; where Congress does not directly indicate its intention in this regard, the court will determine that intention based on the nature and legislative history of the enactment. State legislatures may also preempt local governments in the same way.

Procedure: legal method; the machinery for carrying on the suit, including pleading, process, evidence and practice. The term thus refers to the mechanics of the legal process—that is, the body of rules and practice by which justice is meted out by the legal system—rather than the substance and content of the law itself.

Pro se: Latin: in one's own behalf; for example, one appears pro se in a legal action when one represents oneself without the aid of an attorney.

Prosecutor: a person who prepares and conducts the prosecution of persons accused of crime. It is usually a public official, but in some instances involving minor offenses, it may be the complainant or a private attorney designated by the court to act on the complainant's behalf. In certain cases, the legislature may appoint a SPECIAL PROSECUTOR to conduct a limited investigation and prosecution. The state prosecutors are usually called district attorneys or county prosecutors. The federal prosecutor is known as the U.S. Attorney for a certain district.

The basic role of the public prosecutor is to seek justice and not convictions. His office is charged with the duty to see that the laws of his jurisdiction are faithfully executed and enforced. In the enforcement of laws, the prosecutor has broad discretion in deciding whom and when to prosecute.

The term also refers to the person who initiate the action by "prosecuting" the case.

Quash: to annul, overthrow, or vacate by judicial decision. 162 S.E. 1. Oppressive and unreasonable subpoenas, for instance, can be quashed, as can injunctions, orders, and so on.

Question of law: disputed legal contentions that are traditionally left for the judge to decide. The occurrence or non-occurrence of an event is a question of fact; its legal significance is a question of law.

The resolution of a question of law is paid less deference in an appeal than is a determination of fact. It must be noted that often the line between fact and law is impossible to objectively determine. In those situations, there may be a compound conclusion of law and fact.

Remand: to send back, as for further deliberation; to send back a matter to the tribunal [or body] from which it was appealed or moved. 155 N.W.2d 507, 511.

Remedy: "the means employed to enforce or redress an injury." 272 F. 538, 539. The most common remedy at law consists of money damages.

Repeal: abolish, rescind, annul by legislative act; "the abrogation or annulling of a previously existing law by the enactment of a subsequent statute, which either declares that the former law shall be revoked and abrogated or which contains provisions so contrary to or irreconcilable with those of the earlier law that only one of the two can stand in force; the latter is the 'implied' repeal . . . the former, the 'express' repeal." 139 S.W. 443, 445.

Reversal: as used in opinions, judgments, and mandates, the setting aside, annulling, vacating, or changing to the contrary the decision of a lower court or other body.

Sovereign immunity: a doctrine precluding the institution of a suit against the sovereign [government] without the sovereign's consent. ... The state may nevertheless be held liable where the injurious activity was "proprietary" rather than "governmental" i.e., where the injury was caused by the state acting in its capacity as a commercial entity rather than that of sovereign. This doctrine has been partially abrogated by judicial decisions, 115 N.W.2d 618, and by statutes often called tort claims acts.

Standing: the legal right of a person or group to challenge in a judicial forum the conduct of another, especially with respect to governmental conduct. In the federal system, litigants must satisfy constitutional standing requirements in order to create a legitimate case or controversy within the meaning of Article III of the U.S. Constitution. "The gist of the question of standing is whether the party seeking relief has alleged such a personal stake in the outcome of the controversy as to ensure that concrete adverseness which sharpens the presentation of issues upon which the court so largely depends for illumination of difficult constitutional questions." 418 U.S. 208, 237 citing 369 U.S. 186, 204.

Stare decisis: Latin: to stand by that which was decided; rule by which common law courts "are slow to interfere with principles announced in the former decisions and often uphold them even though they would decide otherwise were the question a new one." "Although [stare decisis] is not inviolable, our judicial system demands that it be overturned only on a showing of good cause. Where such a good cause is not shown, it will not be repudiated." The doctrine is of particularly limited application in the field of constitutional law.

Statute: an act of the legislature, adopted pursuant to its constitutional authority, by prescribed means and in certain form such that it becomes the law governing conduct within its scope. Statutes are enacted to prescribe conduct, define crimes, create inferior governmental bodies, appropriate public monies, and in general to promote the public good and welfare. Lesser governmental bodies adopt ordinances; administrative bodies adopt regulations.

Statute of limitations: "any law which fixes the time within which parties must take judicial action to enforce rights or else be thereafter barred from enforcing them," 116 S.E.2d 654, 657. ... The time limitation is also an essential element of adverse possession, prescribing the time at which the adverse possessor's interest in the property becomes unassailable. The policy underlying the enactment of such laws concerns the belief that there is a point beyond which a prospective defendant should no longer need to worry about the possible commencement in the future of an action against him or her, that the law disfavors "stale evidence," and that no one should be able to "sit on his rights" for an unreasonable amount of time without forfeiting his or her claims.

Substantive law: "the positive law which creates, defines and regulates the rights and duties of the parties and which may give rise to a cause of action, as distinguished from adjective law which pertains to and prescribes the practice and procedure or the legal machinery by which the substantive law is determined or made effective." 192 P.2d 589, 593–594.

Supremacy Clause: popular title for Article VI, Section [2] of the U.S. Constitution, which is the main foundation of the federal government's power over the states, providing in effect that the "acts of the Federal Government are operative as supreme law throughout the Union. They are self-executing, since they prescribe rules enforceable in all courts of the land. The states have no power to impede, burden, or in any manner control the operation of the laws enacted by the Government of the nation. ... [T]he full import of the Supremacy Clause was made clear after John Marshall became Chief Justice. In the Marshall interpretations, the clause meant essentially two things (1) the states may not interfere in any manner with the functioning of the Federal Government; and (2) federal action (whether in the form of a statute, a treaty, a court decision, or an administrative act), if itself constitutional, must prevail over state action inconsistent therewith."

Tort: a wrong; a private or civil wrong or injury resulting from a breach of a legal duty that exists by virtue of society's expectations regarding interpersonal conduct, rather than by contract or other private relationship. 256 N.E.2d 254, 259. "The word is derived from the Latin 'tortus' or 'twisted'." Prosser, Law of Torts § 1 (4th ed. 1971). The essential elements of a tort are the existence of a legal duty owed by a defendant to a plaintiff, breach of that duty, and a causal relation between defendant's conduct and the resulting damage to plaintiff.

Treaty: in international law, a compact made between two or more independent nations with a view to the public welfare, 107 F.2d 819, 827; "an international agreement of the United States must relate to the external concerns of the nation as distinguished from matters of purely internal nature." Restatement 2d, Foreign Relations Law of the United States § 40 (1965). Under the Constitution, the President has the sole power to initiate and make treaties, which must be approved by the Senate before they become binding on citizens of the United States as law. Art. II, Sec. 2. An EXECUTIVE AGREEMENT is often substituted for a treaty. In such agreements the President, without the need for senate approval, may bind the government just as in a treaty. 302 U.S. 324. However, such agreements can reach only narrower topics or be entered into pursuant to formal authority delegated by the Congress in particular legislation. See 69 F.2d 44, 48. Trade agreements for example, are often executive agreements rather than treaties. States may not engage in treaties of any kind, and once a treaty becomes law it is binding on the states under the supremacy clause. Art. I, Sec. 10, C1. 1; Art. VI, C1. 2.

Workers' [workmen's] compensation acts: statutes that, in general, establish the liability of an employer for injuries or sicknesses which "arise out of and in the course of employment." Prosser, Torts 532–33 (4th ed. 19971). The liability is created without regard to the fault or negligence of the employer. Benefits generally include hospital and other medical payments and compensation for loss of income; if the injury is covered by the statute, compensation thereunder will be the employee's only remedy against his or her employer.

APPENDIX 2

A LIST OF SOME OF THE LOOSE-LEAF SERVICES AVAILABLE

Using loose-leaf services is similar to using any other legal resources in that your index-searching skills are crucial to your success (or lack of it). One difference between loose-leaf services and encyclopedias is that a loose-leaf service often has its index in the first volume of its set of volumes. Whenever you're using one of these resources, check the bindings to see where the index is, and then start your search there.

Loose-leaf services can be organized in a number of ways: alphabetically by topic (like an encyclopedia is organized), according to statute, or according to date. However it is organized, start with the index, unless you have a specific cite that you can use.

Americans with Disabilities Act Manual (BNA)
Antitrust and Trade Regulation Report (BNA)
Bankruptcy Law Reports (CCH)
Benefits Coordinator (RIA)
Chemical Regulation Reporter (BNA)
Collective Bargaining Negotiations and Contracts (BNA)
Consumer Credit Guide (CCH)
Consumer Product Safety Guide (CCH)
Employee Benefits Compliance Coordinator (RIA)
Employment Coordinator (Clark Boardman Callaghan)
Employment Safety and Health Guide (CCH)
Environment Reporter (BNA)
Fair Employment Practice Cases (BNA)
Family Law Reporter (BNA)
Federal Tax Coordinator Second (RIA)
Government Employee Relations Report (BNA)
Housing and Development Reporter
(Warren, Gorham and Lamont)

Labor Law Reports (CCH)
Labor Relations Reporter (BNA)
Medicare and Medicaid Guide (CCH)
Occupational Safety and Health Reporter (BNA)
Patent, Trademark, and Copyright Journal (BNA)
Pension Coordinator (RIA)
Pension and Benefits Reporter (BNA)
Pension and Profit Sharing 2d (RIA)
Product Safety and Health Reporter (BNA)
Product Safety and Liability Reporter (BNA)
Real Estate Coordinator (RIA)
Securities Regulation and Law Report (BNA)
Social Security Law and Practice (CBC)
Social Security and Unemployment Compensation (Prentice-Hall Law and Business)
Standard Federal Tax Reports (CCH)
State and Local Tax Service (Prentice-Hall Law and Business)
State Tax Guide (CCH)
State Tax Reports (CCH)
State Tax Action Coordinator (RIA)
Tax Action Coordinator (RIA)
Tax Court Reporter (CCH)
Tax Management (BNA)
Trade Regulation Reporter (CCH)
Toxics Law Reporter (BNA)
Unemployment Insurance Reporter (CCH)
United States Tax Reporter (RIA)
United States Law Week (BNA)
Workers' Compensation (CCH)
Workers' Compensation Law Reports (CCH)

APPENDIX 3

SELECTED LIST OF AVAILABLE CASE REPORTERS

FEDERAL

United States Reports (U.S. Supreme Court cases from 1790 to the present)
Supreme Court Reports, Lawyer's Editions (U.S. Supreme Court cases from 1882 to the present)
Supreme Court Reporter (U.S. Supreme Court cases from 1882 to the present)
Federal Cases (lower court cases up to 1880)
Federal Reporter (lower and intermediate appellate court cases up to 1924)
Federal Reporter, Second Series (lower and intermediate appellate court cases up to 1932, then intermediate appellate court cases from 1932 to 1994)
Federal Reporter, Third Series (intermediate appellate court cases from 1994 to the present)
Federal Supplement (lower court cases from 1932 up to the present)
Federal Rules Decisions (lower court decisions concerning the Federal Rules of Civil Procedure and the Federal Rules of Criminal Procedure)
Federal Rules Service (lower court and intermediate appellate court decisions concerning the Federal Rules of Civil Procedure and the Federal Rules of Appellate Procedure)
Federal Rules of Evidence Service (cases concerning the Federal Rules of Evidence)
Americans with Disabilities Decisions
American Federal Tax Reports, Second Series
Bankruptcy Cases 2d
Bankruptcy Court Decisions
Bankruptcy Reporter

Copyright Law Decisions
Education Law Reporter
Employment Practices Decisions
Environment Reporter Cases
Fair Employment Practice Cases
International Trade Reporter Decisions
Labor Cases
Labor Relations Reference Manual
Military Justice Reporter
Social Security Reporting Service
United State Claims Court Reporter
United States Patents Quarterly
U.S. Tax Cases

STATE

Alabama

Alabama Reports (court of last resort cases from 1840–1976)
Southern Reporter (court of last resort cases from 1886 to the present and intermediate appellate court decisions from 1901 to the present)
Alabama Reporter (court of last resort and intermediate appellate court cases from 1976 to the present)
Alabama Appellate Court Reports (intermediate appellate court cases from 1910–1976)
Court of Civil Appeals and Court of Criminal Appeals (intermediate appellate court cases prior to 1969)

Alaska

Alaska Reporter (court of last resort cases from 1960 to the present, and intermediate appellate court cases from 1980 to the present)
Pacific Reporter (court of last resort cases from 1960 to the present, and intermediate appellate court cases from 1980 to the present)

Arizona

Arizona Reports (court of last resort cases from 1866 to the present, and intermediate appellate court cases from 1976 to the present)

Pacific Reporter (court of last resort cases from 1883 to the present, and intermediate appellate court cases from 1965 to the present)

Arizona Appeals Reports (intermediate appellate court cases from 1965–1976)

Arkansas

Arkansas Reports (court of last resort cases from 1837 to the present, and intermediate appellate court cases from 1979–1981)

Arkansas Cases (court of last resort cases from 1886 to the present, and intermediate appellate court cases from 1979 to the present)

South Western Reporter (court of last resort cases from 1886 to the present, and intermediate appellate court cases from 1979 to the present)

California

California Reports, First Series (court of last resort cases from 1850–1934)

California Reports, Second Series (court of last resort cases from 1934–1969)

California Reports, Third Series (court of last resort cases from 1969 to the present)

California Reporter (court of last resort and intermediate appellate court cases from 1959 to the present)

Pacific Reporter (court of last resort cases from 1883 to the present, and intermediate appellate court cases from 1905–1959)

Colorado

Colorado Reports (court of last resort cases from 1864–1980)

Colorado Reporter (court of last resort cases from 1883 to the present, and intermediate appellate court cases from 1891 to the present)

Pacific Reporter (court of last resort cases from 1883 to the present, and intermediate appellate court cases from 1891 to the present)

Colorado Court of Appeals Reports (intermediate appellate court cases from 1891–1980)

Connecticut

Connecticut Reports (court of last resort cases from 1814 to the present)

Connecticut Reporter (court of last resort cases from 1885 to the present, and intermediate appellate court cases from 1983 to the present)

Atlantic Reporter (court of last resort cases from 1885 to the present, and intermediate appellate court cases from 1983 to the present)

Connecticut Appellate Reports (intermediate appellate court cases from 1983 to the present)

Delaware

Delaware Reports (court of last resort cases from 1832–1966)

Delaware Reporter (court of last resort cases from 1966 to the present)

Atlantic Reporter (court of last resort cases from 1884 to the present)

Delaware Chancery Reports (chancery court cases from 1814–1968)

District of Columbia

Atlantic Reporter (intermediate appellate court cases from 1943 to the present)

Florida

Florida Reports (court of last resort cases from 1846–1948)

Florida Cases (court of last resort cases from 1941 to the present, and intermediate appellate court cases from 1957 to the present)

Southern Reporter (court of last resort cases from 1886 to the present, and intermediate appellate court cases from 1957 to the present)

Georgia

Georgia Reports (court of last resort cases from 1846 to the present)

Georgia Cases (court of last resort and intermediate appellate court cases from 1939 to the present)

South Eastern Reporter (court of last resort cases from 1887 to the present, and intermediate appellate court cases from 1907 to the present)

Georgia Appeals Reports (intermediate appellate court cases from 1907 to the present)

Hawaii

Hawaii Reports (court of last resort cases from 1847 to the present)

Pacific Reporter (court of last resort cases from 1959 to the present, and intermediate appellate court cases from 1980 to the present)

Hawaii Appellate Reports (intermediate appellate court cases from 1980 to the present)

Idaho

Idaho Reports (court of last resort cases from 1866 to the present, and intermediate appellate court cases from 1982 to the present)

Pacific Reporter (court of last resort cases from 1881 to the present, and intermediate appellate court cases from 1982 to the present)

Illinois

Illinois Reports, First Series (court of last resort cases from 1819–1954)

Illinois Reports, Second Series (court of last resort cases from 1954 to the present)

Illinois Decisions (court of last resort and intermediate appellate court cases from 1976 to the present)

North Eastern Reporter (court of last resort cases from 1885 to the present, and intermediate appellate court cases from 1936 to the present)

Illinois Appellate Court Reports, First Series (intermediate appellate court cases from 1877–1954)

Illinois Appellate Court Reports, Second series (intermediate appellate court cases from 1954–1972)

Illinois Appellate Court Reports, Third Series (intermediate appellate court cases form 1972 to the present)

Indiana

Indiana Reports (court of last resort cases from 1848–1981)
Indiana Cases (court of last resort and intermediate appellate court cases from 1936 to the present)
North Eastern Reporter (court of last resort cases from 1885 to the present, and intermediate appellate court cases form 1891 to the present)
Indiana Court of Appeals Reports (intermediate appellate court cases from 1890–1979)

Iowa

Iowa Reports (court of last resort cases from 1855–1968)
North Western Reporter (court of last resort cases from 1878 to the present, and intermediate appellate court cases from 1977 to the present)

Kansas

Kansas Reports (court of last resort cases from 1862 to the present)
Kansas Cases (court of last resort cases from 1968 to the present, and intermediate appellate court cases from 1977 to the present)
Pacific Reporter (court of last resort cases from 1883 to the present, and intermediate appellate court cases from 1895 to the present)
Kansas Court of Appeals Reports, First Series (intermediate appellate court cases from 1895–1901)
Kansas Court of Appeals Reports, Second Series (intermediate appellate court cases from 1977 to the present)

Kentucky

Kentucky Reports (court of last resort cases from 1785–1951)
Kentucky Decisions (court of last resort cases from 1886 to the present, and intermediate appellate court cases from 1976 to the present)
South Western Reporter (court of last resort cases from 1886 to the present, and intermediate appellate court cases from 1976 to the present)

Louisiana

Louisiana Reports (court of last resort cases from 1809–1972)
Louisiana Cases (court of last resort and intermediate appellate court cases from 1966 to the present)
Southern Reporter (court of last resort cases from 1887 to the present, and intermediate appellate court cases from 1928 to the present)

Maine

Maine Reports (court of last resort cases from 1820–1965)
Maine Reporter (court of last resort cases from 1966 to the present)
Atlantic Reporter (court of last resort cases from 1885 to the present)

Maryland

Maryland Reports (court of last resort cases from 1851 to the present)
Maryland Reporter (court of last resort cases from 1942 to the present, and intermediate appellate court cases from 1967 to the present)
Atlantic Reporter (court of last resort cases from 1885 to the present, and intermediate appellate court cases from 1967 to the present)
Maryland Appellate Reports (intermediate appellate court cases from 1967 to the present)

Massachusetts

Massachusetts Reports (court of last resort cases from 1804 to the present)
Massachusetts Decisions (court of last resort cases from 1884 to the present, and intermediate appellate court cases from 1972 to the present)
North Eastern Reporter (court of last resort cases from 1884 to the present, and intermediate appellate court cases from 1972 to the present)

Michigan

Michigan Reports (court of last resort cases from 1847 to the present)

Michigan Reporter (court of last resort cases from 1941 to the present, and intermediate appellate court cases from 1965 to the present)
North Western Reporter (court of last resort cases from 1879 to the present, and intermediate appellate court cases from 1965 to the present)
Michigan Appeals Reports (intermediate appellate court cases from 1965 to the present)

Minnesota

Minnesota Reports (court of last resort cases from 1851–1977)
Minnesota Reporter (court of last resort cases from 1978 to the present, and intermediate appellate court cases from 1983 to the present)
North Western Reporter (court of last resort cases from 1879 to the present, and intermediate appellate court cases from 1983 to the present)

Mississippi

Mississippi Reports (court of last resort cases from 1818–1966)
Mississippi Cases (court of last resort cases from 1966 to the present)
Southern Reporter (court of last resort cases from 1886 to the present)

Missouri

Missouri Reports (court of last resort cases from 1821–1956)
Missouri Decisions (court of last resort cases from 1886 to the present, and intermediate appellate court decision from 1902 to the present)
South Western Reporter (court of last resort cases from 1886 to the present, and intermediate appellate court cases from 1902 to the present)
Missouri Appeal Reports (intermediate appellate court cases from 1876–1952)

Montana

Montana Reports (court of last resort cases from 1868 to the present)
Pacific Reporter (court of last resort cases from 1883 to the present)

Nebraska

Nebraska Reports (court of last resort cases from 1860 to the present)

North Western Reporter (court of last resort cases from 1879 to the present)

Nevada

Nevada Reporter (court of last resort cases from 1865 to the present)

Pacific Reporter (court of last resort cases from 1883 to the present)

New Hampshire

New Hampshire Reports (court of last resort cases from 1816 to the present)

Atlantic Reporter (court of last resort cases from 1886 to the present)

New Jersey

New Jersey Law Reports (court of last resort cases from 1790–1948)

New Jersey Reports (court of last resort cases from 1948 to the present)

New Jersey Equity Reports (equity court cases from 1830–1948)

Atlantic Reporter (court of last resort and intermediate appellate court cases from 1885 to the present)

New Jersey Superior Court Reports (intermediate appellate court cases from 1948 to the present)

New Mexico

New Mexico Reports (court of last resort cases from 1883 to the present, and intermediate appellate court cases from 1967 to the present)

Pacific Reporter (court of last resort cases from 1883 to the present, and intermediate appellate court cases from 1967 to the present)

New York

New York Reports, First Series (court of last resort cases from 1847–1956)

New York Reports, Second Series (court of last resort cases from 1956 to the present)

New York Supplement (court of last resort cases from 1847 to the present, and intermediate appellate court cases from 1988 to the present)

North Eastern Reporter (court of last resort cases from 1885 to the present)

Appellate Division Reports, First Series (intermediate appellate court cases from 1896–1956)

Appellate Division Reports, Second Series (intermediate appellate court cases from 1956 to the present)

North Carolina

North Carolina Reports (court of last resort cases from 1778 to the present)

North Carolina Reporter (court of last resort cases from 1939 to the present, and intermediate appellate court cases from 1968 to the present)

South Eastern Reporter (court of last resort cases from 1887 to the present, and intermediate appellate court cases from 1968 to the present)

North Carolina Court of Appeals (intermediate appellate court cases from 1968 to the present)

North Dakota

North Dakota Reports (court of last resort cases from 1890–1953)

North Western Reporter (court of last resort cases from 1890 to the present, and intermediate appellate court cases from 1987 to the present)

Ohio

Ohio Report (court of last resort cases from 1821–1851)

Ohio State Reports, First Series (court of last resort cases from 1852–1964)

Ohio State Reports, Second Series (court of last resort cases from 1964(1982)

Ohio State Reports, Third Series (court of last resort cases from 1982 to the present)

Ohio Cases (court of last resort cases from 1933 to the present, and intermediate appellate court cases from 1943 to the present)

North Eastern Reporter (court of last resort cases from 1885 to the present, and intermediate appellate court cases from 1927 to the present)

Ohio Appellate Reports, First Series (intermediate appellate court cases from 1913–1965)

Ohio Appellate Reports, Second Series (intermediate appellate court cases form 1965–1982)

Ohio Appellate Reports, Third Series (intermediate appellate court cases from 1982 to the present)

Oklahoma

Oklahoma Reports (court of last resort cases from 1890–1953)

Oklahoma Decisions (court of last resort cases and court of criminal appeals cases from 1931 to the present, and court of appeals cases from 1969 to the present)

Pacific Reporter (court of last resort cases from 1890 to the present, courts of criminal appeals cases from 1908 to the present, and court of appeals cases from 1969 to the present)

Oklahoma Criminal Reports (court of criminal appeals cases from 1908–1953)

Oregon

Oregon Reports (court of last resort cases from 1853 to the present)

Oregon Cases (court of last resort cases from 1967 to the present)

Pacific Reporter (court of last resort cases from 1883 to the present, and intermediate appellate court cases from 1969 to the present)

Oregon Reports, Court of Appeals (intermediate appellate court cases from 1969 to the present)

Oregon Decisions (intermediate appellate court cases from 1969 to the present)

Pennsylvania

Pennsylvania State Reports (court of last resort cases from 1845 to the present)

Pennsylvania Reporter (court of last resort and intermediate appellate court cases from 1939 to the present)

Atlantic Reporter (court of last resort cases from 1885 to the present, and intermediate appellate court from 1931 to the present)
Pennsylvania Superior Court Reports (intermediate appellate court cases from 1895 to the present)

Rhode Island

Rhode Island Reports (court of last resort cases from 1828–1980)
Rhode Island Reporter (court of last resort cases from 1980 to the present)
Atlantic Reporter (court of last resort cases from 1885 to the present)

South Carolina

South Carolina Reports (court of last resort cases from 1868 to the present, and intermediate appellate court cases from 1983 to the present)
South Eastern Reporter (court of last resort cases from 1886 to the present, and intermediate appellate court cases from 1983 to the present)

South Dakota

South Dakota Reports (court of last resort cases from 1890–1976)
North Western Reporter (court of last resort cases from 1890 to the present)

Tennessee

Tennessee Reports (court of last resort cases from 1791–1971)
Tennessee Decisions (court of last resort cases from 1886 to the present, intermediate appellate court cases from 1932 to the present, and court of criminal appeals cases from 1967 to the present)
South Western Reporter (court of last resort cases from 1886 to the present, intermediate appellate court cases from 1932 to the present, and court of criminal appeals cases from 1967 to the present)
Tennessee Appeals Reports (intermediate appellate court cases from 1925–1971)
Tennessee Criminal Appeals Reports (criminal cases from 1967–1971)

Texas

Texas Reports (court of last resort cases from 1846–1962)

Texas Cases (court of last resort cases from 1886 to the present, and intermediate and criminal appellate court cases from 1892 to the present)

South Western Reporter (court of last resort cases from 1886 to the present, and intermediate appellate court cases from 1932 to the present, and criminal appeals cases from 1892 to the present)

Texas Civil Appeals Reports (intermediate appellate court cases from 1892–1911)

Texas Criminal Reports (criminal appellate court cases from 1876–1963)

Utah

Utah Reports, First Series (court of last resort cases from 1855–1952)

Utah Reports, Second Series (court of last resort cases from 1953–1974)

Utah Reporter (court of last resort cases from 1974 to the present, and intermediate appellate court cases from 1987 to the present)

Pacific Reporter (court of last resort cases from 1881 to the present, and intermediate appellate court cases from 1987 to the present)

Vermont

Vermont Reports (court of last resort cases from 1826 to the present)

Atlantic Reporter (court of last resort cases from 1885 to the present)

Virginia

Virginia Reports (court of last resort cases from 1790 to the present)

South Eastern Reporter (court of last resort cases from 1887 to the present, and intermediate appellate court cases from 1985 to the present)

Virginia Court of Appeals Reports (intermediate appellate court cases from 1985 to the present)

Washington

Washington Reports, First Series (court of last resort cases from 1889–1939)

Washington Reports, Second Series (court of last resort cases from 1939 to the present)

Pacific Reporter (court of last resort cases from 1880 to the present, and intermediate appellate court cases from 1969 to the present)

Washington Appellate Reports (intermediate appellate court cases from 1969 to present)

West Virginia

West Virginia Reports (court of last resort cases from 1863 to the present)

South Eastern Reporter (court of last resort cases from 1886 to the present)

Wisconsin

Wisconsin Reports, First Series (court of last resort cases from 1853–1957)

Wisconsin Reports, Second Series (court of last resort cases from 1957 to the present, and intermediate appellate court cases from 1978 to the present)

Wisconsin Reporter (court of last resort cases from 1941 to the present, and intermediate appellate court cases from 1978 to the present)

North Western Reporter (court of last resort cases from 1879 to the present, and intermediate appellate court cases from 1978 to the present)

Wyoming

Wyoming Reports (court of last resort cases from 1870–1959)

Wyoming Reporter (court of last resort cases from 1959 to the present)

Pacific Reporter (court of last resort cases from 1883 to the present)

APPENDIX 4

LIST OF STATE STATUTORY MATERIALS

Alabama

Acts of Alabama
Code of Alabama

Alaska

Alaska Session Laws
Alaska Advance Legislative Service
Alaska Statutes

Arizona

Session Laws, Arizona
Arizona Legislative Service
Arizona Revised Statutes Annotated

Arkansas

General Acts of Arkansas
Arkansas Advance Legislative Service
Arkansas Code Annotated

California

Statutes of California
Advance Legislative Service to Deering's California Codes Annotated
West's California Legislative Service
Deering's California Codes Annotated
West's Annotated California Code

Colorado

Colorado Legislative Service
Session Laws of Colorado
New Statutes Service
Colorado Revised Statutes
Colorado Revised Statutes Annotated

Connecticut

Connecticut Public and Special Acts
Connecticut Legislative Service
General Statutes of Connecticut
Connecticut General Statutes Annotated

Delaware

Laws of Delaware
Delaware Code Annotated

District of Columbia

District of Columbia Statutes at Large
District of Columbia Code Annotated

Florida

Laws of Florida
Florida Session Law Service
Florida Statutes Annotated
West's Florida Statutes Annotated

Georgia

Georgia Laws
Official Code of Georgia Annotated
Code of Georgia Annotated

Hawaii

Session Laws of Hawaii
Hawaii Revised Statutes
Hawaii Revised Statutes Annotated

Idaho

Session Laws, Idaho
Idaho Code

Illinois

Laws of Illinois
Illinois Legislative Service
Illinois Revised Statutes
Smith-Hurd Illinois Annotated Statutes

Indiana

Acts, Indiana
Advance Legislative Service to Burns Indiana Statutes Annotated
West's Indiana Legislative Service
Indiana Code
Burns Indiana Statutes Annotated Code Edition
West's Annotated Indian Code

Iowa

Acts and Joint Resolutions of the State of Iowa
Iowa Legislative Service
Code of Iowa
Iowa Code Annotated

Kansas

Session Laws of Kansas
Kansas Statutes Annotated
Vernon's Kansas Statutes Annotated

Kentucky

Kentucky Acts
Kentucky Revised Statutes and Rules Service
Baldwin's Kentucky Revised Statutes Annotated
Kentucky Revised Statutes Annotated, Official Edition

Louisiana

State of Louisiana: Acts of the Legislature
Louisiana Session Law Service
West's Louisiana Revised Statutes Annotated

Maine

Laws of the State of Maine
Maine Legislative Service
Maine Revised Statutes Annotated

Maryland

Laws of Maryland
Annotated Code of Maryland

Massachusetts

Acts and Resolves of Massachusetts
Massachusetts Advance Legislative Service
Massachusetts Legislative Service
General Laws of the Commonwealth of Massachusetts
Massachusetts General Laws Annotated
Annotated Laws of Massachusetts

Michigan

Public and Local Acts of the Legislature of the State of Michigan
Michigan Legislative Service
Michigan Compiled Laws
Michigan Compiled Laws Annotated
Michigan Statutes Annotated

Minnesota

Laws of Minnesota
Minnesota Session Law Service
Minnesota Statutes
Minnesota Statutes Annotated

Mississippi

General Laws of Mississippi
Mississippi Code Annotated

Missouri

Laws of Missouri
Vernon's Missouri Legislative Service
Missouri Revised Statutes
Vernon's Annotated Missouri Statutes

Montana

Laws of Montana
Montana Code Annotated

Nebraska

Laws of Nebraska
Revised Statutes of Nebraska

Nevada

Nevada Revised Statutes
Nevada Revised Statutes Annotated
Statutes of Nevada

New Hampshire

Laws of the State of New Hampshire
New Hampshire Revised Statutes Annotated

New Jersey

Laws of New Jersey
New Jersey Session Law Service
New Jersey Statutes Annotated

New Mexico

Laws of New Mexico
New Mexico Advance Legislative Service
New Mexico Statutes Annotated

New York

Laws of New York
McKinney's Session Laws of New York
New York Consolidated Laws Service Session Laws
Gould's Consolidated Laws of New York
Michie's New York Consolidated Laws
McKinney's Consolidated Laws of New York Annotated
New York Consolidated Laws Service

North Carolina

Session Laws of North Carolina
Advance Legislative Service to the General Statutes of North Carolina
General Statutes of North Carolina

North Dakota

Laws of North Dakota
North Dakota Century Code

Ohio

Laws of Ohio
Baldwin's Ohio Legislative Service

Page's Ohio Revised Code
Baldwin's Ohio Revised Code Annotated
Page's Ohio Revised Code Annotated

Oklahoma

Oklahoma Session Laws
Oklahoma Session Law Service
Oklahoma Statutes
Oklahoma Statutes Annotated

Oregon

Oregon Laws and Resolutions
Oregon Revised Statutes
Oregon Revised Statutes Annotated

Pennsylvania

Laws of Pennsylvania
Purdon's Pennsylvania Legislative Service
Pennsylvania Consolidated Statutes
Purdon's Pennsylvania Statutes Annotated
Purdon's Pennsylvania Consolidated Statutes Annotated

Rhode Island

Public Laws of Rhode Island and Providence Plantations
Acts and Resolves of Rhode Island and Providence Plantations
General Laws of Rhode Island 1956

South Carolina

Acts and Joint Resolutions of South Carolina
Code of Laws of South Carolina 1976 Annotated

South Dakota

Laws of South Dakota
South Dakota Codified Laws Annotated

Tennessee

Public Acts of the State of Tennessee
Tennessee Advance Legislative Service
Tennessee Code Annotated

Texas

General and Special Laws of the State of Texas
Vernon's Texas Session Law Service
Vernon's Texas Codes Annotated

Utah

Laws of Utah
Utah Code Unannotated
Utah Code Annotated

Vermont

Laws of Vermont
Vermont Statutes Annotated

Virginia

Acts of the General Assembly of the Commonwealth of Virginia
Code of Virginia Annotated

Washington

Laws of Washington
West's Washington Legislative Service
Revised Code of Washington
West's Revised Code of Washington Annotated

West Virginia

Acts of the Legislature of West Virginia
West Virginia Code

Wisconsin

Laws of Wisconsin
West's Wisconsin Legislative Service
Wisconsin Statutes
West's Wisconsin Statutes Annotated

Wyoming

Session Laws of Wyoming
Wyoming Statutes Annotated

APPENDIX 5

SHEPARD'S ABBREVIATIONS*

SHEPARD'S CASE CITATOR ABBREVIATIONS

In the following chart, we give, we hope, more easily understood explanations of what these abbreviations from the case citators mean. We will refer to the case that you were updating as "your case" and the case that later cited to it as the "new case."

History of Case

Later actions involving your specific case. In other words, the cases that use the history abbreviations are all, in some respect, extensions of your case.

a (affirmed) The decision in your case was upheld as the correct decision in the new case.

cc (connected case) This is a citation to a new case that arose from the same circumstances as your case, but it was separated from your case at some point, and therefore, is not affected by the decision in your case, nor is your case directly affected by it.

m (modified) The judgment in your case was modified in this new case. For example, the amount of money in the judgment may have been reduced.

p (parallel) The new case is factually or legally similar to your case.

r (reversed) Your case was heard by an appellate court and the appellate court decided that the decision in your case should be treated as if it was never made.

s (same case) This is merely a citation to your case and not a new case.

Other explanations of abbreviations provided by Sonja Larsen and John Bourdeau.

S (superseded) The opinion in this new case should be used in place of your case. This may happen where the same court that wrote the opinion in your case later decides that it made some sort of mistake in your case and wants this new opinion to be used in place of your case.

v (vacated) The new case, which is a later version of your case, has held that the decision in your case no longer has any legal validity.

U.S. cert den The U.S. Supreme Court refused to grant certiorari to hear the case.

U.S. cert dis The U.S. Supreme Court granted certiorari but then removed the case from the jurisdiction of the Court without taking any other action.

U.S. cert gran The U.S. Supreme Court said it would hear your case.

U.S. reh den One of the parties in your case requested that the U.S. Supreme Court hear an appeal of your case, and the Court said no.

U.S. reh dis The U.S. Supreme Court said it would rehear your case, but then removed the case from the jurisdiction of the Court without taking any other action.

Treatment of Case

Cases that use the treatment abbreviations are not direct extensions of your case, but may have a bearing on the validity of your case.

c (criticized) The new case says that your case was incorrectly decided in some way, but perhaps because the new case is not from your jurisdiction, it can't say that your case should no longer be followed, and says why.

d (distinguished) The new case cites to yours but says that it does not have to follow what your case decided because the new case is presented with a different legal or factual situation.

e (explained) The new case goes into some depth to explain the reasoning behind the decision in your case.

Ex (Examiner's decision) Your case was cited in a new case heard by an administrative agency.

f (followed) The new case says that it must follow in the footsteps of your case and decide the issue before it in the same way as your case did.

h (harmonized) The new case took your case and another case, which may have seemed as though they came to different conclusions, and explained how they could both be followed without upsetting either.

j (dissenting opinion) Your case was discussed in the new case, but by a judge who disagreed with the rest of the judges on the court who heard the new case.

L (limited) The new case recognizes that your case may have come to a valid decision, but only in the exact situation that occurred in your case, and therefore, it refuses to follow your case.

o (overruled) A higher court in the same jurisdiction says in the new case that the decision in your case was wrong and should no longer be followed.*

q (questioned) The new case says that either the decision or the reasoning in your case is incorrect but doesn't necessarily say why.

SHEPARD'S STATUTORY CITATOR ABBREVIATIONS

Operation of Statute

Legislative

A (amended) Statute amended.

Ad (added) New section added.

E (extended) Provisions of an existing statute extended in their application to a later statute, or allowance of additional time for performance of duties required by a statute within a limited time.

GP (granted and citable) Review granted and ordered published.

L (limited) Provisions of an existing statute declared not to be extended in their application to a later statute.

R (repealed) Abrogation of an existing statute.

Re-en (re-enacted) Statute re-enacted.

Rn (renumbered) Renumbering of existing sections.

*The terms *overruled*, *reversed*, *superseded*, and *vacated* are very similiar in that they basically indicate that you shouldn't use your case because it is no longer valid law.

Rp (repealed in part) Abrogation of existing statute.

Rs (repealed and superseded) Abrogation of an existing statute and substitution of new legislation therefor.

Rv (revised) Statute revised.

S (superseded) Substitution of new legislation for an existing statute not expressly abrogated.

Sd (suspended) Statute suspended.

Sdp (suspended in part) Statute suspended in part.

Sg (supplementing) New matter added to existing statute.

Sp (superseded in part) Substitution of new legislation for part of an existing statute not expressly abrogated.

JUDICIAL

The following abbreviations are used, preceding the citation, to indicate the citing court's holding with respect to the cited provision's constitutionality or validity:

C Constitutional.

f (followed) The statute you are Shepardizing was expressly relied upon as controlling authority.

i (interpreted) The statute you are Shepardizing was interpreted in some significant manner. This may include a discussion of the statute's legislative history.

na (not applicable) The statute you are Shepardizing has been found to be inapplicable to the legal or factual circumstances of the citing case.

rt (retroactive/prospective) The retroactive or prospective application of the statute you are Shepardizing has been discussed by the citing case.

V Void or invalid.

Va Valid.

Vp Void or invalid in part.

U Unconstitutional.

Up Unconstitutional in part.

SHEPARD'S CODE OF FEDERAL REGULATIONS (C.F.R.) CITATOR ABBREVIATIONS

Operation (Judicial)

The following abbreviations are used, preceding the citation, to indicate the citing court's holding with respect to the cited provision's constitutionality or validity:

C Constitutional.
V Void or invalid.
U Unconstitutional.
Va Valid.
Up Unconstitutional in part.
Vp Void or invalid in part.

Special Symbols for Dates of C.F.R. Provisions

The following symbols indicate the meaning of the date that is included with each C.F.R. citation:

* Followed by a year refers to the C.F.R. edition, if cited.

Δ Followed by a year indicates the date of the citing reference (date of C.F.R. provision not cited).

SPECIAL SYMBOL REGARDING PUBLICATION STATUS OF CERTAIN DECISIONS

# Indicates that review or rehearing of the California citing case has been granted, or that it has been ordered not published, pursuant to Rule 976 of the California Rules of Court (publication status should be verified before use of the citing case in California).

INDEX

Note to reader: In the following index, page numbers in italics refer to pages containing figures or charts related to the subject heading; page numbers in bold-face type refer to discussions of the subject in the Chapter Highlights.